PRAISE

Birgitta, is undoubtedly the most wonderful, kind-hearted, out of this world (in a nice way) and genuine person we have ever met. We have never come across someone who has been through so much in one lifetime, to come across as genuine and full of love.

The knowledge and wisdom that Birgitta holds and channels is pure source and never to be doubted or questioned. She has chosen to work through her dark times, whereas most people on this planet run and hide. She has learnt to trust not only herself but her wonderful spirit team and has managed to keep wearing that smile. This shows true strength and power.

Birgitta has written some beautiful books, and I would highly recommend everyone to take time out to read these. Her latest book, *Child of the Sun: Enroute to Enlightenment in India,* is a particularly poignant and powerful read, drawing from Birgitta's own profound personal experiences to guide readers on a transformative journey of self-discovery and healing.

Her book is a delightful buffet of hard-earned wisdom, serving lessons on reclaiming your power and mustering the courage to toss aside the heavy baggage of past traumas. For those seeking deeper meaning and heartfelt advice from a fellow 'earthly' traveler, Birgitta's latest work is a gem and an absolute must-read that profoundly uplifts and inspires.

Birgitta is a naturally gifted healer to all who cross her pathway and walk with her along life's journey.

We are extremely lucky to have her, as not only our friend, but as someone we also look up too.

Garry Edwards – Psychic Medium, Trance Medium Psychic
www.garryedwardsspiritconnections.co.uk
Leone Edwards – Psychic Medium, Healer & Spiritual Teacher
www.leoneedwards.com

This book truly resonated with me in so many ways.

I loved the authentic self-reflections woven throughout, and the blend of channeled mediumship and automatic writing is so powerful. You've done an amazing job at presenting complex spiritual ideas in a way that feels clear, approachable, and grounded in plain English—especially helpful for neurodivergent readers like me. The visual analogies are fantastic for seeing the bigger picture, and I found myself deeply inspired by the cosmic adventure you invite readers on.

It was also refreshing to feel the unique personalities of the communicators shine through their teachings, bringing a lively energy to each lesson. Altogether, *Child of the Sun* is enjoyable, thought-provoking, and a wonderful contribution to your body of work.

Revd. Ashley Robinson – Spiritualist Minister, Medium, Counsellor Sharing wisdom, laughter, and evidence of Life After Death & Spiritualism truths with love
www.facebook.com/AshRobinsonMedium

Child of the Sun is ultimately a journey about returning home; to love. It is mesmerizing, heart activating, enlightening and uplifting. A book that holds codes to living life consciously, with intention and joy.

As Birgitta shares her unique and fascinating story, interspersed with powerful channeled guidance, she takes you the reader on a parallel journey of your own, steering you to clear out the garbage of the mind, to laugh at life and the meanderings and distractions you can so beautifully place upon the path to prevent you from embodying your divine and unique light.

The words in Chapter 7 of The Basic Course are filled with valuable insights, and simple truths.

Each breath we take is a blessing. Though life may not always be easy, we must remember that the very act of living is a privilege denied to many. Our circumstances do not define us. What matters most is how we choose to see the world—with eyes of gratitude or resentment. This moment is a gift. This breath is a miracle. You are alive, and that alone is reason enough to rejoice. So, open your heart, spread your arms wide, and give thanks for the immeasurable gift of simply being here.

Birgitta's authenticity, wit and loving heart shine through the pages inspiring you to take hold of the reins of your life, to be present, to live courageously and joyfully.

Siobhan Purcell – Quantum Consciousness Healer and Guide
www.siobhanpurcell.net

Birgitta Visser has crafted a remarkable narrative in *Child of the Sun*, inviting readers into a deeply personal and transformative exploration of her spiritual journey. This book is not just a memoir; it is a relatable guide through the intricacies of modern life, where the challenges of trauma and the beauty of growth intertwine.

From the first page, Birgitta's story is captivated by its authenticity and vulnerability. She shares her experiences with an openness that feels both refreshing and comforting. It's as if she is sitting across from you, sharing the lessons learned from her struggles and triumphs. Each chapter unveils a new layer of her journey, resonating with anyone who has ever faced adversity or sought deeper meaning.

What makes *Child of the Sun* particularly powerful is how Birgitta weaves her personal stories with universal themes. Her insights on navigating pain and finding purpose in the chaos of modern existence are profound and accessible. Readers will find themselves reflecting on their own experiences and drawing parallels between her journey and their own.

The prose is poetic and insightful, making complex emotions and spiritual concepts tangible. Birgitta's ability to articulate the lessons learned from her traumas offers a sense of solidarity to those of us grappling with similar struggles. She shares her wisdom and encourages readers to embrace their journeys, reminding us that every experience—good or bad—holds the potential for growth.

Overall, *Child of the Sun* is a heartfelt and inspiring read that resonates long after turning the last page. Birgitta has created a roadmap for anyone seeking clarity and connection in a rapidly changing world. This book is a testament to her resilience and a beacon of hope for those on their own spiritual paths. I highly recommend it to anyone looking for guidance, inspiration, or a beautifully told story of one woman's journey through life.

Furkhan Dandia – MBA, Counsellor, Author,
Speaker and Podcast Host of EZ Conversations
www.eunoiazen.com

Birgitta has one of the most beautiful souls I have ever met. She reminds me of bottled sunshine. If she were a colour, I would say she was a very bright gold, with silver rays running through. She has a mixture of wisdom, humbleness, vulnerability and an eagerness to learn and soak up as much as she can. She is one of those rare individuals who walks the walk; in other words, she lives her truth, with honesty and integrity. She maybe in a 3rd density bodysuit, but her soul shines brightly through, giving the impression that she is in the world, but not of it.

In *Child of the Sun*, Birgitta takes you on her journey to the discovery of the very core of her being. It is colourful, enjoyable and extremely readable - I could not put it down. I laughed with her and felt the emotions that were playing out during different parts of her journey. It is a totally honest account of her discovery of self. There is no sugar coating of her adventures, it is what it is!

Dispersed throughout the book are beautiful messages from the divine, offering wisdom, healing and hope for all our futures.

This is a book to read over and over again, to keep at your bedside and delve into when you need peace, inspiration or any other encouragement for the soul.

Thank you, dear friend, for birthing this book and sharing it with us all.

Nicola Taylor – Psychic Medium, Level 2 QHHT Practitioner,
StarSeed Traveler & Reiki Practioner
www.healingtreetherapy.co.uk

Child of the Sun, hmmm! I find the synchronicity of Birgitta's words in alignment with my life and messaging. We both embarked on a similar journey in the same year. No coincidences that we found our way to each other. I have heard and spoken about what she writes my whole life. It took my whole life to fully understand it! If that is even possible. These are universal truths. We live in an illusion. I have often said, what if our "waking" state is the dream and our dreams are reality?

I love how Spirit works, when it's time for a message to come out, it will find those willing to pick up the sword and slay the dragon. I've come to know Birgitta and I believe we are Soul Sisters. We have similar messages and we deliver them in our unique style. This is what working in cooperation is like. We support each other because there is enough to go around. Her words are beautifully written to help those seeking the truth. We truly are Children of the Sun. This is a must-read for those who are seeking the truth. Your pain is real. You have to face your demons, but what is on the other side is worth facing the illusion to discover your truth and beauty. Well done, Sister.

Kathleen Flanagan – International Multi-Award Winning Author,
Transformational Expert & Coach, Aromatherapist,
Sound Therapist & Podcast Host of the Journey
of an Awakening Spirit
www.kathleenmflanagan.com

Child of the Sun is delightful! It is a book to read slowly as it commands one to savour, contemplate and digest every page before moving on to the next. Birgitta shares deep transformational truths through playful, witty, humorous stories, metaphors and channeling, illustrated further by her personal experiences. Her vulnerability and brutal honesty can only inspire us to embrace our own journey called life. The practical exercises and mantras are priceless to support us in finding our way Home. Truly a profound, enlightening read.

Dina Marais – Founder of Soul Purpose Publishing
coaching.dinamarais.com

Child of the Sun is a mesmerizing journey into the heart of a world rich with spiritual depth, emotional complexity, and vivid storytelling. From the very first page, I was captivated by the way the story intertwined elements of myth, culture, and human experience, weaving them into a narrative that both entertains and enlightens.

The author's ability to craft such a unique blend of characters and world-building is nothing short of remarkable. Each chapter left me with something profound to reflect upon, and I found myself drawn deeper into the protagonist's quest for identity, belonging, and purpose. This is not just a novel; it's an exploration of the human spirit, universal truths, and the connections that bind us all.

What sets this book apart is its seamless fusion of ancient wisdom with modern-day relevance, creating a story that resonates on multiple levels. The language is beautifully lyrical, and the themes of self-discovery and transformation will speak to anyone who has ever questioned their place in the world.

As a reader who had the privilege of experiencing this story before its publication, I wholeheartedly recommend "*Child of the Sun*" to anyone seeking not just a story, but an unforgettable journey that will linger in your heart and mind long after the final page.

This is a book to treasure, one that will undoubtedly leave a lasting impact on anyone who reads it.

Caroline Biesalski – M.Sc. International Economics & Finance, B.Sc. Psychology, Bestselling Author Inspired Choice Coach & Podcast Host of Inspired Choice Today
www.inspiredchoice.today

Child of the Sun draws you in from the first pages to the adventure that is the life of Birgitta Visser as she travels to India to find herself. Love the way she paints the picture for us of life in India, one almost feels as if they are right there with her, experiencing their own transformation in the process.

Jill Hart – The Coach's Alchemist & Host of the You World Order Showcase Podcast
www.hartlifecoach.com

A cosmic journey through self-discovery and spiritual awakening, *Child of the Sun* offers a transformative experience that will leave you inspired and enlightened. It radiates positivity and strength throughout.

Rutuja Ramtake – Doctor of Ayurveda and Book Blogger
www.instagram.com/rutuja_ramteke_

CHILD OF THE SUN

CHILD OF THE SUN

Enroute to Enlightenment in India

BIRGITTA VISSER

Copyright © 2025 by Birgitta Visser.

All rights reserved. No part of this book may be reproduced or used in any manner without written permission of the copyright owner except for the use of quotations in a book review. For more information, contact: birgittavisser@hotmail.com.

Published by

Universal Light Press

PowerSoulHealing.com

Book design by Journey Bound Publishing

Paperback ISBN: 978-1-7396389-3-1

Ebook ISBN: 978-1-7396389-4-8

Audiobook ISBN: 978-1-7396389-5-5

Library of Congress Control Number: 2024923098

This is a work of creative non-fiction. All of the events in this memoir are true to the best of the author's memory. Some names and identifying features have been changed to protect the identity of certain parties. The author in no way represents any company, corporation, or brand, mentioned herein. The views expressed in this memoir are solely those of the author.

First Edition

"Regardless of the mud puddles you may wade through, as long as you have the breath of life, be humble and bow in the mere awesomeness of deep gratitude, for every waking morning is another chance for you to change your yester sorrows, by creating in the very presence of today for infinitely better morrows."

Keep that spark going and that light ever flowing, weaving a little magic and sprinkling a little fairy dust along the way, whilst dancing in the suit of your hue-manness, enriching your life with the flavorsome experiences to reach those penny dropping moments of understanding the richness of life's served dishes, rather than remaining stuck in the ever-thickening broth of a bubbling stew."

—The Divine

CONTENTS

ACKNOWLEDGMENTS XIX
FOREWORD XXI
INTRODUCTION XXVII

PART I: SEEKING ENLIGHTENMENT 1
1. FLYING OUT TO INDIA 5
2. FIRST IMPRESSIONS OF BANGALORE 13
   A BRIEF HISTORY OF BANGALORE 14
   REDISCOVERING SIMPLICITY 14
   GAU: GENTLE TEACHERS AND HEALERS 17
   A CULTURE OF COMPASSION 19
3. LORD DIVYA KRISHNA 23
4. MANTRAS 29
   KRISHNA MANTRAS 31
5. THE ART OF LIVING CENTER 35
6. GURUDEV SRI SRI RAVI SHANKAR 41
7. THE BASIC COURSE 45
   FORMING CONNECTIONS 47
   SELF-REFLECTION AND ASPIRATIONS 50
   SATSANG 51
   TOURING THE GROUNDS 52
   LITTLE HANDS, HEAVY BURDENS 55

    THE ORPHANS OF KASHMIR 58
8. THE ADVANCED COURSE 63
    THE JOY OF SILENCE 69
    A KALEIDOSCOPE OF COLORS: HOLI DAY FESTIVAL .. 73
    CONTINUING CHALLENGES 76
    REFOCUSING ON GRATITUDE 78

PART II: LESSONS FOR AN ENLIGHTENED LIFE 81
9. EXPLORING THE WISDOM OF SRI SRI RAVI
    SHANKAR 85
10. EXERCISES AND TECHNIQUES 93
    MEDITATION AND BREATHWORK 93
    THE SUDARSHAN KRIYA BREATHING TECHNIQUE ... 99
    SIMPLE BREATHWORK MEDITATION EXERCISE 108
11. THE ASCENDED MASTER GANESHA 111
12. THE AILMENTS OF MODERN SOCIETY 123
    TECHNOLOGY, SOCIAL MEDIA, AND PEER
    PRESSURE 123
    CRITICISM AND STRESS 128
    FEAR, DEPRESSION, AND MENTAL HEALTH 134
    Q&A WITH SOURCE 140
    MY JOURNEY THROUGH DEPRESSION 145
    OVERCOMING CHALLENGES AND FINDING
    INNER STRENGTH 152
13. WHY THE PAIN AND SUFFERING? 157
    Q&A WITH THE RAINBOW WARRIORS FROM
    THE GALACTIC FEDERATION OF LIGHT 162
14. FINDING HAPPINESS AND EXPLORING OUR
    IDENTITY 171
    SEEKING HAPPINESS: Q&A WITH THE
    ASCENDED MASTER ST. GERMAIN 171
    SEEKING IDENTITY: Q&A WITH THE ASCENDED
    MASTER ST. GERMAIN 180

CONTENTS

15. RELATIONSHIPS AND LOVE **185**
   THE ART OF LIVING MATRIMONY SERVICES 190
   FALLING IN LOVE 190
   WHEN RELATIONSHIPS BECOME TOXIC 192
   NEEDINESS 194
   CONFLICT 196
   "I CAN FIX THEM" 198
   LEARNING SELF-LOVE 199
   THE GODDESS KALI MA 201
   HEALING WOUNDS, BOTH OLD AND NEW 210
   WHAT ABOUT SOULMATES? 214
   SELF-ACCEPTANCE AND SELF-FORGIVENESS 216
   CREATING A LOVING MINDSET 217
   WHAT IS "TRUE LOVE?" 220
   THE DEPTHS OF LOVE: Q&A WITH MASTER
   DJWHAL KUHL 222
   ASCENDED MASTER HANUMAN ON LOVE AND
   DEVOTION 226

**16. SHATTERED REFLECTIONS: THE TWIN FLAME
EXPERIENCE** **233**
   THE EFFECTS OF TRAUMA ON THE EARTH 242
   HELPING YOURSELF HEAL 243
   THE POWER OF LIGHT LANGUAGE HEALING 244
   THE HO'OPONOPONO PRAYER 246

17. KARMA AND PAST LIVES **249**
   WHAT IS KARMA? 249
   KARMIC GUIDANCE FROM LORD MAHA
   CHOHAN AND MASTER DK 250
   THE DEATH AND REBIRTH CYCLE 254
   LEARNING FROM MY PAST LIVES 256

18. NADI ASTROLOGY **263**
   WHAT IS NADI ASTROLOGY? 263

    HOW DOES PALM LEAF READING WORK? 266
    KARMA AND DESTINY 268
    MANIFESTATION 269
    EMBRACE THE PLAN OF THE UNIVERSE 270
19. **HEALING WITH AYURVEDA** 275
    THE MIND, BODY, AND SPIRIT CONNECTION 275
    WHAT IS AYURVEDA? 278
    LISTENING TO YOUR BODY 281
    THE THREE DOSHAS: VATA, PITTA, AND KAPHA 283
    MY VISIT TO AN AYURVEDIC DOCTOR 286
    MY EXPERIENCE WITH AYURVEDIC TREATMENTS 290
    GRATITUDE FOR THE EXPERIENCE 294
20. **CONCLUSION: THE ROAD TO BETTER TOMORROWS** 297

RESOURCES 305
ABOUT THE AUTHOR 307

ACKNOWLEDGMENTS

A HUGE SHOUTOUT TO MY incredible Mum, the original architect of my existence! Your unwavering love and support have been the foundation of my journey, and without you, I'd probably just be another lost sock in the chaotic laundry of existence. To my Dad, the unsung hero, watching over me from the great beyond, who contributed the essential ingredient to my creation—thank you. And to my sister, I'm grateful for having you as a treasured part of my journey!

A massive thank you to my publishing team at Journey Bound Publishing for believing in this dream, and to my brilliant editor, Ashten Luna, your magic has truly shaped this book into something special.

I'm grateful to everyone who has been a part of my journey—your lessons have been invaluable, helping me reflect and heal into the person I am today. Here's to the woman I've become through this incredible process.

A heartfelt thanks to everyone at the Art of Living Centre; without your wisdom and my time spent at the ashram, these pages would have remained blank! To my Guides and all the cosmic beings out there, your gentle nudges have been the fuel for my creative fire. And to you, dear reader, thank you for picking up this book and giving my words a chance.

Lastly, I owe the biggest thank you to God, because without that divine spark, none of this would be possible.

FOREWORD

"**E**XUBERANCE!" IT'S NOT A word that I use often, if at all, but it is the word that comes to mind when I think of my very first meeting with Birgitta almost 10 years ago. She bounced into my world like a ray of sunshine looking for a place to land.

That's when she found a special place in my heart!

After years of witnessing her journey, I know that she walks her talk and speaks her truth. And she does it her own way without concern for how another will see her. She has reached that stage of "self-acceptance" that is authentic, even when she's tripping her way through another tender stage of perpetual self-discovery like the rest of us.

I admire her boldness in living freely! When she dreams, she makes those dreams a reality. Step by step, she moves closer to making the unimaginable a very real reality in her life.

In this book (that I'd prefer to call a "heart sharing"), Birgitta takes you along on the eye-opening journey of discovering her soul. Through all the highs that remind her of how empowered and free she is, and the unexpected "pitfalls" of life that do the same. She brings vibrance (and a bit of comedic wordplay) to all the learning experiences that life brings.

She weaves lighthearted and playful humor into each story, and I easily smile because Birgitta's refreshing sense of humor often catches me off-guard. While explaining a deep spiritual truth, you'll often find wildly unexpected similes describing that esoteric truth perfectly. These creative wordplays stretch my mind to think in new and colorful ways. They push me to imagine fanciful imageries that delight my soul.

Throughout this book, Birgitta inspires us to accept the wild and unique beauty within ourselves and every soul we meet—and she teaches us through example. She lets her authentic nature shine brightly because anything else would be a distortion of truth.

I find great beauty in this.

This book is for lovers of poetry, symbolism, and clever use of thoughts and words.

I particularly enjoy the messages she channels from the Divine. They include wisdom, humor, inspiration, and a healthy dose of "tough love" when needed.

Birgitta offers us an intimate view of her channeled communications with the Divine. She generously shares whole channeled messages, without shifting a word, to keep the encoded energy of the original message true to its source.

I often paused to reread the channeled messages because I knew there was more insight hidden between the words that were written. I knew my soul could respond to that wisdom on a much deeper level.

As an example, in these poetic words channeled from the Divine in Chapter 8, I see so much beauty and potential.

"Faith blooms in the stillness of the mind, where doubt's shadow cannot linger. As the morning sun burns away the mist, faith arises and illumines all things."

These words are filled with so many nourishing seeds that speak to our soul.

Birgitta has a beautiful way of connecting the sacred knowing we hold within to the Source of truth in all things— to that which is divine presence.

FOREWORD

Her relationship to timeless masters of truth and love, like Archangel Michael, Lord Shiva, and St. Germain teaches us to trust our own intimate relationship with these sources, too. Birgitta reminds us that all we once considered a "separation" between ourselves, and Divine Source was merely an illusion—a distorted view of reality.

As witness to the words shared, as I was with each page that I turned, I saw Birgitta's truth as the greatest gift she shares. A pure expression of heart and soul!

I bow to the light of a thousand suns within her! To that which encourages her to always share her truth with the fire of personal soul knowing.

Birgitta says it many times within the book. She continues to learn, remember, and understand more about herself and all life, every day. This assures me that this is not the last of her great musings. For we will all continue to marvel at the radiant eclectic mind of Birgitta Visser through her many future endeavors.

I trust her creative spirit has no bounds.

Thank you, Birgitta, for sharing your sacred journey with me.

We have danced through the cosmos together and will continue to do so, I'm sure.

—Alania Starhawk, Divine Channel, Inspired Author,
Spiritual Mentor, Sacred Visionary
www.alaniastarhawk.com

Birgitta is an amazing person, a true gem who has soared beyond the mundane and now dances in the realms of deep spiritual insight. Her presence is like a warm light in a dim room, illuminating the path for those fortunate enough to cross her way. Having known her for many years, I can't help but feel a fatherly affection for her, as if she were my own daughter. This connection is rooted in a profound respect for her journey and the remarkable person she has become. She possesses a wealth of wisdom, her mind operating on a higher frequency than most that allows her to see the world through a lens of almost magical clarity. It's as if she has access to a deeper understanding of life's mysteries, effortlessly weaving together the threads of knowledge and intuition. Birgitta doesn't just live; she thrives while uplifting others, embracing the beautiful tapestry of mind, body, and spirit in all her endeavors. Her approach to life is 'wholistic,' recognizing the interconnectedness of all things and nurturing each aspect with grace and intention. With an empathetic heart, she has an extraordinary knack for listening, often grasping the essence of people better than they do themselves. In her presence, one feels seen and understood, as if she has the ability to peer into the depths of their soul. Life has thrown some serious curveballs at Birgitta, yet she has emerged from the storm with her warmth and kindness shining brighter than ever. Her resilience is inspiring; she transforms challenges into opportunities for growth, embodying the very essence of strength and perseverance. There's a fire within her that might baffle those who can't quite grasp the depth of her spiritual beliefs, but Birgitta stands firm, pouring her heart into every venture she undertakes. She is unapologetically herself, embracing her unique path with courage and conviction. While her dreams don't always unfold as she envisions, she trusts that the universe has a plan, providing her with what she truly needs. This unwavering faith in the greater design of life is a testament to her spiritual maturity and understanding. Her healing gifts are remarkable; just having a chat with Birgitta can wrap you in comfort and peace. She has an innate ability to create a safe space for others, allowing them to express their fears and hopes without judgment. She has been a fountain of wisdom for me, gently guiding me to see the beauty of the angelic realms, even when I was a non-believer. Her patience and understanding have opened my eyes to possibilities I never considered, enriching my own healing journey.

    Birgitta has transformed from a classic people-pleaser—often at her own expense—into a powerhouse of believing in herself and radiating far more confidence. She's discovered the magic of self-acceptance and the importance of prioritizing her own happiness. With her infec-

FOREWORD

tious spirit, she encourages everyone around her to embrace their true selves and pursue their dreams with unwavering determination. She is a true believer in the power of the human spirit, and I am honored to know and love this wonderful human being. Her presence in my life is a constant reminder of the beauty of personal growth and the importance of self-love. In a world that often pressures us to conform and seek approval, Birgitta shines as a beacon of empowerment and authenticity, and I am grateful to witness her incredible evolution.

—Martin Allum

Birgitta, my big sister and bestie, even though it took us many years to find our way back to another I wouldn't want to miss her for the world.

Most of you know how hard she has worked on her inner self, her soul to reach her level of enlightenment.

She has shared her story, her messages from amongst others the Ascended Masters and Archangels. She helps people with Light Language, but she has a natural ability to put others ease and heal them.

This book is not only about spirituality, it is a journey through India– the most dominant DNA in our bodies–it is about her adventures, the people she met, the teachers she found, the places she went, but most of all the feelings and lessons she learned.

Get swept up in a colorful journey!

—Barbara Visser
www.powersoulhealing.com/work-with-barbara

In the boundless journey of life, there exists an often overlooked but profoundly transformative path—one that leads beyond the physical, into the depths of our spiritual essence. These pages read as a delicate tapestry woven with threads of wisdom, insight, and transcendent experiences, invites you to embark on a voyage of the soul. It is a call to awaken, to rise above the mundane, and to ascend into higher realms of consciousness.

As you turn these pages, you will encounter characters who grapple with the same existential questions that have puzzled humanity for millennia: Who am I? Why am I here? What lies beyond the veil of material existence? Through their trials and triumphs, you will witness the unfolding of spiritual growth, the shedding of illusions, and the embrace of divine truths.

This story is a reflection of a universal journey. Each chapter, each moment of awakening, mirrors the potential within us all to transcend our limitations and connect with the infinite source of love and wisdom. It is an exploration of the inner landscapes where the soul's light shines brightest, even amidst the shadows of doubt and fear.

In a world that often prioritizes the tangible and the seen, this story serves as a gentle reminder of the unseen forces that shape our existence. It beckons you to look within, to listen to the whispers of your heart, and to recognize the sacredness of your own path. As you immerse yourself in this tale, may you find inspiration to elevate your consciousness, to seek the truth that lies within, and to embrace the spiritual awakening that awaits.

Let this book be a guide, a companion on your journey toward enlightenment. May it stir your spirit, expand your awareness, and ignite the flame of ascension within your soul. For in every page, in every word, there is a seed of transformation, waiting to blossom into the fullness of your divine potential.

Welcome to a journey of spiritual awakening. Welcome to the ascent of consciousness.

Get ready to face your soul in these pages. Trust me, you will never be the same again.

With all the love there is within me for it flows through each one of us,

—Nic Nierras, Fellow Soul Sister of the Universe, RTT Practitioner, Certified Hypnotherapist, Wholistic Coach and podcast host of *You're Worthless*.
www.thenicnierraswholisticlifestyle.com

INTRODUCTION

As the wintry Spanish Costa Blanca sun sets on the final days of 2023, I find myself lost in quiet contemplation of the winding and often rocky road my life has taken. Tears well up in my eyes as I recall the dizzying highs and gut-wrenching lows along this emotional rollercoaster ride of life. Though the rough patches most certainly knocked the wind out of me, leaving me bloody on that battlefield of my life's experiences, often going one step forward, two steps back, each time I emerged from the fight just a wee bit wiser, allowing me to move forward and, eventually giving me a better understanding of life.

My heart overflows with gratitude for those who have walked beside me, hands clasped in mine; and for those I have had to let go of whose paths diverged from my own, allowing them to follow their own path and experience life in all its essence according to the song of their own heart. How can I not be grateful for the time we shared? How can I not love them for all they taught me? Who would we be without the reflections of others, that help us heal the unhealed wounds within ourselves? I have come to understand that each of us must follow our own path to savor all the different flavors life has to offer, to truly grasp the beat and flow of our own soul, no matter where it takes us. Though our hands may unlink, the bond remains. Each companion lights the way for the next, and I will carry their spirits and their love with me in my heart as

I continue onward. This life is made meaningful not by one soul alone, but by all those we meet on our unfolding earthly journey.

The often hard-wrought trauma cast upon me, allowed me to re-evaluate my own life, befriending the darkness, shaking hands with my demons, lifting me from dark valleys. Yet intertwined with the pain, there were also sweet moments of joy that lifted me to euphoric heights. As I gaze upon the sea's beckoning horizon over the terracotta rooftops from the quiet solace of my terrace, I am enveloped in a sense of peace that washes over me like the gentle lapping of the waves miles away. The rhythmic swaying of the palm trees, their leaves rustling in the soothing breeze, fills me with a profound calm that seems to quiet the chatter of my mind. In this moment of still contemplation, I am acutely aware of my own breathing, each inhalation and exhalation connecting me to the very essence of life that surrounds me. I smile, knowing more plot twists and enchanting discoveries await me all whilst climbing the Jacob's Ladder, and with each step I become more aware and conscious of the very essence of life. But here on my secluded terrace, I am content to just be, to appreciate the beauty of this fleeting moment, and to let go of the worries of the world, replaced by a deep sense of appreciation for the simple yet powerful beauty of nature. With the garnered wisdom of understanding, I appreciate each experience as a poignant thread in the tapestry of my current embodied human story, enriching itself through the light and dark nuances of duality alike. The fading sunlight illuminates every stitch: the friendships, the heartbreaks, the triumphs, and the failures, all shimmering with significance. I welcome what is yet to come, carrying within me the love that makes this journey meaningful.

Spirituality has always intrigued me, even as a child. My father, a devoted follower of Rosicrucian teachings, meditated daily and lived with one foot in the mystical realm. Though his spiritual devotion was admirable, he struggled to find balance between the ethereal and earthly planes. I sometimes wished he had been more present with our family instead of spending so much time exploring inner dimensions. His passing in 1988 left an ache in my heart, but also a longing to connect with the wonder he had found. India called to that searching part of my soul, just as my father's teachings had planted the seed years before.

I have the soul of a nomad, a wanderer, a seeker. Throughout my life, I have willingly created and chosen many difficult experiences to help enlighten me along life's journey. I have moved more times than my age, and my travels have led me through many storms of hardship, each trauma another mile marker on the map of my life. I chose this path knowing the risks, for better or worse. But we are not defined by what happens to us. It is the lessons we learn, the wisdom we gain, and how we allow those experiences to shape us that determines who we become. Every trial can refine us and every setback can be an opportunity to grow if we keep taking steps forward on the journey. These scars and stories have marked my soul, but my spirit remains unbroken. The road continues to unfurl ahead, and I walk on, weathered but wiser, never losing sight of the horizon.

As a Soul Empowerment Coach, Divine Channel, and Light Language Healer, my mission is to help others heal their wounded minds and thrive in every aspect of their lives. Drawing from my own journey of transformation, I've poured my heart and soul into my first book "BE-com-ing Authentically Me," which is filled with channeled messages from the many Master Teachers that offer a fresh and humorous perspective on self-discovery and spiritual growth. I've also co-authored two empowering books. "Become Empowered" shares the stories of fifteen incredible women who have triumphed over trauma and adversity, providing hope and guidance for those looking to break free from their own limitations. In "I'm So Glad You Left Me," I delve into the themes of overcoming challenges and embracing change. My goal is to inspire others to embrace their pain, practice forgiveness, and ultimately heal, coming back to a place of self-love. Remember, you must feel at home in your skin, for your body is the only given home to your soul. I'm merely here to help guide others towards a life that is more abundant, authentic, and spiritually aligned.

We live in transformational times, with many sensing a deep shift within themselves and seeking the true meaning of life. As Michael Caine famously stated in the final moments of the movie *Alfie*, "You know what? When I look back on my little life and the birds I've known, and think of all the things they've done for me and the little I've done for them, you'd think I've had the best of it along the line. But what have I got out of it? I've got a bob or two, some decent clothes, a car, I've got me health back and I ain't attached. But I ain't got me peace of mind—and if you ain't got that, you ain't got nothing. I don't know. It seems to me if they ain't got you one way they've got you another. So, what's the answer? That's what I keep asking myself—what's it all about? Know what I mean?"

Why are we all here, you ask? What is the point of this whole living anyway? It's to play the most epic game of all time: the game of LIFE! This ain't no board game or *Jumanji*, though; it's the real deal. We're here to grow, to learn, and to help each other level up as we are incarnated, taking in this wild ride called existence. The goal? To unlock our true potential, shake off the societal conditioning, remember who we are, and become the brightest, most sparkly versions of ourselves!

We're all divine, cosmic double agents learning life's light and dark nuances through the created recipes of our lived experiences. In this earthly burger joint of existence, we're like sizzling patties on the grill of duality, getting flipped up and down, and back and forth by the spatula of karma. Some flips bring us together, merging our essences and sharing wisdom, like basking in the warm glow of the buns of love, feeling wrapped in acceptance. Other flips separate us, leaving us to wonder when we'll reunite for that perfect bite. Each flip of the spatula brings new flavors–the spicy zing of excitement, the rich umami of purpose, the tangy pickle of adversity, the fiery peppers of burning our arse and a dash of Cajun flair that has us shrimping like a shrimp at a seafood buffet. Like alchemists, we experience each flavor until we transform into perfect patties, infused with the wisdom of all seasons. Until then, we wait patiently, sizzling sacredly under the heat of life's grill, trusting each flip will lead us to greater wholeness rather than burning us into oblivion. The divine spatula keeps flipping, and we keep learning and growing one blissful bite at a time.

How do we play this game of cosmic evolution, you wonder? Simple: by embracing it *all*; the good, the bad, and the downright nitty-gritty ugly. Every experience is a chance for us to heal, become lighter, brighter, and wiser. I daresay, bring it on! The universe is throwing all kinds of adventures our way, and we get to decide how we respond. With an open heart and a sense of humor, we can, if we choose to accept, turn any obstacle into an opportunity to grow. This game's got endless levels, countless quests, and the most amazing graphics you've ever seen. Time to roll the dice and play!

In 2008, my journey to enlightenment started in India, the land of my ancestors. Even though it took me many more years of chosen hardships and perilous experiences to uncover the light hiding within, India sparked a flame. It was the first step toward knowing myself and realizing that life's not about having all the answers. It's about asking the questions, and stumbling in the dark until we see the glow within.

Healing hurts. It's not pretty. It's not easy. To heal means facing the uncomfortable truths we've tried to ignore—the parts of ourselves we thought were strong but are actually broken. Real healing requires tearing down walls and stripping away facades to expose our wounds to the light. It's painful to look at our own brokenness. But only by acknowledging where we are hurting, only by letting light into those dark places, can we truly begin to mend. I know full well that the process is difficult, but let's be real, healing brings relief as we shed what is false and make room for what is real. If we endure the necessary pains of healing, we emerge wiser, lighter, and ready to walk the way home to the unfolding lotus within ourselves.

CHILD OF THE SUN

This book's title, *Child of the Sun,* refers to all people being rays of light from the Divine Orchestrator, the Creator. Walking through our journey of life, we may forget our divine essence, if only for a while. Do not despair when lost in the maze of this mystery, simply tune in and follow your inner compass back home. The universe whispers to those who listen—you are a Child of the Sun. Though illusion clouds your path, reality awaits within. Stay true to the light of your soul and you will find your way.

The sun shines in each and every one of us. Some of us may have simply hidden our sunlight beneath the darkness of the heavy clouds dancing across the vastness of our mind, waiting to be released by the impending rain, to free the soul back to the light of the sun within.

We are all rays of the cosmic sun, sparkling gems rebirthing time and again through our experiences, unfolding petal by petal like the beautiful lotus flowers we are, having sprung from the Ohm of creation, without beginning nor end, for we are and always have been.

"You are a radiant celestial Child of the Sun, feel the light of your inner light shine bright.

Feel your heart pulsate with the magic of your hue-manness, for you are all brilliant rays beaming from the Divine Creator. You have been blessed by the cosmos with your spirit encapsulated in a wondrous meat-covered suit to create and weave your magic as you see fit. Let your talents blaze like the eternal warmth of the summer sun. Craft each day into a masterpiece, much like the delightful spread of peanut butter, spreading joy and flavor across the canvas of life, illuminating the world with your uniquely crunchy creamy delicious vision. Why be ordinary when you are extraordinary? Allow your spirit to glow as you leverage your experiences, alchemizing these from the clouded meatball heaviness, into the perkiness of the clear blue skies, constantly creating and mastering the impossibles to possibles. Blow life into the dreams imagined in the Charlie Chocolate Factory of your mind, and be that wondrous cosmic soul surfing renegade

INTRODUCTION

rock star that you are, revving across the shimmy shakin' skies, a ray of sparkling bubbly, bubblin' with soul and purpose.

You've always been an eternal Child of the stars, woven into the fabric of the cosmic-conscious Sun. Are you ready to play in this celestial playground and bust out some funky dance moves with the Universe and create some dazzling masterpieces?

—*The Divine*

Remember that your path is not my path, nor is your direction my direction. My truth is not your truth, for we see life through the lens of different perspectives. This book reflects my personal experiences and perspectives, which may differ from your own. My intention in sharing these experiences is not to offend anyone, but rather to offer a snapshot of how I've maneuvered through the challenges of my own life. We all walk our own journey, allowing our consciousness to blossom in our own divine, sweet time, through the reflective experiences we cast upon one another within the dueling dualities on this plane called earth; and yet, in the end, we walk one another home. Your soul, your journey, as much as the journey is a return to a love for your own soul in turn embracing others sparking the light of hope within the tempests of their own hearts.

You must have been drawn to this book for a reason, as nothing ever happens by 'chance.' Whatever you may be looking for, I hope that the words and teachings contained within these covers will uplift your soul and support you on your life's journey.

Allow the vibrant deities of the Indian spiritual tradition to become your steadfast companions as you explore the rich tapestry of this mystical realm. Invoke the mighty Hanuman, whose boundless strength and devotion can inspire you to overcome any obstacle. Bask in the playful, beloved energy of Krishna, whose teachings on the nature of the divine and the human experience can awaken the joy within your own heart. Face the fierce and transformative power of the goddess Kali, who can help you shed the layers of illusion and step into your authentic self. And let the gentle, benevolent presence of Ganesh guide you, removing obstacles and paving the way for your spiritual growth.

Let the wisdom of the Master Teachers like St. Germain, Archangel Michael, Lord Sananda, Master Djwhal Kuhl, Lord Maha Chohan and others be your guiding lights, illuminating your path with their profound insights, wit, and humor, empowering you to navigate life's journey with greater clarity and courage. Immerse yourself in the transformative mantras, meditation practices, and rejuvenating breathing techniques woven throughout these pages, allowing them to become your tools for self-understanding and healing. Dare to dive into the depths of pain, fear, and depression, for it is in these vulnerable spaces that the true nature of relationships and the healing power of love can be revealed.

Let the insights contained within these covers take your hand and light your way, kindling your spirit and nourishing your soul as you continue on your path of self-discovery. For in these pages, you will find not just words, but a living, breathing invitation to embark on a transformative journey—one that has the power to awaken your deepest potential and guide you towards a more fulfilling, meaningful life.

May the words help stir something deep in your soul, uncovering the true colors hidden beneath layers of societal expectations and conditioning you have so brush stroked yourself with. For too long, you may have tried squeezing yourself into the wrong mold, like an ill-fitting suit, merely trying to cope with life as is. My hope is that through self-healing, you'll find the tools here to break free from the past, heal your inner spirit, and inspire others to do the same. Together, we can strip away society's suffocating expectations to reveal the unique beauty within us all. My aim is that you find within these pages the tools to help you nurture your growth and live a life fully and freely—and inspire others

INTRODUCTION

to do the same. These words are an invitation to rediscover your authentic self and share your light with the world.

It's time to discover your inner glow. So, let's link arms, beautiful souls, and walk this path of reading and absorbing the words written here together. The journey starts here.

"You hold the rays of a thousand cosmic suns within you.

The I AM Power of my I AM, shines forth into the I AM of you as much as you are the I AM of Me.

Stop chasing the sun without, and start shining those beautiful rays from within, illuminating the world without.

Maybe you wonder, my Child, if you are lost, but you merely need to wander the wonder within, for 'lost' is a mere wording of seeking to transform the tumultuous inner, to know that you were never truly lost to begin with.

Maybe you have merely forgotten who you were in le bazar et le grand cirque de la vie, that you have surely so forgotten that you are le soleil d'or shining from within?

Maybe now is the time to walk the Divine wonder of the inner hues of you, returning to the radiance of the magnifique BEing you are and have always been.

Shine on beautiful StarLight particles of the cosmiclicious ever-expanding Universe, and let the games begin."

—*The Ascended Master St. Germain*

PART I
Seeking Enlightenment

"We are all flickering lights of a delight in this delightful experiment of life enroute to the light of enlightenment."

"I AM Surya, Master Creator and Elohim of the Sun

Walker of the lands of foregone fathers of the founding shores, the grounds upon which you have chosen to tread and walk the worlds, remembering the conscious spark of the light that you so divinely are.

I AM the Light, I AM the spark of the infinite wisdom, shining but ever so brightly within the hues of the human embodiment that is the incarnation of the very hue of you.

I AM the churner of evolution, the key holder to the consciously turning water wheel of incarnate souls.

I AM consistent of the fiery enlightened star light particles, transcended from the Sirian Cosmic star belt

And yet I AM as much as who you are and choose to be

I AM a Ray of the Eternal Cosmic Consciousness, the Creator Sun, as much as you are a Ray carried within the beauty of the encapsulated embodied shell of beautifully molded organic clay you have given yourself home to whilst suited and booted, finding your way on the lands of field o' play.

You are the light of hope to the world, for how can you not be when you carry the hue of the stars within your beating heart?

Peace comes from the bless-ed inner mother of oneself, for the earth was created out of the womb of the Cosmos, as much as Mankind was created out of the womb of the Mother.

One is the Earth as much as the Earth is one with thee.

One is reborn time and again to enlighten the very soul of oneself and ignite the flame of cosmic remembrance into the heart of oneself and of Man.

This game of cosmic evolution is not mere for selfish reasons, but to lose the egotistical settled dust one has impounded upon oneself, and the bearer of the cross, the Mother.

PART 1: SEEKING ENLIGHTENMENT

For how one treats the self is a direct reflection of how one treats others, and in turn how one treats the nurturer of all that graces beneath thy feet.

Accept yourself as you would want others to accept and appreciate the light that is you.

Unfold in the flame of peace, allowing for hurt to seep back out of the mind into the gracious enfolding cosmos, who will wipe your tears, alchemizing the droplets into the vastness of the stoic ocean of consciousness.

I AM the rainbow to the reflection of your Spirit

I AM the rain gently striking your cheeks

I AM the wind easing you to move forward in life's ever-evolving ocean

I AM the clouds hovering over the landscape of your soul, whilst you ease through the created burdens of life

I AM the All, as much as you are the All in the drop of the Ocean of All.

I am the ray to the sunshine you hold within the raindrop of your soul.

Let us dance the dance of eternal knowing, of consciousness divine, of everlasting love, so that the cup within thee may overfloweth to the hearts of the downtrodden, blowing life back into their spirit, of seeing the world and all of life in all its majestic infinite wisdom, bathed in nothing but the cradle of love.

In all of life's experiences, let love be the pearl of wisdom to guide thee along the many tides of change, turning inward to the warmth and bless-ed inner radiance of the heart of the Sun, connecting back to the cosmic grid of convergence and thus to thyself and the One in All."

—Surya, God of the Sun

CHAPTER 1
FLYING OUT TO INDIA

IN MARCH 2008, MY life was in dire straits and I felt pretty lost within myself, as my long-distance relationship was in a funk. Even at the age of thirty-three, I was still a green bean, naïve and always wanting to see the good in people rather than cutting ties. I didn't yet understand that it is best not to cling on to people that are acidic to my own soul. (I've since written at length about my beautifully toxic relationships in my first book, *BE-com-ing Authentically Me)*. At that time, the romantic contender in my life was unreliable, disappearing sporadically without explanation. Feeling a need for change, I hoped to break my own destructive cyclical patterns that I had so blissfully cultivated. Our guides, who spur us on from the sidelines, will all too happily push us over the edge of a cliff, making our lives deliberately uncomfortable, so that we feel the pain of our experiences and wish for nothing but to heal the unease we feel within ourselves. We unconsciously seek out situations reflecting old wounds until we understand the lessons held within these experiences, allowing ourselves to heal.

India has long fascinated many people, myself included. My ancestry is diverse, with Indian heritage flowing through my veins. My father was a half loaf of stoic German and cheerful Dutch, while my mother is a vibrant mix of Indian, Indonesian, 'waffly' Belgian, and 'moutarde' French. India beckoned me with its promise of spiritual awakening.

While working in The Hague, the Netherlands, I crossed paths with a kindred spirit who spoke of an oasis of inner peace: the Art of Living Center in Bangalore. Founded by the renowned spiritual leader Sri Sri Ravi Shankar, this center was calling me to embark on a journey of self-discovery. Though content in my job, I felt drawn to India, land of ancient wisdom, where I hoped to heal and reconnect with my true purpose. The Art of Living Center represented a doorway to transformation, and I was ready to step through and see where it would lead me.

My inner spirit was searching for something more—an inner peace, a calling that resonated deep within. I was searching for meaning in this life when I stumbled upon this path. It called to me, resonating with something deep inside me, and I knew this was exactly what my soul had been yearning for. This marked the beginning of my spiritual journey, one that was not without challenges. Over the years, I endured more trauma, incinerating myself to a fine crisp repeatedly, only to rise again from the ashes like a phoenix reborn. We have to be willing to face our demons within and do the shadow work, in order to truly heal and evolve.

I was one of these sadomasochists who, through her extensive, unhealed, and accumulated trauma, attracted broken birds. Yet I was still a broken bird, clinging to unhealthy relationships, thinking I could fix and mold others, much like kneading and shaping clay. I was so focused on healing those around me that I neglected my own bleeding wounds.

Over the many years that followed, I had to learn that the journey begins within. We must learn to heal, love, respect, and appreciate ourselves, letting go of the excess weight, before we can fully embrace the vigor of life. By walking with open hearts, we can transform our pain into strength; if we understand that pain, our experience can also be the remedy to the malaise we carry. Letting go meant stepping into the unknown, and that terrified me. I feared that without this relationship, I would lose my sense of self and be left adrift with no anchor. Though it was time to move on, I stubbornly resisted, preferring the familiar pain to the uncertainty of change. My identity had become so enmeshed with this other person that I couldn't imagine surviving alone. But deep down, I knew I had to find the courage to leave the past behind. Only then could I discover who I was without my old habits and routines. The path forward wasn't easy, but I figured if I faced my fears, I could somehow emerge stronger, wiser, and more whole than ever before. Looking back many years later, I now understand that the answers lie within ourselves, not in others. Like attracts like. When we raise our own vibration, we attract healthier relationships. As we show ourselves love, we find inner peace. The holes in our mind can only be patched from the inside out, allowing for our soul to breathe a bit lighter.

My life felt like the movie *Groundhog Day*—my days were an endless repetition of the same old challenges, getting the same old results. I was stuck in a rut, repeating patterns over and over. My guides were having a field day with me, watching me spin my wheels. But you know what? Looking back, I'm grateful for those repetitive experiences. They were opportunities to learn, evolve, and become more aware of how life works. Those tough times helped me take back my power and break free of my old ways and patterns, along with those that kept me trapped within them. I'm still on the road to enlightenment, but I've come a long way from that hamster wheel. Life keeps teaching me, and like you, I am still a work in progress.

My flight from London Heathrow to India was long but fairly comfortable. I left a rainy and windy London behind to swap it for the welcoming warmth of India. I flew with Air India on a nearly empty plane, having three seats all to myself. Perhaps the low passenger count reflected the airline's less than stellar reputation, even though all airbuses originate from the same manufacturers, differentiated only by their exteriors. Negative airline safety reputations are perhaps not deserved, since when flying, the risk of a crash is the same regardless of the airline.

While emergency protocols aim to save lives, a catastrophic crash leaves little chance for survival.

On the plane, turbulence jostled us like dice in a cup. An adventurous uncle grinned as he bounced down the aisle, nearly knocking his head on the ceiling. The cabin crew gently shepherded him back to his seat. In that instant, a profound realization dawned on me: beneath the superficial variations between us there lies a timeless spirit that unites us all. Though oceans and traditions may separate us, our inner light forever seeks kinship with others. Our core essence transcends the body's impermanent vessel, whispering of an eternal oneness waiting to be discovered. Though we each wear our own unique body suit to experience our humanity, our inner light, the energy encapsulated within in each of us, remains the same, and shines just as brightly. This truth would further occur to me amidst the vibrant hues of Indian culture. There, diversity is celebrated in all its technicolor splendor.

After an interminable ten hours of being tossed around in the skies like a rag doll, I thought I might lose my tandoori lunch. Cramming my gangly thirty-four-inch legs into the tiny economy seats was pure torture. To make matters worse, the chatty cabin crew kept forcing tea and muffins on me when all I wanted was to be left alone to sleep off my airsickness. Every time I started to drift off, another violent bout of turbulence jolted me awake. My only respite was watching the cheesy Bollywood flick, *Jab We Met*, which provided a welcome distraction from the hellish flight. How can you resist the infectious beats and melodies of Bollywood films? These movies offer more than just entertainment—many explore deeper themes about life, love, and humanity. But for sheer entertainment value, my all-time favorite has to be *Om Shanti Om*. This rollercoaster ride stars the legendary Shahrukh Khan as a young artist besotted with a leading lady. When he perishes tragically in a fire trying to save her, he is reincarnated decades later with hazy memories of his past life. As his surroundings trigger flashbacks, he sets out to uncover the truth behind his death. Of course, *Om Shanti Om* is just one of many gems. For thought-provoking stories, you can't go wrong with *3 Idiots*, *Ghajini*, the *Doom* franchise, and other films that stay with you long after the credits roll. Bollywood has a captivating way of blending music, drama, comedy, and meaning into irresistible cinematic feasts.

When we finally touched down in a sunny, muggy, and polluted Mumbai, I'd never been so happy to have my feet on the ground. My first time in the chaotic yet glamorous home of Bollywood was off to a rocky start, but at least I survived the trip without vomiting up my airplane meal all over the cabin.

Mumbai (originally called Bombay) has origins that trace back centuries, through the hands of explorers and emperors. In *Lendas da Índia*, written in old Portuguese by the historian Gaspar Correia (1492-1563), the city was called *Bombaim*, meaning "good bay." When King Charles II of England married Catherine of Braganza in 1661, Bombay passed to the British as part of sweet Catherine's dowry. The British anglicized *Bombaim* to *Bombay*, and so the city entered the annals of the British Empire. Her bay may have been good, but under colonial rule, Bombay transformed into something greater. She became the beating heart of British India, a center of culture and commerce.

The city also has a rich history as a fishing town. The local Koli people, skilled fisherfolk, were already calling it home back in the 16th century. Mumbadevi, the patron goddess of the city, watched over the Koli as they cast their nets and protected the local salt collectors. Mumbadevi was like a mother to these early residents, and her spirit lives on in the soul of the metropolis. Though the city has transformed over time, its heritage as a haven for fishermen endures. The call of the sea still echoes through the busy streets, a reminder of the Koli people and their beloved goddess Mumbadevi.

India achieved independence in 1947 due to the powerful protest movement spearheaded by Mahatma Gandhi, which lasted for decades. In 1995, when the regional political party Shiv Sena came to power, it changed the city's official name from Bombay to Mumbai. The party saw *Bombay* as a legacy of the British colonists that once occupied the city and wanted a new name to reflect the city's Maratha heritage by paying tribute to the goddess Mumbadevi.

If you listen closely, you can still hear Mumbai's sweeping history whispered in the streets—tales of Portuguese sailors, British merchants, and Indian workers who toiled to build the city into the legendary and vibrant, breathing metropolis she remains today.

After my long, arduous flight, I stumbled wearily out of the stuffy metal tube they call an airplane and into Mumbai's sultry embrace. The heat wrapped around me like a sweaty hug as I stood there, bleary-eyed and disheveled, fantasizing about nothing but a refreshing shower. But alas, the magic of India would have to wait—first, I had to endure five more tedious hours until my connection to Bangalore. Oh, the glamorous life of travel! Stinky planes, endless layovers, and an ever-present layer of grime—truly the stuff dreams are made of. At last, my terminal bus arrived. As I hauled my suitcase aboard, a helpful teenager offered to stow my bag. In that moment, his kindness touched my heart. I longed to tip him generously for his trouble, as is custom. But in my befuddled state, I failed to calculate the currency exchange rate from euros to rupees. The best I could mutter was "God bless you," though the words felt hollow without a gift to back them. I vowed then to be better prepared on my return flight, so I could show proper appreciation to the good people of Mumbai. God bless indeed—may the city forgive my ignorant tourist's blunder.

The airport was a bustling mess as I waited in the lounge, sinking into the dull tedium of the airport terminal. People jostled past with no regard for lines, impatient to check in. Amid the chaos, I met an intriguing couple from Cape Town, South Africa, who were on their way to Hyderabad. Though Muslim, they were on a quest to consult a Hindu priest in hopes of improving their lives and relationships. It was a fascinating glimpse into the human desire for meaning that transcends religious boundaries. The couple was willing to push aside preconceived notions in pursuit of inner peace. I wished them well as we parted, swept up again in the swirling crowds. India was already working its magic, drawing seekers from afar, and pulsing with an energy that stirred transformation.

Though my flight to Bangalore was short, it was once again disrupted by severe turbulence that made sleeping difficult. I held onto the armrests tightly and prayed, fearing this time that the violent shaking might damage the wings and doom us all. Finally, after a grueling twenty-four hours of travel, I was relieved to escape the airport at last. All I craved was a steamy hot shower. Subramanyam, a colleague from the India office scooped me up and took me to the Art of Living Center, my journey's end. The center is an ashram, a spiritual hideaway led by a guru, serving up a buffet of zen, peace, and tranquility.

CHAPTER 2
FIRST IMPRESSIONS OF BANGALORE

"Each one has to find his peace from within. And peace to be real must be unaffected by outside circumstances."

—*Mahatma Ghandi*

DRIVING THROUGH BANGALORE WAS a total trip. This bustling capital of Karnataka state makes London and New York City seem tame. It's a crash course in road rage! But beyond the chaotic streets lies a cosmopolitan city blossoming into a major tech and cultural hub.

Home to over twelve million people, Bangalore, also known as Bengaluru, is the Silicon Valley of India and the byte-basket powering call centers worldwide. It's also earned the nickname "Pub Capital of India" thanks to its swanky restaurants and nightlife. You might just spot a Bollywood star at one of the many upscale eateries.

Even so, I wasn't there for any of that, as I had too many demons running round in my head, tormenting my quest for inner peace. These triggers were my teachers, arising to reveal wounds and needing tenderness, not the fists that had been my strategy for most of my life. (Trust me, I wasn't done giving myself a battering, and I would give myself many more down the road). Rather than continuing to play whack-a-mole with my emotions as I had over the many tumultuous years, I learned to welcome their messages with deep gratitude. This path was the start of leading me more to feeling *at home* within myself. By embracing my demons as guides, I was able to find stillness within the turbulence.

Bangalore also seemed to have a softer side. It's known as the "City of Gardens," with lush parks and serene lakes nestled between the glass high-rises. This fusion of nature and urban energy makes it a fascinating place to explore and find an oasis of peace on the outskirts of the hustle and bustle.

A BRIEF HISTORY OF BANGALORE

Bangalore beautifully blends old and new, traditional and modern. It's an exhilarating contradiction—a sanctuary hidden in plain sight. Legend goes that in the late 14th century, King Veeraballa of Vijayanagara, mighty ruler of the kingdom, once got lost while hunting in the forest. Exhausted and famished, he stumbled upon a humble hut where an elderly woman lived. She took pity on the weary king and offered him a simple meal of boiled beans, known as "benda kalu" in the local tongue. The king, unaccustomed to such plain fare, found it more delicious than any feast he had enjoyed in his palace. To show his gratitude for the woman's kindness and the delicious beans that had saved him, King Veera Ballala named the area *Benda Kalu Ooru*—the "town of boiled beans." Though only a legend, the tale shows how a humble act of kindness (even just offering a bowl of beans) can mean more to someone in need than the greatest of riches. The flavors we savor most are not always the fanciest, but those that nourish the soul.

REDISCOVERING SIMPLICITY

As I explored Bangalore, I was struck by the poverty surrounding me. Despite their humble means, the people seemed content with what little they had. I found their ability to embrace life's simplicity beautifully inspiring, and I began to reflect on my own way of living.

We live in a materialistic world that values possessions over presence. But do we truly need all the things we collect? I've never understood the frenzied shopping, excessive feasts, and mindless consumerism of gift-giving holidays in the Western world, like Christmas. The spirit of Christmas has become the spirit of overindulgent "shopaholism." To me, the greatest gift is acceptance and loving each other as we are.

The words *woke* and *spirituality* have seemingly become "dirty" words, triggering an almost allergic reaction in many. What was once simply about raising consciousness and awareness now feels tainted by negativity. "Woke culture" has become toxic, and a label for anything deemed too progressive or liberal. Those being actively aware and attentive to significant issues, particularly those relating to racial and social justice, are now often ridiculed. Meanwhile, spirituality gets a bad rap and is shunned by many as some flaky, pseudo-religious fad. It's a shame how awareness and enlightenment have become so politicized and polarizing.

For some, "spirituality" conjures images of mysticism, new age crystals, or a joyless existence devoid of worldly pleasures. But true spirituality is far from the esoteric stereotype. It is simply the pursuit of meaning, purpose, and connection with something larger than oneself. A spiritual life is about living mindfully, consciously, and with compassion. It is not antithetical to happiness or enjoyment. In fact, spirituality can enhance our capacity for fulfillment. When we cultivate inner peace, we become less attached to the ephemeral. We gain perspective on what truly matters. Spirituality is a journey toward understanding ourselves, others, and the sublime. Rather than something to avoid, it is a wellspring of insight and vitality. Spirituality deserves an open mind, not closed doors. It deepens life's richness for those brave enough to explore it.

Perhaps we need to get back to the pure meaning behind these concepts of wokeness and spirituality: keeping an open mind, uplifting others, and seeing all humans as spiritual brothers and sisters. There's nothing dirty about wanting equality, acceptance, love, justice, and inner peace for all. If we can move beyond the egos, toxicity, and "allergies," maybe we can have an honest dialogue about the issues that really matter.

Happiness is an inside job. When we cultivate inner peace and embrace each moment as it comes, life flows much more heartily—like a scoop of beautifully smooth, heavenly, cucumber and vanilla-flavored ice cream on a hot summer's day. But without that inner connection—and by living from the outside in rather than from the inside out, with the ego firmly in place—life can feel jagged, like a thorny popsicle made of chunks of hardened rocky road. The choice is ours: do we savor the present or freeze up around it? By living consciously and finding joy within, every day can be a delicious new experience.

Bangalore helped me rediscover the beauty of simplicity. Then again, I have never cared for having many earthly possessions, and I live in a rather basic way, knowing that when my time comes to drop my worn-out physical body, memories and experiences are all I'll take on my journey homebound. Too much stuff clutters the space, and thus the mind. I believe that the less with have, the clearer the mind, and the easier it is to breathe through the journey of life. (Of course, the choice is yours. If you choose to remain in the slurped-up cyclone of that 3-D reality, doused with the illusion of fear and the material, tone-deaf to what truly matters, then by all means, live according to that disassociated frequential timbre). In some ways, my sparse surroundings let me cherish each moment, unencumbered by the material. Life's meaning isn't found in things, but in how we touch each other along the way.

As my Guides say, *"Be more consciously spiritual to understand the material, for merely living in the status quo of the material leaves one but rather dainty and superficial in the spiritual. Humanity often accumulates so much coal, coughing in the dis-ease of their 'tainted' selves, forgetting to uncover the accumulated dust of the gem that is the light within their own souls."*

GAU: GENTLE TEACHERS AND HEALERS

Cows, called "gau" in Sanskrit, roamed freely around Bangalore, grazing on sparse patches of grass and picking through piles of garbage for scraps. Despite the less-than-ideal conditions, the animals seemed unbothered by the crowds and noise, blissfully going about their day. Seeing the poor, neglected state of some of these cows broke my heart. Bones protruding from their ragged hides, they still retained an inherent dignity and grace. They are such peaceful, nurturing souls, possessing wisdom we humans often lack. I just wanted to hug them and give them the appreciation they deserved. Perhaps the temples that take them in understand what gentle teachers they can be to the human spirit.

In the West, cows are viewed through a more utilitarian lens, and valued mostly for their meat and milk. The contrast speaks to a fundamental difference in how life is regarded in the East and West. To the Hindu, the cow embodies the giving spirit of Mother Earth. For others, cows represent little more than hamburgers and steak. When I look into the eyes of a cow, I see a soul that, like ours, emanates from the divine.

Have you ever wanted to find Krishna? Look no further than a cow! Gopastami, or the "Cow Holiday," celebrates the day when Krishna and his brother became cowherders. On this magical day, cows are treated like royalty. People decorate them with flowers, say prayers to them, and shower them with gifts—all in hopes that the cows will bring prosperity into their lives. After all, cows are where Krishna resides. By honoring these gentle bovines on Gopastami, people connect with Krishna's loving presence. If you're seeking Krishna, seek out a cow. Tend to her with care, appreciate her divine nature, and you just may find Krishna smiling back at you.

The Vedas, ancient Hindu scriptures, encourage vegetarianism. They say abstaining from meat brings great rewards. Cows are considered sacred in India, not to be worshipped, but to be protected for their practical benefits. They hold an exalted status in Hindu religion. Their place in Hinduism traces back centuries, to a time when these docile beasts plowed fields and gave milk—providing essential, life-giving service. To harm or kill a cow would be unthinkable. These gentle creatures are still seen as God's gift, providing nourishing milk, cheese and yogurt. Even their dung has value. When dried, it serves as a fuel source in households, ghee oil for lamps, and keeps flies at bay (unlike human stool, which does the exact opposite). Burning it creates a mosquito-repelling smoke. Cow dung is used in religious rituals too, and applied as a tilak mark on the forehead. Since cows give so much, their lives are precious. Killing one for food means losing a provider. The Vedas inspired India's tradition of cow protection and vegetarianism. Reverence for cattle arose from gratitude for all they offer humanity.

The ancient, healing science of Ayurveda has long revered the curative properties of cow urine. Dating back thousands of years, Ayurvedic texts like the *Charaka Samhita* (written and revised by Maharishi Charaka, known as the "father of medicine," and possibly dating back from the 2nd to the 6th century BCE), describe how this unlikely elixir can improve health and wellbeing. While it may seem unconventional, cow urine contains a treasure trove of vitamins, minerals, and other nutrients that can nourish us from the inside out. Studies show cow urine can lift depression, calm the mind, slow aging, and strengthen the brain and heart. Cancer patients have experienced benefits, as have those seeking help with weight loss, cholesterol, memory, liver function, colds, headaches, thyroid issues, constipation, acne, and eczema.

This practice of "cowpathy" continues today, with people worldwide discovering the soothing, restorative effects of cow urine. Cow urine and blood have been used in traditional medicine for centuries, revered for their healing properties. According to ancient wisdom passed down through generations, cow urine contains Pran Shakti—the vital life force energy in yogic philosophy that governs all bodily functions. *Prana* represents the breath of life, while *Shakti* relates to feminine creative power. Cow blood was seen as an elixir capable of curing even the most stubborn diseases. The forefathers spoke of its incredible Pran Shakti, attributing near-mystical healing virtues.

While modern medicine may not fully endorse these historical claims, the cultural legacy remains strong. For centuries, cow urine and blood have been integral to traditional medicinal practices and tied to concepts of primal energy and the Sacred Feminine. Their use continues today, a testament to the enduring wisdom of the ancestors.

As we drove down the dusty road, an astonishing sight met my eyes—endless rows of chicken coops stretched as far as I could see. Rows of cages were stacked high, each containing a live chicken that could be purchased on the spot. It was peculiar yet fascinating to see the chickens peering out from their cages, awaiting an unknown fate. It was a bit unsettling to me to see them in their cages. It looked like an endless along the road 'marketplace' of poultry, with hundreds of clucking birds ready to be purchased on the spot by hungry customers. I couldn't look away from the rows and rows of feathers fluttering behind metal bars. It was a like a live conveyor belt of chickens destined for dinner plates. I was reminded of the time I visited a Chinese family in Seremban, Malaysia, and met their chicken farmer grandmother. At first it was endearing to see her lovingly tend to her backyard chickens. That is, until she calmly chose one, swiftly chopped off its head, and declared chicken was on the menu. I stood speechless as the headless chicken manically flapped about in its last throes before crumpling lifeless to the ground. Though it was only a fleeting moment, the distress of that chicken's abrupt end was seared into my young mind. Of course, I understand it is the cycle of life, but as a child it was a traumatic peek into the reality of farm-to-table. Even today, I feel a twinge of sadness when I recall those chickens stacked in cages, their destiny resting in the hands of those that bought them.

A CULTURE OF COMPASSION

As we continued traveling through Bangalore, I saw a curious sight: little children being bathed at the roadside. My colleague explained that water is scarce here, arriving for just a short time each day from a single pipe. The women collect their share in pots which they carry home, balanced perfectly on their heads. This was a stark reminder of how we take simple things for granted back home. Turn on any tap, anytime, and out flows a stream of clean water. Not so in this arid landscape, where every drop is precious.

We passed ramshackle huts crammed tightly together, with plastic sheets for roofs to keep the rain out. There was the occasional solid brick house in between, spacious and grand in comparison. Side by side, poverty and prosperity called this place home.

And driving in Bangalore, well, that was an adventure in itself! The half-finished roads were rough and rocky; a two-lane motorway was made into a four-way with cars, motorbikes, bicycles, and auto-rickshaws alike, all jostling for space, horns blaring in one mad chaotic dance. You'd travel faster on a bike than by car.

Many people clearly struggled just to clothe themselves. They make do with what they have and persevere with hard work; no government handouts here. The Divine Shakespeare Club whips up a witty and thought-provoking quip on the cleverly created government benefits and social welfare programs for countries that do have them. They pose the question, *"People think they benefit from benefits, but truly the benefits benefit from them, so are these benefits beneficial and actually benefitting the growth of one's soul?"* It made me reflect on how easy it can be back home to live off benefits, losing motivation and having laziness instilled within. How do we progress when we remain as we are? While benefits provide a crucial safety net for those in genuine need, on the flip side they're just a fancy name for some soul-stunting con, a cozy trap that stifles our spirit. Here, people strive each day just to survive—powerful reminder that progress takes grit and graft. We're on this journey to really live, to find joy in all we do and to awaken the flame of our spirits within. It is time to make our lives count, rather than just drifting aimlessly. As my Guides have always said, "If you don't do life, life will do you. You can sit and wait for an eternity for things to magically happen, or you can get up and unleash the magic within to make things happen, the choice is yours."

I really admired the people and culture of Bangalore; they touched my soul with their resilience and compassion. Despite their humble means, they work each day to put food on the table and keep a roof over their head. Neighbors lend a helping hand not because they're friends, but because it's the right thing to do. A deeper sense of awareness lives within them—they know we're all kindred spirits on this journey, no matter our status. Their selfless acts and open hearts warmed my own. We'd do well to follow their lead, to appreciate the blessings we have and to extend kindness to others, rather than buying into false divisions. For in the end, we're all cut from the same cloth. When we live from the heart, as these folks do, we just may heal this fractured world.

CHAPTER 3
LORD DIVYA KRISHNA

I LOVE KRISHNA, BUT WHO exactly is this blue-hued wonder, spreading joy like sunshine peeking through the clouds? Even as a child in the 1980s, flipping through my father's book in Kuala Lumpur, I was captivated by the images of the blue man playing the flute, oozing nothing but playfulness and joy. Though life may often serve up cloudy meatballs stuffed with challenges, Krishna reminds us to reach deep within, see our experiences with humor, and find that happiness that we have tucked so far away.

I have channeled Krishna on numerous occasions, and you cannot help but feel giddy in his infectious energy, for he truly ignites this within your soul. He says, *"Stop running! Take a breath, breathe, and relax, laughing through the idiocrasy of the created cinematic dramas you have spun inside your beautiful mind. Ah, is it not just sheer madness how one concocts the world within conjuring la vie grande without? Rather, my Child, reach inside, and uncover your inner happy you've kept hidden under lock and key in a treasure chest, somewhere in the archived parlors of your compartmentalized mind."*

Like a ray of sunshine on a gloomy day, Krishna's presence sparks up your soul in absurdly sweet ways. He reminds us we have the power to transcend whatever we go through in life and to choose joy! Why take life so seriously? Life's too short to spend it frowning and worrying, and to live with the many swirling "what ifs" that crowd the mind. Dance and play your flute like Krishna, laugh through the cosmic comedy of life, and savor all your experiences like a decadent bite of chocolate bliss! Every day is a sweet surprise filled with creamy caramel moments, dark chocolate drama, and nutty adventures. Go ahead, take a bite out of life's candy coating and let the smooth, rich flavors of your experiences melt in your mouth. This wild ride is packed with sugary peaks and bittersweet valleys, so savor each morsel as you unwrap all that life has to offer. With its endless assortment of tasty treats, life is a chocolate lover's paradise just waiting to be devoured.

LORD DIVYA KRISHNA

"I AM Lord Divya Krishna, one of the Arcturian Council of Supreme Light.

A Ray of the Sun God and of the Supreme BEing, Vishnu.

I AM the Lord of Light, of joy, and of happiness, reflecting and refracting these like iridescent light particles within the loving space of your blossoming kaleidoscopic essence of a butterfly heart.

I AM the Master Healer to the hidden inner child within and a brother in arms to the Great White Brotherhood.

I AM the duality to your darkness, carrying but a torch and a pendulum of hope.

I AM a hierophant and a sage of sacred ancient wisdom.

Where I was, and where I AM now, is no different to where I started and to what I have become and am still becoming, for like you, I AM a drop in the vast ocean of pure God consciousness, each wave an octave to reaching higher dimensional frequencies of that divine illumination.

For I AM, and I remain, a cosmo-naut of the principles of all expansive matters, dancing but fluticiously a la musica to the tune of my own harmonic cosmic flute.

I AM a spark to the Source of All, as much as you are a spark from that same Source, plugged within the embodiment of the zipped-up physical.

You are made of the clay of the earth and made of the stars in the masterfully created eclectic celestial heavens, creating a symphony of the atomic stardust particles in the given hue-man embodiment.

You have to awaken the inner sleeping giant of your enraptured mind through the nurturing of the divine heart space within, to awaken the spark of awareness into seeing the beauty of all in the outer world.

You have cocooned yourself so much into this sugar spun, pink cotton candy floss, you have forgotten to live through the beauty of the space *of the heart, having become drunk on the 3-D sugar drizzle that has intoxicated your mind, and thus the bubble of your created reality that you have so duly manifested, having lost all sense of self. It is often the mind that has been eagerly overfed with these worldly, tripe, bite-sized, hallucinogenic party nuggets, that one has become high on the illusion of what life is supposed to be, which in reality, is but merely an illusion and thus one has been had. What you believe to be true is merely a perception of your pertained reality.*

I am the demon slayer to your rattled caged joy

Unleashing the torrent that has kept you imprisoned in the fear of your own walls.

I am the joy to your very own concocted and created 'rain on my parade' of heaviness.

The laughter to your many shed tears that have rolled down your beautiful cheeks.

A cornerstone to your squirrely, deeply buried, and innate wisdom.

The light to your cloaked soul of having shrouded the mind in darkness.

And I will always be the sun to the warmth of your heart, thawing the experiences that have kept your mind iced in sub-zero temperatures, allowing you to see the light of day, through the reflective rays of change duly reflected within.

Call on me to bring back music to thy wayward Mind that has inhibited thy Soul

To sing, laugh and dance with the rhythm of thy true nature, surrendering to the embrac-ed soul of the you in YOU, bringing out thy inner child of playfulness.

Be present in the moment, for conscious creating on a 'soul-lular' level, allows for the molecular god particles within your body and within your energy field to move and shake those sleepy atoms like shakin' those salt 'n pepper shakers, creating the imagined-in-your-mind dreams into the musical symphony of blowing life into manifesting your creations.

In other words, my Child, you are an atomic god particle within the seas of consciousness, and what you decide to do with the Power of the I AM atom that you are is entirely up to you.

All the I AM in You is the You in the I AM of Me

And through the cycles of rebirth, experiences become moot and a breeze to walk, for lightness in thy step is the key to the quickening of one's evolution, a la carte of one's chosen experiences on the menu of life in that welcoming restaurant called Earth.

Remember that life is a blessing, a wondrous journey and you, my Child, are a cosmic spark of eternal consciousness, ascending to a crescendo of ever spiraling new heights.

Remain not on the going round in circles of a merry 3-D carrousel, getting lost and confused by the repetitive imagery imprinted upon the mind.

Hop off, catch your breath, shaking hands with the unhealed demons, walking the journey to your own spiritual nirvana.

Always see the joy, in all that you do.

Be that joy and feel that joy.

Laugh at life's little ironies, and relish each moment like a spoonful of "vanilicious" honey heaven. Every day's an adventure if you sprinkle a little fun on top. With a carefree spirit and playful heart, you'll find life as sweet as a chocolate, hot fudge-drizzled sundae. Dig in!

Be blessed, feel blessed, live blessed, for thou art blessed.

Faithfully I remain, a humble servant of a return to the joy of the bless-ed self."

—*Lord Divya Krishna*

CHAPTER 4
MANTRAS

YOU WILL FIND VARIOUS mantras throughout this book. Let the soothing rhythm of the mantras wash over you like the warm ocean waves. Feel the calming vibrations resonate deep within as you chant these powerful phrases. Imbue each syllable with positive intention—let this be your guide. Mantras are simple, yet profound. They open the channels to higher states of awareness and align you with the energetic flow of the cosmos.

Much like the *I AM* and *Violet Flame* invocations by the Ascended Master St. Germain, mantras elevate our frequency. These exercises are simple yet powerful, turning negative vibes into positive ones and transforming the energies within our auric field. Modern science confirms what the ancients knew all along: the sound and language of mantras can profoundly influence our mind, body and spirit.

So, ride the cosmic waves through the power of a mantra. Let the repetitive melodies open your consciousness to new depths of inner peace, clarity, and lightness of being, and feel yourself becoming one with the universal flow.

The most famous mantra is probably "Om," or "Aum," also written in Sanskrit as ॐ, meant to be said slowly and out loud. This is done by taking a deep inhale for eight counts and then chanting it on the exhale for eight counts. The vibration represents the original sound of the universe. *A* symbolizes creation, *U* represents manifestation, and *M* refers to destruction. Om resonates at 432 Hz, assisting in harmonizing our energy with that of the earth and nature. Chanting aligns us with the cosmos, alleviating stress and negativity. Om is the whole universe consolidated into a single sound, unifying body, mind, and spirit. Let its gentle hum draw you inward to your center. Feel the vibration connect you to all of creation.

Let us turn our minds to the sacred, ancient Buddhist mantra, "Om Mani Padme Hum," or the "Praise to the Jewel in the Lotus." Below, the phrase is written in Tibetan:

ཨོཾ་མ་ཎི་པདྨེ་ཧཱུྃ

Om is the sound of the universe, the vibration of creation connecting us to the cosmos.
Ma instils morals, freeing the heart from envy's grasp.
Ni cultivates patience, releasing these clinging wants and desires.
Pad sparks diligence, dispelling ignorance and judgement.
Me focuses the mind, and helps us let go of attachments.
Hum unifies all, embodying wisdom that liberates us from hatred's bonds.

Sure, muttering mystical mumbo jumbo may seem silly at first (like you're speaking a language only goats can grasp), but slap me thrice and call me Namaste—truth be told, a lotus blossoms within us all! Inside every petal of our souls hides an enlightened little gem, a glowing glimmer ready to make our hearts soar and giggle. I dare you to get chanting. Let that ancient Om Mani Padme Hum roll off your tongue, and make your inner light chuckle.

With each Om Mani Padme Hum, visualize your heart opening like a laughing flower, its jewel center sending tickling beams of wisdom and self-love through your whole being. Let your inner lotus bloom and soon you'll be grinning at the glimmer within. Om Mani Padme

Hum—praise the truth that dwells in all of us, waiting to fill our lives with beauty and laughter!

Each mantra syllable rings with transformative potential, guiding the spirit to enlightenment. By chanting these sacred sounds, we tap into divine wells of peace, compassion and bliss.

KRISHNA MANTRAS

Below, you will find some simple mantras for Krishna. It does not matter how many times you chant them or when you choose to, as long as you do so with intention (not half-arsed!). My father always used to say, chant the same thing twenty-eight days in a row. Tradition states to get up at the crack of dawn, because the mantra magic happens between 4 a.m. and 6 a.m. For the desired effect to take place, repeat your chosen mantra 108 times. To avoid losing count, grab a tulsi mala—those handy prayer bead thingies you may have seen before—and *ommmm* to your heart's content. Send that positive energy out into the universe and, like a proverbial boomerang, it will jolly well bounce back to you. Connect with your inner Krishna and become one with the cosmic consciousness!

Changing our mindset is kind of like going to the mental gym; it takes time and effort to reshape our thinking. Working out in the gym is hard work, am I right? You can't just show up once and expect to look like The Rock the next day. Nope, it takes dedication and consistency to see results. But instead of bench-pressing thoughts, we're doing reps of positivity. And rather than targeting our quads, we're strengthening our optimism and flexibility. So why not take ten to fifteen minutes each day to pump up those mental muscles? Flex that inner motivation to break out of the stale thinking patterns you may find yourself lost in. Let those feel-good endorphins flow through the dusty corners of your mind, breathing life into dried-up perspectives. Release the heaviness of doubt and negativity, and return to that state of joy and lightness.

With consistent mental workouts, you'll gradually reshape your mindset. Don't expect an overnight six-pack abs of wisdom, but know that over time, and if you are willing to put in the effort, you will see results. Flex those inner stagnant particles that have had you set in your ways of thinking, allowing the rivers of energy to move and flow through the dried-up river beds of your mind. Release the heaviness and return to a state of joy. Lace up those mental sneakers and get ready to elevate your outlook, one rep at a time!

The most well-known Krishna mantra is, "Hare Krishna Hare Krishna, Krishna Krishna Hare Hare. Hare Rāma Hare Rāma Rāma Rāma Hare Hare." The spiritual sound vibration this mantra creates nourishes the inner-self. Personally, this mantra doesn't do much for me, but what resonates with one does not have to resonate with another.

I've had my run-ins with Hare Krishnas on the streets in Holland and the UK. With their orange robes swishing, tambourines jangling, and chants filling the air, they make quite a spectacle. But, as per my experience, beneath the display lies an often-aggressive sales pitch for their Bhagavad Gita. I found them rather pushy, which put me off. Still, they've got nothing on the fire-and-brimstone Christian Street preachers I've encountered. Armed with their microphones and Bibles, these zealots accost passerby with shrill warnings of sin and damnation. "Only through accepting Jesus," they scream, "can one enter the kingdom of heaven." I tend to give these fanatics a wide berth to avoid their ranting, politely declining their pamphlets when approached.

In the end, I think these public displays of faith have more to do with how the preachers feel within themselves than any true attempt at outreach. The street becomes their stage as they act out their inner turmoil, less concerned with making converts or saving souls, and more concerned with reaffirming their own shaky beliefs. Much like the door-to-door "evangelical salespeople" who aim to keep their existing customers in line, not necessarily win new ones. You can't scare your followers away or rather keep your followers devoted if you don't remind them of hell every now and then.

Hare Krishna Hare Krishna, Krishna Krishna Hare Hare. Hare Rama Hare Rama, Rama Rama Hare Hare. I often heard my father recite this infectious chant. I too have chanted it at holistic workshops, but as earlier stated, it never really vibed with my soul; not all are enchanted by its mystical allure. The Hare Krishna mantra has permeated popular culture with its catchy tune and unmistakable lilt. The beauty of mantras is that their power comes from resonance, not doctrine. What enchants one heart may leave another utterly untouched. The Hare Krishna melody's transformative potential differs for each listener.

Krishna Mantra for Success
Om Sri Krishnah sharanam mamah

I love this simple mantra, and whether you choose to sing it or speak is entirely up to you. As Krishna says, *"It is a powerful cleansing agent, a rub-me-on detox agent, clearing the encapsulated pockets of toxins you have garnered within the dry creeks of your mind, leaving you in a state of misery and limited beliefs. Call on me to help alleviate the heaviness and to see the lighter side of life."*

Krishna Gayatri Mantra
Aum Devkinandanaye Vidmahe Vasudevaye
Dhi-Mahi Tanno Krishna Prachodayat

The Gayatri mantra packs a punch when it comes to spinning negatives into positives. This tricky tongue-twister of a mantra will have you feeling like a superhero as you chant your way to a sunnier outlook on life. So, dust off your cape, settle into your power stance, and get ready to chant yourself from gloom to gleam! Give this mantra a whirl and spin those frowns upside down.

As Krishna says, *"A mantra for those that have fallen out of love with themselves, to rejuvenate, replenish, and lift the fugue of the tired and over-*

run mind, that has gotten you in a state of imbalance, having taken its toll on you, leaving you in a taxing state of affairs with oneself. Is life not a return to a love for oneself, returning home to the bliss of one's inner blowing bubbles and bluebells of joy, allowing for these magical musical notes of happiness to trickle into all areas of one's life, rather than remaining in a sheer dis-ease and state of despondency? Life is about creative thinking, not about creating a problem to every solution."

CHAPTER 5
THE ART OF LIVING CENTER

After several grueling hours on the road, we finally rolled up to the ashram. My legs were jelly and my butt was numb from bouncing around on those rocky roads; if I'd had a bike, I surely so would have gotten there sooner. To make matters worse, between the crazy turbulence on the flights here and navigating the chaos of Bangalore, I was feeling a little light in the head.

In sharp contrast to my previous leg of the journey, the ashram was an oasis of zen. No trash, no stench, no noise—just peaceful vibes. The beautifully landscaped gardens were straight out of a postcard, pumping out the most intoxicating floral scents: sweet, spicy, woodsy...... my nose was on a magic carpet ride. They say smells can bring back memories, and I swear every whiff took me on a mind vacation.

As is custom in India, upon entering the reception area I was politely asked to remove my shoes. The area was basic yet tidy, with photos of Sri Sri Ravi Shankar and the *Art of Living Center* plastered on every wall. I filled out some forms, forked out 150 USD for the Basic Course (which they calculated using the local pricing of the country you reside in, called the "domestic green grass policy"), and was handed a room key and map. My new home was in the creatively named Nandi Building. They also gave me a list of house rules: lights out at 11 p.m. sharp, clean up after yourself, and return all linens and blankets when leaving the center. This was going to be an interesting stay.

My room was located in a different time zone from the reception desk. After schlepping my overstuffed, nearly sixty-pound suitcase up countless stone stairs (thank you work-out sessions), I finally arrived at my room, sweaty and gasping for breath. Alas, the padlock combo they gave me didn't work, so I had to hoof it all the way back downstairs to get a new one.

When I finally got inside, "basic" seemed to be an overstatement. We're talking two rickety bed frames with mattresses thinner than my paycheck. The "pillow" was really just a folded napkin. There were more holes in the walls than a slice of Swiss cheese. It was clear they hadn't quite finished building this room yet. There was no TV and no radio, just the sweet sounds of nature coming through those handy wall holes. Oh, and they left candles in case the power went out, but no matches to light them. Real smart.

No smoking or drinking was allowed on the premises. This was a given, seeing we were on the grounds of an ashram to change and improve our lives, not leave pollution and remain stuck like a broken record within our old programming. The cupboards were bare except for a few spiders. At least there was a bathroom (albeit with a not-so-legit toilet and shower) rather one of those wretched "squatty potties." You can't even sit on those suckers—enough said. The shower area consisted of a little shower hose, not to be used for drinking water, as the locals use this for a post-potty rinse. In layman terms, we use toilet paper and they use a water hose.

Overall, my accommodations were not exactly the Ritz, but trust me, I've stayed in worse over the years. I don't mind, as long as I have a pillow to lay my head on to sleep. A little incense helped mask the smell of mildew. I told myself it also added to the authentic ashram experience. Namaste!

Instead of unpacking, I caught up with Subramanyam and followed him to the main and Annapurna dining hall, built to serve up to 3,000 hungry souls. I felt like I'd stepped into a boisterous temple of flavor as I gazed upon the crowds sitting cross-legged, scooping up mouthwatering curries and stews with their bare hands. This was Indian dining at its authentic best. They served three meals a day: breakfast, lunch and dinner. Indian food is generally meant to be eaten with the hands, and Indian foods such as dosa, roti, and chapati (types of thin, cooked dough, sort of like pancakes or flat bread) are eaten with the fingers and usually dipped in a vegetable curry. The cuisine reminded me of my days at Sayfol Schools in Kuala Lumpur, Malaysia. Here, too, some mornings we were served chapatti with vegetable curry. I loved it, except for the dreaded papaya. I could never stomach its sickly-sweet stench, which reminded me of vomit. Even though the teachers would come round to make sure we ate our meals, I'd either give my slice of papaya to someone else, or cover it with a napkin and then quietly walk to the bins, dumping it and scurrying off down the stairs.

Eating in India is a full sensory experience. Sight, smell, touch, taste—all the senses get a workout. I noticed that the locals only used their right hand for eating, and I learned that the left hand is reserved for serving food or passing dishes. These folks took dining etiquette seriously.

I was offered a refreshing glass of buttermilk, but one whiff of that sour, curdled stench was enough to make me gag. I'm not a fan of milk, unless it's piping hot and drowning in my cereal. They say buttermilk (the liquid leftover after churning butter out of cream) is supposed to be some kind of health elixir. People claim it tastes just like yogurt, but let me tell you, after bravely dipping my finger ever so slightly into this weird concoction, my tastebuds begged to differ. That rancid, gag-inducing buttermilk was disgustingly sour, nothing at all like the sweet tang of yogurt. No thank you! It's a churned disaster best avoided by the spoonful.

Traditionally, Indians don't drink alcohol. It's just not culturally accepted in most parts. No booze or cigarettes were allowed at mealtimes. If you broke this rule, you'd be slapped with a severe warning. But I didn't need any liquid courage to enjoy the feast of flavors. My right hand was busy enough scooping up delicacies with naan!

Having grown up in Malaysia, eating with my hands was as normal as breathing to me. However, sitting cross-legged on the floor on a thin mat wasn't so easy, especially with my long, gangly legs. My knees jutted up sharply as I struggled to fold myself into a neat little pretzel. But the discomfort was worth it for this authentic ashram experience. When my colleague plopped a heaping plate of curry down in front of me, I dove in. The spices immediately attacked my tastebuds like a hoard of angry fire ants. The food itself wasn't half bad, aside from the face-melting spices. My stomach can't handle spicy food—it makes me a frequent flyer to the loo.

Once we finished our dinner, we dumped the leftovers in the designated blue bins. Then, we proceeded to a remarkable sight—not just one sink, but six sinks, all filled with water. To our delight, two of these sinks were equipped with organic soap, ensuring a gentle and eco-friendly cleansing experience. With great care, we washed the trays, diligently scrubbing away the remnants of curry and rice mush that had become stubbornly stuck. Finally, we rinsed the trays in the remaining four sinks, leaving them sparkling clean and ready for their next use. I'm used to cleaning up after myself. It may not be glamorous to some, but it's part of the deal when you want an authentic experience.

Years later, many independent reviewers and bloggers have praised the ashram's meals, describing them as a warm hug for the body and soul. These dishes, rooted in Indian culinary traditions, enhance both meditation and spiritual journeys. Today, the ashram also offers a diverse array of international options, ensuring every palate is satisfied.

The ashram stay was shaping up to be quite the adventure, even with the uncomfortable legs and molten mouth, but I had a feeling there were many more challenges and laughs to come.

THE ART OF LIVING CENTER

After dinner, we ventured to the Vishalakshi Mantapa, a marvel of ancient architecture and design. A magnificent five-story structure, it rose up 108 feet into the night sky. Eighty-one ornate pillars support its domed ceilings, leading the eye upward to an impressive fifteen-foot kalasha perched on top. These metal spires were traditionally placed atop temples and buildings in Ancient India, and meant to absorb the cosmic energy from the heavens above. As this spiritual force flows through the kalasha and into the building below, it blesses all those who gather within for prayer and meditation. Walking through the Vishalakshi Mantapa, one can't help but feel a sense of wonder at its grand scale and mystical purpose. The soaring heights transport you back through centuries to a time when architecture was imbued with sacred geometry and intent.

Stepping into the ancient hall, the building took my breath away. As I gazed upward, the ceiling blossomed with intricate, pink-hued lotus petals carved out of stone (known as "the thousand-petalled lotus"). Each petal contained a zodiac symbol, and Hindu deities danced across the walls. It was truly a marvel to behold.

The day suddenly caught up with me, and I realized I was exhausted. The heaviness of my eyelids soon betrayed me, and I found myself nodding off where I stood. After scarcely an hour, I walked back to my modest monk quarters, wanting to get some sleep. I unpacked the necessary things, but *yowza*—upon closer inspection of the room, I realized it had not been properly cleaned. It was like a dust bunny family reunion in there. The "hairy" floor hadn't seen a mop since the Stone Age. I cannot for the life of me sleep in dirt. My space needs to be clean so I can breathe. I dropped to my hands and knees, armed with my dispensable washcloth, and I scrubbed away the grime until the tiles on the floor were clean. My back was aching, but cleanliness is next to having that lightened enlightened mind, right?

A shower was next, to rinse the sweat and dirt from my skin. I hopped in the shower, turned the knob and... ice water! I shrieked, but decided to hold my breath and brave the cold temperatures for the quickest shower imaginable. Finally clean, yet shivering like a wet pup, I collapsed onto the paper-thin mattress, which felt about as cozy as a wooden table. Thankfully, there was one anti-mosquito plug in the room, which secured me for a "good" night's sleep. My training started at the crack of dawn, so I welcomed the rest, though it was far from peaceful.

After the first few restless, back-aching nights, I adjusted to the modest lodgings. I guess you could say that hardship is the price to finding enlightenment. This was all just seasoning for the soul, or, at least that's what I told myself as I drifted off to sleep each night, dreaming of my soft bed back home. I did tell the receptionist that the water was colder than the Arctic. Several days later, they claimed to have "fixed" it, but the only time I would be able to get a lukewarm shower was between 5 and 7 a.m. Fat chance of that happening! And even within that time frame, it was about as hot as a penguin's bath water. Thank goodness I brought my disposable washcloths with me, or I would've looked like I just crawled out of the sandbox. I used the cloths to wash my skin, and only stuck my head under the icy tap to wash my hair. After a while, I got used to the cold water. Thankfully, years later the Art of Living Centre installed hot water so guests can now enjoy a warm shower.

Furthermore, the ashram has undergone significant improvements to its facilities, while still maintaining a strong emphasis on simplicity and spiritual purpose over luxury. The fundamental principle of living simply is highly valued here, upheld by committed volunteers who demonstrate a deep commitment to service.

CHAPTER 6
GURUDEV SRI SRI RAVI SHANKAR

"Fear is lack of love. Only one thing can eliminate fear and that is love."

—*Sri Sri Ravi Shankar*

I WANT TO INTRODUCE YOU to the founder of the Art of Living Center, Sri Sri Ravi Shankar—or as his followers affectionately call him, Guruji. His wisdom and teachings are woven throughout my own story of visiting India, but who exactly is this mystical figure?

Born in Southern India in 1956, Sri Sri Ravi Shankar's journey began humbly, yet his message of inner peace and service has spread worldwide. His spiritual journey commenced at the tender age of four. His teachers were gobsmacked when this young boy effortlessly recited the ancient Hindu scripture, the *Bhagavad Gita*. Clearly, he was no ordinary child. Under the tutelage of his first teacher, Pandit Sudhakar Chaturvedi, a close associate of Mahatma Gandhi, Sri Sri's wisdom grew far beyond his years. He immersed himself in the study of Vedic literature while also pursuing a degree in modern science, straddling spirituality and rationality with ease. His quest for knowledge then led him to the renowned Maharishi Mahesh Yogi, pioneer of transcendental meditation. Transcendental meditation aims to help one reach a state of inner peace and pure consciousness through silent Sanskrit mantra repetition and deep meditation.

The Art of Living Center was founded in 1981 and over the decades, Sri Sri Ravi Shankar has been honored with accolades across the globe for his spiritual leadership and humanitarian work. He has received the highest civilian awards of Mongolia, Paraguay, Guatemala, and Colombia, along with India's prestigious Padma Vibhushan award. Sixteen international institutions have granted him honorary doctorates. For a man who began his life's work at four years old, it has been an incredible journey, yet he remains utterly humble to all that cross his path. Through meditation, yoga, and inspirational talks, he guides millions to discover their highest potential. Revered as a spiritual master, Sri Sri's gentle presence and sparkling eyes radiate an inner light. His infectious joy and acceptance touch all who cross his path.

Sri Sri Ravi Shankar illuminates the path to inner peace and joy. As a spiritual leader, he inspires us to embrace our shared humanity and awaken to the divinity within. He has inspired millions around the globe with a vision of a stress-free, violence-free world. His teachings reveal the beauty of our existence when we let our inner Krishna play freely in the earthly fields of life. Stress and violence melt away as we connect to the wholeness underlying our illusion of separation.

In India, Sri Sri has united people across traditions and faiths, evoking a unifying light not seen since Mahatma Gandhi. His message still rings clear today: together we can achieve so much more; by uplifting our communities as one, we uplift our world.

We are all One, yet we believe ourselves to be separate from the whole. In truth, that is an improbability, merely created by that wonderful feature called the mind. Sri Sri beams the light of our connectedness. Through his grace, we find inner fulfilment and spread peace.

For over thirty years, Sri Sri Ravi Shankar's Art of Living Foundation has brought transformative programs to prisoners around the world. From India to the U.S., Europe, South America, South Africa, and Russia, the Art of Living has helped over 700,000 inmates rediscover their inherent goodness. Instead of perpetuating cycles of violence and self-loathing, prisoners learn techniques like yoga, meditation, and breathing exercises to gain serenity and self-control.

Rather than punishment, the Art of Living emphasizes rehabilitation. In Denmark, judges now send juvenile offenders to Art of Living workshops instead of sentencing them to jail time. Sri Sri has also pioneered recreational activities like music, theatre, and dance to engage inmates' creativity. Vocational programs provide valuable skills for life after release. With Sri Sri's encouragement, prisoners have started production units in select jails to gain a sense of purpose.

Most inspiringly, the Art of Living has rehabilitated 4,500 former insurgents and extremists. Through trauma relief workshops and vocational skill training, these once-violent individuals have discovered nonviolent ways to improve their lives. After three decades of humanitarian service, the Art of Living continues bringing light into the darkness of the prison system worldwide.

I think it is so amazing to see the incredible work Sri Sri has done to uplift communities and help people overcome addiction. Through the 5H Program, which focuses on Health, Hygiene, Homes, Human Values, and Harmony in Diversity, Sri Sri has empowered thousands to break free from drugs, alcohol, and other substances. From the villages of India to the streets of the U.S., Mongolia, and Bahrain, people have been deeply touched by Sri Sri's compassionate wisdom and found the strength to let go of dependencies that once chained them. Domestic violence has decreased as more find inner peace by releasing their pain. It is a beautiful sight to see lives transformed, families reunited, and communities healed. Sri Sri's initiatives spark hope in the darkest of circumstances. His work is a testament to the power of love and education to create positive change, even in the most challenging of times. I'm filled with admiration and awe seeing how he is making our world brighter, one step—and one person—at a time.

CHAPTER 7
THE BASIC COURSE

THE BASIC COURSE WAS a three-day, life-changing experience that transformed my outlook and daily practices. Over those three illuminating days, I dove deep into a dynamic blend of exercises, profound spiritual wisdom, and deep meditation with fellow participants. I emerged renewed, with cherished lessons that continue to guide my journey today. The insights I gained cut to the heart of what matters most. My experience was a gateway to living life more fully awake and aware. Every day I'm grateful for the profound awakening the Basic Course sparked within me.

At its core, the Art of Living is simply about living your best life. It's not a religion or cult; there's no doctrine to follow. The approach uses ancient breathing techniques to help you reduce stress, increase energy, and enhance your overall wellbeing. Developed by Sri Sri Ravi Shankar, these practices aim to tap into your inner strength and wisdom. The idea is that you can find peace and joy within, regardless of your external circumstances. Sri Sri states that all the created worldly religions can be compared to a banana skin, and that spirituality is the inner fruit of the banana itself. So, whether you choose to pray to a deity, to nature, or to just focus inward, it doesn't matter. The goal is always to connect to your true essence and realize that beneath our differences, we're all one. Through mindful breathing and meditation, you can begin to shed layers of accumulated stress, awaken your body's natural healing abilities, and align your life with your true purpose. The Art of Living simply provides the tools to help you enhance your life from the inside out. Hand on my heart, I can testify that through breathwork and inner reflection, you can discover new levels of vitality, clarity, and calm.

When considering spiritual practices and organizations, you may think of the term *guru*. But what exactly is a guru? While there are often many misconceptions, a guru is not meant to teach or "convert" you. Rather, their role is to help shed light upon the layers that cloak the light within your soul. These layers come from unhealed wounds absorbed within the haze of our pre-programmed mind. You could say gurus are here to throw light on your inner shadows and triggers, much like a torch revealing unhealed wounds you've yet to mend. As the author Landon Parham said, "Life isn't just about darkness or light, rather it's about finding light within the darkness."

So, how does the Basic Course fit into all of this? The course is a breath of fresh air in the world of personal development programs. Don't let the simplicity of its approach fool you—this course has the power to profoundly shift your consciousness if you open your mind to it. Even the biggest skeptics among us can benefit from the Basic Course if they are willing to release their preconceived notions and conditioned ways of thinking. The program encourages you to "tune out" the mind's limiting beliefs and "tune in" to the wisdom of your heart and intuition.

Rather than getting caught up in expectations (something I avoid, along with over researching), you enter with an open mind and heart, and allow the flow of your own energy to guide you in the moment. You may be surprised by the insights and "aha moments" that emerge when you suspend judgment and lean into this experiential journey of life with trust. The magic of the Basic Course is that it meets you where you are with compassion and plants seeds that can blossom into lasting transformation for how you decide to live your life.

THE BASIC COURSE

The adventure started bright and early on the first day of the course. We were up with the sunrise, which meant getting up at 5:30 a.m. and being on time for class. If you were late, chances were you would get kicked out unless you had a damn good reason. By 6:30 a.m., we had rolled out our yoga mats, ready to bend and stretch before the day's lessons. Laughter filled the room as we followed the instructor's lead, giggling through our sun salutations. Though I may go to the gym, I'm not exactly known as "Ms. Plastic-elastic." I did, however, feel energized starting the day with joy and movement.

Little did I know that after an hour of yoga filled with laughter, we would recharge with a delicious breakfast before immersing ourselves in lectures that that lasted until dusk. The compound's lights clicked off promptly at 11 p.m., although I was fast asleep by 9 p.m., allowing myself plenty of rest in preparation for another early rise.

"Once you release the potted-up genie of an alchemist you've kept hidden in plain sight out of the bottle, you create magical moments through the sheer expression of your untamed soul, as you have released the barriers of the mind that have kept you imprisoned in the conditioning of your so-called reality."

—*The Divine*

FORMING CONNECTIONS

There were forty-two participants in the Basic Course, but don't believe for one minute that it was cozy. Forget comfy chairs and tables; all we got were flat little square cushions to sit our arses on. Chairs were reserved only for those with severe health issues. Our humble learning space was right by the Vishalakshi Mantap building. Leading the charge were Sangita Gujrati, a director of the Association for Human Values, and Dr. Divya, a dentist. Most participants were of Indian descent, with only a few travelers from abroad. Besides me, the foreigners present consisted of a Russian girl, a Canadian lady, and two women from the UK.

"I belong to you, you belong to me," sang Lenny Kravitz, and that's exactly how we felt after a fun icebreaker introduction. To get to know each other, we had to get up, look each other in the eyes, say our names and where we were from, and then state, "I belong to you." At first it seemed a bit strange, but it quickly had us all laughing and chatting like old friends. The informal atmosphere helped make everyone more comfortable and allowed knowledge to begin flowing freely between us. Though an unusual exercise, it worked; we bonded as a group and got to know each other on a deeper level. I belong to you, you belong to me, and we all belong together. We're all chipped from the same block of ice, and our chipped ice crystals have landed in hue-man bodies to experience the warmth of life.

We are all 'hue-man'; we are all walking 'light-man' wandering the earth, trying to find our way back to the light within by peeling away the layers of our conditioning through the richness of our many diverse and flavorsome experiences.

Next, we were split into six groups of six and had to pick a voluntary lead. My little group was a motley bunch, and we christened ourselves the "Bollyhood Dodgers." I was chosen as the group lead, and it was my job to keep tabs on everyone and make sure we were all on time to our events and activities. All was well until I noticed a girl was missing. Her name was Renu, and she was a sweet soul who had flown in from the UK with her mother. She was battling a bad stomach bug and could barely sit still due to horrendous cramps, let alone meditate with the rest of us. I asked Dr. Divya if I could pop by her room with some crackers from Holland, thinking it might help settle her stomach so she could rejoin us the next day. But Dr. Divya said to let her be, and that rest was the best medicine. Renu was a little diamond, and I say was, because tragically, in the autumn of 2010, two years after we first met, Renu chose to end her life, freeing her beautiful soul from the constraints she felt within her physical essence. I will discuss Renu in more detail in the chapter on fear, depression and mental health, but during our brief time together, she brought a sparkle to our merry band of Dodgers.

THE BASIC COURSE

The Basic Course drew quite a mixed bag of folks. Most were engineers or students, with disciplines ranging from zoology to the liberal arts. There were also a few housewives looking to shake up their routine and retirees seeking more meaning to life. But the attendee who amazed me most was a seventy-year-old gentleman who I swore appeared to be in his early fifties! He radiated vitality. When I asked his secret, he revealed it was the Art of Living Basic and Advanced Courses he'd taken over the years. He firmly believed they kept him looking and feeling young. Clearly the courses and their teachings on breathwork had worked wonders for this inspiring septuagenarian.

The focus of the course was on mastering the art of active listening, going beyond simply hearing what others have to say. We were introduced to the three different types of listening techniques.

- **intellectual listening**, where we analyze and let others know whether we agree or not.
- **emotional listening**, where we connect through shared feelings.
- **open-minded listening**, where we drop our biases and focus on understanding and holding space for others.

I then wondered, do people actually listen like that in real life? Most of us are lost in our own heads, distracted and disengaged. We're all talk, no ears. Talking comes easily, but *true listening*, not just hearing, takes skill.

We were supposed to remember it all without taking notes. "Your brain will store the information," Dr. Divya assured us. Yeah, right. Her words went in one ear and out the other. It was like, talk-to-the-hand, because this face ain't listening.

If you think about it, life is an endless conversation. To truly connect with one another, we must learn the art of listening. When someone speaks to us, we should be fully present. Tune your senses to their words, tone, and body language. Understand their perspective with empathy. Make them feel heard. It's easy to be distracted, allowing our minds to wander or get hijacked by notifications and other devices. If you cannot be authentic with others, how can you be authentic with yourself? If you cannot listen to others and are constantly distracted, that is a direct reflection of how you treat yourself. Distractions from true listening disconnect us from others and ourselves.

You know how it is—some days at work we can be up to our eyeballs, trying to juggle ten things at once. So, when mum rings me then, I have to be straight and tell her that I am busy and will call back later when things quiet down. She's good like that, and she understands. If someone else calls me, I either ignore it or send a quick text hours later. Thankfully, I can live without my phone, unlike most folks these days. Half the time I don't even answer when that dang thing rings (on silent mode, I might add), as I am a bit of an anti-social shit bird who'd rather keep to myself. It's true, I may not be the most sociable bird in the flock, but at least I ain't peckin' at my phone 24/7 like an addict desperate for their next fix. I'll take being an oddball hermit over a "tech zombie" any day. No hard feelings, my time is precious, but I always make sure to phone my mum back once I have a free minute.

SELF-REFLECTION AND ASPIRATIONS

During the course, we were asked to reflect on what we want out of this one precious life we've been given. When we gaze into the future, what dreams fill our hearts with hope and purpose? What obstacles trip us up or hold us back from realizing our potential? What wisdom, skills, or community, do we seek? What do we expect from the course that might help unlock doors and light the way forward?

I went into the course with an open mind and no expectations. I've always believed it's best to approach new experiences like a blank slate. It's no secret that researching and anticipating outcomes ahead of time only limits what you might experience. Rather than capping the energy, like expectation does, it's better to let it flow naturally, allowing the experience itself to guide you. That way, you remain open to the joy and wonder. Always go into anything with an open mind, unless your insides scream at you that something is off. If it doesn't agree with your spirit, trust that instinct. Our egoic mind can be a devious little trickster, but our soul will always know the way to oneself. We should always follow our inner compass—it points to our true north.

"Mind can be our greatest enemy or our best friend."

—*Sri Sri Ravi Shankar*

SATSANG

Class was great, but that dreaded nightly ritual after class, called satsang that we were all forced to attend, not so much. Satsang is derived from Sanskrit, with *'sat'* meaning true and *'sang'*, meaning company. It's simply being in true company, or being in the company of people seeking the highest truth. They told us it was a form of meditation, a chance to unite our minds through music, meditation, and wisdom. According to the great Guruji himself, it was about "celebrating life," and one that does not do *satsang* is like a wild animal. Don't get me wrong, I'm sure satsang really gets some people going. I could see the appeal of singing, dancing, and chanting to "rejuvenate" your mind, body, and soul. But let's be real—it wasn't everyone's cup of chai. As for me, I might as well have been a wild animal for all the good it did my soul. I just didn't vibe with all that kumbaya stuff.

So, what did I do? I made a beeline for the back row every night. That way, I could sneak out after thirty minutes without disrupting the blissed-out dancers up front. I wasn't about to sit there in silent misery just to please Guruji & co. We all have to find what resonates with our soul, and if it doesn't, don't be sitting there like the people pleaser you are, unable to move, plotting a thousand escapes in your mind, because you'd feel guilty for getting up and doing your own thing. Call me crazy, but mindlessly following rituals that don't resonate with you seems less "truthful" than tuning into your own nature. When Guruji was not traveling the world inspiring people with his talks, and at the ashram, that hall was more packed than a Mumbai train at rush hour. People came from everywhere just to hear him speak. Me? I'll take a good book over a packed chant-fest any day. To each their own path to truth, I say. I'm sure satsang lit up some people's chakras like Diwali fireworks. For me? Not so much. But that's the beauty of finding your own way.

TOURING THE GROUNDS

On the last day of the life-changing Basic Course, we were gifted an inspiring tour of the ashram. I could hardly contain my excitement. Finally, a chance to see beyond the walls that had cradled our journey of self-discovery! We piled into two tiny yellow buses, their shocks no match for the uneven dirt roads ahead. As we jostled over potholes and swerved around muddy ruts, I felt gratitude for the opportunity to fully immerse myself in ashram life. One of the other participants managed to snap a photo of Renu and I, laughing as we bounced in sync with the rattling bus. Though the ride was bumpy, our spirits remained high, uplifted by the community we had found within these grounds. The place had seeped into our souls, and now we got to witness its entirety.

As we rolled through the lush greenery, nature's beauty surrounded us. We passed by vibrant schools filled with eager students: the Heritage School, Sri Sri Junior College, and the Kannada School with its 1300 pupils. We passed by the gleaming research laboratories, their pristine white walls and glass windows shimmering in the sunlight. These state-of-the-art facilities are dedicated to the ancient science of Ayurveda, India's traditional system of natural healing. As we drove on, I felt a swell of inspiration. Here, scientists are rediscovering the wisdom of the ancients, combining age-old remedies with modern technology. Who knows what breakthroughs lie ahead? The potential to alleviate suffering through safe, effective, natural medicine feels boundless.

A small farm came into view, with cows grazing away lazily. This was the Gaushala Project, created by Sri Sri Ravi Shankar. The farm started with just four cows, but now houses over 100 indigenous cows across fifteen exotic breeds. Their milk is packed and distributed to nourish the community. Everything here serves a purpose. Even the cow dung fertilizes the soil and the cow urine aids healing at the Ayurvedic Hospital. At the Panchakarma Clinic, time-honored treatments harness nature's wisdom. Witnessing the symphony of life unfolding filled me with inspiration. This was a land of ancient knowledge and modern innovation, where nature and progress worked hand in hand.

Sri Sri has a humanitarian spirit that shines through his tireless work uplifting the poor and disadvantaged. In 2001, he established the Sri Sri Rural Development Program (SSRDP) to train rural women in skills that lead to self-sufficiency. With cotton and jute, these artisans craft beautiful, eco-friendly bags. Their talents bloom through tailoring, cutting, stitching, embroidery, and block printing. Guruji empowers not just their livelihoods, but their inner strength. The Women Empowerment Program nurtures creativity and courage in women from disadvantaged backgrounds. With newfound confidence, these women step into their power and grace. Guruji's projects are countless—he is an inspiration. His vision uplifts communities and his wisdom inspires human potential. Through his teachings, Guruji empowers lives with purpose and meaning.

As we ventured from the schools to the old ashram near Gate 1, we were greeted by a troop of mischievous macaque monkeys. These clever creatures roam the ashram grounds freely, searching for any scraps of food they can find. In Bangalore, they've become true pests, terrorizing humans who get too close. (I once witnessed a monkey poking holes in an empty juice packet just to get every last drop—they can be quite determined! I damn straight made sure to keep my distance).

We climbed the stairs past the old amphitheater, which now lies in ruins, though the grounds remained filled with vibrant flowers in full bloom. At the top of the hill stood the majestic old ashram, a breathtaking sight. The center contains a quaint garden, and the views of the surrounding landscape are spectacular. It's an inspirational place, where one can't help but feel at peace amidst the natural beauty and tranquility. Though the macaque monkeys run a bit wild, they seem to fit into the lush environment. Visiting this historic ashram and its serene grounds was truly a magical experience.

Two majestic elephants roamed the grounds, creatures of wonder carrying an air of ancient wisdom. One hailed from the sweeping savannas of Africa. I never saw this particular elephant, as she was spirited and untamed, with only Guruji able to control her. The other, an Asian elephant named Indrani, was a gentle soul. Without the mighty tusks of her counterpart, she moved with quiet grace. Her footsteps rang with the tinkling of bells, and you'd hear her playing the harmonica with her trunk as she walked on by. Each morning her soulful music never failed to inspire joy in all who heard it. With each note, she spread a little magic across the ashram. Between 9 and 10 a.m., you could find her at the Vishala canteen, where she welcomed chapatti and roti from eager hands. To behold an elephant is to experience a living antiquity, a being sculpted through uncounted generations into a towering incarnation of poise and power. Indrani was no exception. Her massive yet careful form radiated the dignity of her kind, even as she delighted in simple snacks and scratches behind the ear. To cross paths with one of these elephants was an incredible joy and privilege, reminding us that beauty can be found in the most unexpected of places.

I enjoyed strolls through the lush gardens of the ashram in the early morning light, surrounded by brilliant flowers and tranquil trees. The beautiful flora and fauna were a sight to behold. I reveled in the peace and quiet—no music or blaring TV screens here. The stillness was inspiring. My mind became as calm and clear as a serene pond. It was a magical place, and wandering those paths was the highlight of my time there.

The journey through the surrounding areas of the ashram opened my eyes to the possibilities ahead for humanity overall, with the various flourishing projects bringing light to the community. Kids laughed and learned, farmers and volunteers got their hands dirty, planting seeds and harvesting nutritious crops. Everything was a testament to the spirit of service that guided this place. Though the tour eventually came to an end, it was truly inspiring to see people coming together—fully alive in mind, body, and spirit—to create positive change. May others follow in their footsteps of working and creating something together selflessly for the betterment of the community. Working joyfully as one, we have the capability of making not just our neighborhoods, cities, and the world a little bit brighter, but to lift up humanity as a whole and heal our shared home, Mother Earth.

LITTLE HANDS, HEAVY BURDENS

My heart broke when I witnessed the injustice of child labor still rampant in Karnataka. Tiny, innocent children who should be playing and learning were instead forced to work long hours without proper food or fair pay. Their bright eyes that should be filled with joy and possibility are instead clouded by exhaustion and despair. Child labor is a reality that persists in India seeping into countless corners across the nation.

The Care for Children Art of Living Schools, established by Sri Sri, shine as a symbol of hope and opportunity, offering free education to children across India. However, many from the older generation, shaped by their own life experiences, do not always recognize or appreciate these educational opportunities they themselves were once denied.

Sri Sri firmly believes that by giving these children access to education, healthcare, and proper nutrition, the schools can help break cycles of poverty, inequality, and poor health. By advocating for education as a fundamental human right, the schools empower young minds, allowing them to reshape their futures and ignite transformative change in their communities.

Dedicated to the welfare and dignity of marginalized children, particularly in rural and tribal areas, the Care for Children schools are a lifeline for nearly 100,000 underprivileged students. With over 1,262 free schools across more than 2,050 villages, these institutions achieve an impressive 90%+ attendance rate with no recorded dropouts—a testament to the profound impact of this initiative.

Even amidst hardship there is beauty to be found. One such example were the gorgeous smiles of the young girls selling flowers outside Gate 2 each night. Though filthy and covered with dust, their faces lit up each time they saw me. "Auntie, auntie," they would call in their sweet voices. I never bought their garlands of marigolds, jasmine, and roses, knowing the blossoms were not mine to take; I would rather they sell them to others. But I gave those girls ten rupees each—a tiny gift for their beautiful spirits. It made my heart melt just to see them smile. I hoped their days would soon be spent at school desks, not dusty curb sides. With education's light, today's flowers can bloom into tomorrow's leaders. Even the smallest act of love nurtures that growth.

I'll never forget a little boy I met during my time in Bangalore. His tiny hands worked a hammer with expertise beyond his years. This beautiful boy, no more than eight years old, toiled away, fixing the room two doors down from mine.

"Shouldn't you be in school?" I asked.

"I'm carpenter," he replied softly.

My heart broke for this little kid, as I repeated the question, only to get the same response: "I'm carpenter."

When I asked his age, he didn't understand. Instead, he said, "I'm Hindi, Karnataka State."

It saddened me, because he was just a child, already fixing things and learning his father's trade instead of enjoying a carefree childhood. I rummaged through my suitcase, searching for a gift to brighten his day.

I settled on a wooden model chopper I'd bought in Holland. When I presented it to him, his eyes opened wide with wonder. His face lit up with the most radiant smile. He was speechless, overwhelmed by this simple act of kindness. I told him to enjoy it and then left to meet my friend Sangita, wishing the boy a wonderful rest of his day. He deserved so much more.

Sangita later explained that carpentry skills are passed down in families like his. At a tender age, he was already earning a living to support his loved ones. While this may be all he knows, it pains me that this bright, beautiful child cannot revel in a worry-free childhood like so many other children across the globe. His situation is heartbreaking, yet inspiring. I will never forget that smile lighting up his precious face.

Through simple acts of kindness, I found beauty and heartbreak during my time at the Art of Living Center. Another child I met, Kamala, was just twelve years old and cleaned in the Human Resources area. Whenever I saw her, I always made a point to say hello and sit with her, just to see how she was doing. I checked my suitcase to see what I could find for her, and decided to give her the bunch of pink, girly hair wraps I'd gotten in Holland. Her smile when I presented them was one of pure joy. It's incredible how these kids appreciate the smallest things.

I was crushed when Kamala told me she didn't go to school. I asked a kind groundskeeper to translate so I could understand why. He explained that her mother had received the enrolment forms but pulled Kamala out after sixth grade to work. The HR manager, Meera, told me Kamala's mother refused to listen to reason. I begged Meera to keep trying, even offering to pay for Kamala's schooling myself. Education is free, Meera reminded me, but she promised to ask the mother again. My only hope was to send Kamala books so she could keep learning. I'll never forget seeing her scrub floors on her hands and knees and lugging heavy buckets of water—such difficult work for a child. Before I flew back to Holland, I left a little bag of treats and 100 rupees (equal to about $2.50 USD at the time) with reception to give to Kamala. Though I couldn't give it to her myself at 5:30 a.m., I prayed it brought a smile to her face. Kamala's situation was heartbreaking, but also gave me insight into the generational gap that still existed.

Even when life challenges us, we can spread warmth through tiny gestures. The beauty and spirit of the children I met will stay with me forever. Though life was hard, their spirits remained unbroken. I'm inspired by their resilience and ability to find joy in the smallest of things. They empower me to appreciate everything I have.

Each breath we take is a blessing. Though life may not always be easy, we must remember that the very act of living is a privilege denied to many. Our circumstances do not define us. What matters most is how we choose to see the world—with eyes of gratitude or resentment. This moment is a gift. This breath is a miracle. You are alive, and that alone is reason enough to rejoice. So, open your heart, spread your arms wide, and give thanks for the immeasurable gift of simply being here.

THE ORPHANS OF KASHMIR

When I hopped on the plane to India, the extra weight in my suitcase came from the materials I bought for the orphans at the ashram in India. The lady at the British Midland Airlines check-in counter was unmoved by my explanation. She just shrugged her shoulders when I told her about the toys, books, and other stationery for the orphaned boys from Kashmir. With a deep sigh, I paid the fee for excess baggage weight and got my boarding pass.

The ashram stands as a beacon of hope for these children, who have endured unspeakable trauma and hardship. It works tirelessly to bring a little sunshine into their lives, which have been overshadowed by the dark clouds of violence and conflict. These displaced children, from a militancy-ridden home state, were living in unimaginable conditions, with little access to basic necessities, let alone the care and support they desperately needed. Yet, the ashram has taken on the noble quest of creating a sanctuary—safe space where they can start to heal, both physically and emotionally, from their harrowing experiences.

With a holistic approach that addresses their need for shelter, education, food, and emotional support, the ashram strives to restore a sense of normalcy, stability, and hope to these young lives. It is a vision of pure compassion and healing, as the dedicated staff pour their hearts into nurturing these children and empowering them to rise above their pasts. One step at a time, the ashram is lighting the way to a brighter future, providing the love and guidance necessary for these kids to reclaim their childhoods and reach their full potential.

Tucked into the northern reaches of India, Kashmir has long been a place of conflict. Generation after generation has grown up amidst the sound of gunfire and the boom of explosives. For the orphans, days that should have been filled with play and family instead brought loss and turmoil.

The once-disputed region of Kashmir sits nestled in the towering Himalayan mountains, caught between the tense borders of India, Pakistan, and China like a precious jewel coveted by rivals. Its stunning natural beauty and strategic location made it the apple of discord between India and Pakistan ever since their independence from the British in 1947. Each claimed the land as their own, though ceasefire lines divided it.

The Kashmiri people themselves have resisted Indian occupation since 1989, taking up arms against their overlords. India responded by flooding the valley with troops to crush the Kashmiri Freedom Movement. Meanwhile, Pakistan-backed Islamic militants slipped across the border to fight the Indian forces and launch attacks, further destabilizing the region at the time.

Kashmir was the Gordian knot in relations between India and Pakistan, the sacred ground over which blood has been spilled for decades. Its mountain passes echo with the cries of those yearning for independence as three nations stared each other down over the fractured land.

The Indian government declared the Kashmir conflict resolved in 2019 when Jammu and Kashmir's autonomy was revoked and became part of India. But this "resolution" failed to ask the Kashmiris what they thought justice looked like. Their sovereignty was broken, their voices went unheard, and though they were the people most affected, they were never consulted. Effective resolution requires listening to everyone, including those longing for peace. Today, Kashmir still waits for the conflict to truly end.

I'll never forget the day I met the thirty-two boys at the orphanage. Their ages ranged from five to fifteen. With sweet, cherubic faces and spirited laughter, they lit up the ashram with joy. I found it odd that there were no girls in the group. Where were the Kashmiri girls who had lost their parents to the conflict? What circumstances led to this blatant gender inequality? I felt sure that some of the boy orphans must have had sisters. Their absence raised more questions than answers. It was a topic I should have queried, but in that moment, it simply slipped my mind.

As I walked onto the orphanage grounds, I noticed the school buildings differed vastly from those in Europe. They were barren, with no decorations or learning materials in sight. There were no windows, just bamboo roll-up shades to keep out the wind and rain. Inside, there were no blackboards, tables, or chairs, and the boys sat cross-legged on the floor during their lessons.

As my eyes wandered to the first floor, I caught sight of the sleeping quarters. I was amazed to see rows of bunk beds lining the walls as far as the eyes could see, with only two fans hanging from the ceiling. Though the buildings showed cracks and needed fresh paint, at least the boys had a roof over their heads.

As I stepped into the courtyard, lugging my heavy backpack and two big plastic bags, I noticed the makeshift clotheslines strung across the patio. Laundry fluttered in the breeze. I found the teacher, a woman named Rupa, in the courtyard, helping three boys with their homework while the others played nearby. Rupa welcomed me with open arms, though I could tell she already had her hands full with this rambunctious bunch. She quickly ushered me inside a nearly empty storage room, where shelves were poorly stocked with necessities like slippers, pants, white shirts, soap, and cleaning detergent. I unpacked stacks of coloring books, crayons, pencils and pens, and other supplies. I had also brought marbles, puzzles, bubble blowers, animal stickers, books, and Smurf figurines—characters they'd never heard of. I included some kid-friendly DVDs among my gifts, hoping the orphanage would be blessed with a generous donation of a television and DVD player, allowing the children to enjoy these films together. My heart sank as some of the children eventually gathered round; eyes full of longing as they stared at the colorful DVD covers. Though they tried to hide their disappointment, I could tell they were wishing they could experience the magic of movies.

After unpacking all the materials and stacking them neatly on the shelves, we headed back outside. Rupa told me that seventeen more boys were set to arrive at the orphanage from Kashmir, and I wondered how she would manage them all. Her love for the boys shone through, despite the difficult job. She was truly inspirational.

"Do you think the boys would mind if I stayed for a bit?" I asked Rupa. "I'd love to sit with them, listen to their stories, and get to know them better."

Rupa's face softened into a smile. "Of course," she said. "I'm sure they'd enjoy the company."

I nodded, thankful for her kindness. If I could offer the children even a moment of warmth, I was eager to stay.

During my visit, one of the boys got himself into quite the pickle! He'd ripped his pants right on the zipper seam. When he asked the ever-patient Rupa for a new pair, she refused, saying she had just given him a new pair recently. He'd have to make do. So, what does this little rascal do? He wrapped a tea towel around his waist to hide the tear. When Rupa saw his makeshift skirt, she just shook her head and asked if I could patch up his pants, seeing she was busy helping some other boys with their homework. The boy handed them over a bit sheepishly, and I neatly sewed up the rip for him. When I was done, he thanked me profusely.

Afterward, I sat with the boy for a bit and stressed how important it was to study hard, even if he didn't love school. I told him that school had been a drag for me most days, but education was the key to achieving his dreams and seeing the world one day. I asked what he wanted to be when he grew up, and he said maybe a policeman. I assured him that was a noble goal, and reminded him he'd need to do all his schoolwork and pay attention in class if he wanted to make it happen.

I told him where I was from, and about some of the places I'd traveled to and lived in, trying to open his eyes to the possibilities out there for him. I could tell my words resonated by the thoughtful look on his face. After we talked, he dutifully went back to finish his geography homework.

Before dinner, I helped line up all the chatty, energetic boys for dinner in the Annapurna Hall. They may have come from difficult circumstances, but their hopefulness and joy were infectious. Bellies full, the boys then ran off outside, soccer ball in tow. After play, the boys went to satsang every night, clapping and singing along with such gusto, you'd think they were at a rock concert! (This is more than can be said for me, as I did a Houdini every night).

I was grateful to connect with these inspiring young souls. It made me happy to see these boys had a safe home, healthy food, an education, and a roof over their heads. They truly seemed to make the most of what they had.

CHAPTER 8
THE ADVANCED COURSE

AFTER FINISHING THE BASIC Course, I moved on to the Advanced Course. It was turbulent yet illuminating. At the same time, a severe stomach bug struck, leaving me doubled over in pain and dashing to the bathroom. I lost weight I couldn't afford to lose and had several crying fits. Despite the health challenges and physical suffering, the Advanced Course proved to be an eye-opening journey of healing and self-discovery.

After the first day, we observed complete silence for the duration of the retreat—no talking allowed! We communicated only through meditation and reflection. The quiet brought unexpected peace. During early morning yoga and long walks, I drank in nature's tranquility. Without idle chatter, I became more aware of my surroundings and inner world. Though illness battered my body, my spirit appreciated the nurturing silence.

"Faith blooms in the stillness of the mind, where doubt's shadow cannot linger. As the morning sun burns away the mist, faith arises and illumines all things. When the clamor of thoughts grows quiet, faith sings its silent song. Doubt flees before faith's radiance, vanishing like dew in the dawn. In faith's warm glow, the impossible becomes possible. Mountains move, seas part, darkness turns to light. Faith is the sunburst that scatters

the night, the lamp that guides the way. It springs from within, a seed germinating in the heart's fertile soil. Tend to it with tender care and it will bear fruit beyond measure. Faith transforms life into a vibrant luminous garden, each moment bursting with meaning and purpose."

—*The Divine*

The silence allowed me to tune out the noise of daily life and tune into the whispers of my soul. This ancient practice of silence has been used for centuries across cultures to revive energy, restore enthusiasm, and provide rest for body and mind. The silence can be challenging at first, but leaning into the discomfort reveals truths about yourself you may have never known. If you're ready to dive deeper and discover who you really are behind the mask you wear in the world, the Advanced Course will take you there.

I had my room at the center all to myself until a girl named Lilliana, bless her heart, barged in at 11 p.m. one night. This Bolivian girl, who lived in Bangalore, was originally meant to stay at the Aparna, but her roommate there had been throwing hissy fits. Instead, she was sent my way. I was already knocked out with a nasty cold when she came knocking. I could barely peel my eyes open as she plopped her bags on the floor. Little did I know the deafening nightmare that was about to unfold.

Liliana was lovely, but she could saw logs with the best of them. As soon as she drifted off, the chainsaw impersonations began. The snores were so jarring I nearly levitated off my bed. I pounded my pillow over my ears, but nothing seemed to help mute her snoring. She sounded like a rhinoceros—I kid you not! By some miracle, I managed to snooze here and there amidst the snorting and snuffling. Come morning, I gently brought up her snoring situation. Liliana was very apologetic and mentioned she'd had nasal surgery that left her snoring like a bear in hibernation. She offered to move to another room, but I told her not to be silly—there was no need for such drastic measures. She insisted

THE ADVANCED COURSE

I give her a nudge if it happened again so as not to disturb my sleep. I told her not to worry about it. We both had to be up at the crack of dawn, or around 5 a.m. to get to our 6 a.m. class on time.

Classes were a bit of a mess this time around. They stuffed us above the Annapurna cafeteria—not exactly the peaceful shala I was hoping for, but with 3000 people on campus, I guess there was nowhere else for us. We started as usual with some yoga and breathing exercises before grabbing breakfast downstairs. Our new teacher was a character who went by the name Swami B (or something like that—I never quite caught his name). The first day was totally bizarre. There must have been over 100 students crammed in there, and my roommate Lilliana and I were the only clueless foreigners trying to decipher his Hindi-English mashup. Let's just say his spiritual ramblings got lost in translation and sounded like total gobble-dee-gook to us! Even so, the things I did pick-up in English, when Swami B happened to speak it, were definitely little gems that made perfect sense. One message that stuck with me is that the crow sings for the joy of song, not because it has a good voice. In other words, the crow sings not to impress, but to express its delight in the day.

During class, we gathered in small groups, sitting cross-legged on the floor, and shared glimpses into our lives for ten minutes each. One woman, thirty years old, went on and on about her problems, and fretted that time was running out for her to find a husband and get married. She rambled on while precious minutes ticked away. By the time she finished her diatribe, barely two minutes remained for me. I gave the glazed nutshell version of my life, omitting most of the gritty details—it wasn't important. I understood the need for this woman to unburden herself. The exercise itself was still worthwhile, forcing us out of our shells and to speak from the heart.

Another great exercise we did on this course was to sit in pairs and let one person unload all their problems and complaints in life. The purpose was to allow them to get it all out of their system, leaving them feeling lighter after offloading their baggage. My partner really took advantage of this opportunity. He unleashed a flood of issues about work, his family, and trying to find a wife. I learned his family had started a charity, but he felt too unmotivated to get it going, hence the work backlog. The passion and joy had fizzled out for him, like a soda can left open too long. He'd been practicing the Art of Living for two years and wanted his stubborn mother to try it, too. Because she refused, there was a rift between them, with endless arguments about how he lived his life. My advice to him was to be honest with his mother and to accept her the way she was. I never got the chance to share my story as his story lasted the entire session. When he finished, I said, "Everything changes, so this, too, will change."

It's true, life ebbs and flows like the tide. Each moment washes in, bringing something new—a fresh burst of joy, a twinge of sorrow, a flicker of insight. Everything flows, nothing ever remains the same for long. The sandcastle you built with such delight will soon be erased by the crashing waves. The pain that gripped your heart will dissipate as the water recedes. Change is the only constant. Though it may seem scary at times, change also brings new beginnings. If you open yourself to it, change can lead you to growth. So, when life shifts in unexpected ways, take a deep breath and surf those waves, knowing that this too shall pass.

Once we got to the meditation part of the class, I was so excited! But that excitement quickly turned to frustration. The speakers had such bad, hollow, echoey sound quality that I could barely understand what the teacher was saying. It was incredibly frustrating, to the point that I honestly felt like choking the life out of him! Meditation is supposed to be a wonderful, Zen, experience. This was the complete opposite. I sat there on the verge of tears, wondering what the point of it all was. This course was turning out far worse than the Basic one. At least the Basic teachers (like Sangita and Dr. Divya) had stuck around to answer questions. Swami just left after class.

I walked out of the class with Lilliana, tears streaming down my face. We ran into Sathiye near the reception area, and I just broke down crying again. Even though Sathiye had studied engineering, he was helping out with the administration at the ashram for a few months. He told me to take a walk with him to the elephants and explain what happened. He listened to me patiently. His response really resonated with me. He said, "Even if you don't understand much, once you're meditating, you're meditating." In other words, acknowledge the outer worldly sounds but focus on the breath. The outside world will fade to the background as you find your center. Inhale, exhale. Stay present, stay grounded. Let the noises float on by as you sink into this moment. Your breath is an anchor amidst the chatter, a refuge within the storm. Return to it again and again, and discover that inner stillness. He promised to talk to Swami B about remembering to teach some parts in English, too, and I appreciated both his empathy and help.

Lilliana and I bounced on satsang that night. No, thank you—singing, dancing and clapping just weren't our thing. I was exhausted after that harrowing first day of the Advanced Course, and I just wanted to get some sleep.

The next morning, I woke up bright and early for the 6 a.m. class, expecting the usual crowd of eager students. But when Lilliana and I arrived, the halls were empty—just a few stragglers wandered about.

"Where is everyone?" I asked one woman, bewildered. She simply shook her head and pointed to her name badge, which read: I AM IN SILENCE.

"Silence?" I looked at Lilliana, confused. As it turns out, the announcement about mandatory silence beginning that day had been shared at the previous night's satsang, which we'd skipped. There we were, chatting away, oblivious to the fact that the whole class was deep in contemplation. Oops! I clasped my hand over my mouth, as did Liliana, to stop laughing. I guess we'd have to quietly join the silence now, too.

During the Advanced Course, we were required to perform *seva* every day—a Hindu concept of selfless service for the greater good, without expectation of recognition or reward. My first seva assignment was sweeping the floors of the Aparna building using a rickety old handheld broom that did my back no favors. As I swept in silence, people walked right through my freshly cleaned floors, kicking up dust again. One little boy even barged past me, shoving me aside without so much as an "excuse me." I was in silence mode, and couldn't call after him, so of course the little bugger ignored me completely.

The next day, Liliana and I waited in the smoky kitchen area for our next seva assignment. After ten minutes of waiting, the guy working in the kitchen still hadn't returned. We began snapping some pictures of the kitchen, fascinated with how meals were cooked for the masses. When the head of the kitchen saw us, he demanded we delete the photos. Both being the little rebels we were, we didn't. Instead, we tiptoed out quietly and darted back to the classroom upstairs. Maybe not the most selfless service, but at least we found our seva entertaining!

The kitchen was a hive of activity, capable of feeding up to 3,000 hungry mouths three times a day. With the holidays of Good Friday, Holi Day, and Easter all converging, the kitchen staff worked tirelessly to prepare the traditional vegetarian fare. Chapatti dough was rolled out in industrial quantities while gigantic pots bubbled away with aromatic vegetable curries and spicy sauces. The kitchen blended modern equipment with time-honored techniques for maximum efficiency. Despite the controlled chaos, cleanliness was paramount. The kitchen was fairly clean, but there were several flies hovering right next to me over the chapatti dough. I couldn't believe they were touching the food that people would later eat. I did notice some staff periodically swatting away flies, but my guess is they were so busy, they let it be. Personally, I found the traditional spicy cuisine too hot for my palate. Instead, I opted for the plain dosa for breakfast and chapatti or roti for lunch. For dinner, I visited the nearby Vishala canteen. Still, witnessing the kitchen's orchestrated efforts to nourish thousands was impressive.

Dosa, for the uninitiated, is a mouthwatering South Indian crêpe that can satisfy you morning, noon, or night. This carb-and protein-packed delicacy is nothing like the sweet, vanilla-kissed, French crepes many of us know and love. No, dosa is a savory affair, with a pleasantly sour taste that comes from being made with a fermented batter of rice and lentils. The batter is spread thin on a hot griddle until the edges crisp up like lace. Then the dosa is served alongside little bowls of spicy chutney, earthy sambar stew (dhal), and a potato curry, the latter which I loved. After two weeks straight of Indian food, I'll admit my body was craving the familiar flavors of a Big Mac and fizzy soda. But alas, those indulgences were nowhere to be found in the strict, healthy confines of the ashram. My only recourse was drinking small cartons of apple juice and bottled water.

By day two of the Advanced Course, my stomach was suddenly in full revolt. I couldn't even look at food without making a beeline for the bathroom. Apparently, this is common, as the intense meditation flushes toxins and old residues from your system. Even substances from many years ago can still linger within and need to be purged. I was told to drink plenty of water to help cleanse my body, but I've never been a fan of the tasteless stuff. I managed to chug down just under a liter a day, mixed with some fruit squash when I could sneak it. I know consuming water every day plays an important role in maintaining a healthy body, and you know what they say—hydrate or "die-drate." I'm aware that water flushes out all those nasty toxins like a human Brita filter, preventing your skin from shriveling up like an old, wrinkly apple and banishing gnarly aches and pains from dehydration, but I've always needed it flavored.

After a day and a half of feeling sick and not eating, I was desperate enough to try some Marie biscuits that Lilliana had bought for me at the convenience store opposite the reception area. As we weren't allowed to speak during the course, we passed notes on scraps of paper to communicate. There was no contact with the outside world, no phones, no internet—just inner reflection with yourself in silence. My stomach was still touchy, but those biscuits gave me the strength to push through.

THE JOY OF SILENCE

The joy of silence has a cleansing, restorative power, allowing us to realign with our true selves and uncover the rich gifts it has to offer—inner peace, clarity, and profound insights that would otherwise remain hidden in the noise. Silence is a faithful companion, always available to transport you into a state of tranquility and *being*, rather than endless *doing*. When you heed the call of silence and allow yourself to simply be, without agenda or distraction, you open the door to a realm of blissful stillness that has the power to heal, renew, and illuminate. The silence will wait patiently, ever-present, for you to discover the transformative magic that arises when you surrender to its serene embrace.

"Did Depeche Mode not sing, 'enjoy the silence?' Sometimes words are unnecessary as lashing out like a smashing pumpkin, can only do harm; so stop crashing into your world.

Flying off the handle like an out-of-control Hulk, hiding behind the 'I'm always angry,' syndrome, is merely flicking your inner issues away, non?

Silence is your friend, it robs you not of joy, but gives you the very gift of just that!

Silence is golden, but your eyes still see, n'est-ce pas?

Diminish the chatter of your own drowned-out voice. Take a deep breath and allow your soul to revel in the joyful silence and gentle warmth of yourself.

Let the quiet enfold you like the breath of a warm summer's embrace.

Listen to the gentle whispers of your soul knocking on the windows of your mind.

What dreams lie dormant, sleeping tightly under the covers of your heart and mind, waiting to be awakened?

Breathe life into your dreams, rather than keeping them jarred up, giving yourself permission to want more and to be more, recovering the very radiance of the covered-in-muck hue in you.

THE ADVANCED COURSE

You are a multifaceted being, and dare I say, a multi-faucet, for either you turn the tap and flow with the universal stream, or you keep it shut tight, causing your soul to debilitate. You are an infinite wellspring of potentialities, of probabilities and possibilities. Rather than depriving your beautiful spirit of the beauty of all it can be, drink deeply from these wisdom-held waters and watch your soul soar.

The past has melted away like the mist at dawn, so why remain ever so fixated on things that were once, but are no longer?

The future blossoms from seeds planted in the present moment, overflowing with a hive of possibilities or the breaking-out-in-hives of no-can-do implausibilities.

Feed your mind with the munchies of joy, water them with that sweetened tea of eternal gratitude, and cultivate flowers of richly warm spicey and honey-like hope.

When fear casts its shadow, breathing down the base of your neck, know that it is merely a smooth disillusioned criminal imprinting its illusion within the screen of your mind. Breathe through it. Meet that darkness with the flickering candle of eternal light, and hold its quivering hand, gently telling fear to stop huddling in the cold, remaining frozen like that poor wee popsicle, unable to move forth. Hold hands with fear, let it talk of its bothersomeness, and softly tell fear that it's okay to let go, and to be free.

You are the sun, radiant and whole, there is nothing that cannot be warmed with the touch of your sun-kissed bliss-ed soul.

There is nothing that cannot be resolved with a warm cup of chai or a brew of hot cocoa and a droplet of vanilla essence causing a simple ripple of change within the field of dreams and possibilities.

Center yourself in this knowing.

With each breath, dissolve the illusions that bind you, and know that you are free.

Rise renewed and refreshed, ready to hop upon your Alladinian carpet, weaving your magic threads in the tapestry of your life. One step at a time, keep moving forward. Even when the path may seem wobbly and weary, you have wings. You can fly.

Learn to dance ever so gracefully with the universe and the universe will dance ever so gracefully in the flow of all that is to be.

It's much like the show, dancing with the stars. If you keep kicking your poor dance partner the universe, is it any wonder that she starts limping, eventually falling over due to the inflicted bruises, causing an energetic malarkey, as much as you will start limping, causing a right malarkey in your own life.

If you won't shush and listen, then indeedly so you two cannot and will not dance in sync, and you will keep tripping like a bumbling Clumsy the Smurf in your own worldly earthly life. So, boomshakalaka—take a breather, breathe and be in tune with your inner dance hall moves in order to be in tune with the outer dance hall bravado of life.

Runnin' through this strange life, you can keep chasin' those green lights, like a poor lil' old me out-of-breath gerbil on a burnt-out treadmill, but what good will it do you? If the light in your life turns red, then stop, collaborate, and listen……

Be less of an ice ice shady, and more in the flow of a hot shot coffee.

Rather than shifting gears, revving it up living in the fast lane, enjoy the silence as much as the silence enjoys spending time with you.

Be not like a deer in the headlights, but bask in its serenity as much as it delights in the light of your company. Let the hush wash over you, soothing your soul like the quiet of a film noir.

Ouvrir ton coeur, to the joy of wordless communion, and know that stillness will embrace you like a long-lost friend, patiently waiting in a diner called 'Quiescence', allowing you to sit there with just you and your thoughts pouring your heart out to silence.

Cherish these precious moments of togetherness, before you take your leave, having fed your mind with a hearty meal of wonderfully stacked different possibilities and drank but a hearty warm brew to soothe the ailing spirit, relieving the shivering stress and anxiety it was so embroiled in. And if you want to dance with somebody, then let it be with that enigmatic and stylish beaut of a caped crusader called Silenzio, moonwalking you back to the la bamba beat of your vivacious inner groove in the heart of your dancing soul, knowing that you and silence will have had the time of your lives.

There is joy in silence, that sweet sound of nothing, yet everything. Silence speaks its own language, one of serenity and restoration. Listen close and you'll hear it—the gentle rhythm of your own heartbeat, the soft whisper of your breath. Joy lives here, in the spaces between the noise. All you must do is pause and feel it."

—*The Ascended Master St. Germain*

A KALEIDOSCOPE OF COLORS: HOLI DAY FESTIVAL

Holi Day fell during the Advanced Course. Holi, the festival of colors, is a springtime celebration of good triumphing over evil. I got to experience this colorful festival firsthand, and in complete silence no less! People see it as a time of rebirth and new beginnings, which normally involves lots of joyful noise and spraying of vibrant powders. Not for me! I was sitting quietly next to a stray dog while crowds of people swarmed around me to get to Guruji. They really worship and respect him. The sights and energy were wild, even if I couldn't yell along with the crowds. Holi Day through the lens of silence was an experience I won't ever forget.

"Holi" means "burning" in Hindi. The name itself comes from the ancient story of Holika, the demon aunt of Prahalad. According to the story, the demon king Hiranyakashipu was desperate for revenge against Lord Vishnu for killing his brother. The tyrant demon king wanted to replace Vishnu as the king of heaven, earth, and the underworld. Consumed by anger, Hiranyakashipu performed intense prayer and penance for years. Eventually, he was granted a boon, gaining enough mystical power to become nearly invincible. Drunk on his newfound strength, he demanded that his subjects worship him instead of the gods. Hiranyakashipu's young son Prahlada refused, remaining devoted to Lord Vishnu despite his father's threats. Enraged, the demon king turned to his sister, Holika, for help. Immune to fire, Holika sat in a blazing pyre, clutching Prahlada, seeking to burn the boy alive. Despite this, Prahlada emerged unharmed while Holika herself burned to ashes. Prahlada's pure devotion to the gods protected him, affirming the triumph of good over evil.

Modern celebrations of the festival of Holi trace back to the legend of Holika. On the eve of the full moon, people gather to celebrate Holika Dahan—the night when Holika's pyre is relit in the form of crackling bonfires. As the flames dance into the night sky, it is said that the evil spirits of the past are burned away. The soulful celebration fills the air with joy and camaraderie. Holi commemorates the triumph of light over darkness, the victory of young Prahalad over his wicked aunt Holika, and how devotion and righteousness will always prevail, lighting up the world with hope.

When the full moon rises high over India on March 21st, it signals that winter's gloom and northerly, blustery winds bow out, and the invigorating breezes of spring caress our cheeks and stir our souls. As nature blooms once more, an era of color blossoms. Trees and bushes bloom in vivid hues, shaking off their winter slumber. Birds return from long migrations to bask in the warm sunshine. Squirrels and other creatures peek from their burrows, bones soaked in the sun's nourishing rays. The fields are ripe for harvest, and the air is filled with promises of lengthening days and nature's bounty. Our hearts, too, are reawakened after winter's long hibernation. The depression of short, frigid days melts away in spring's radiance, and the need to stand under a lightbulb to catch some rays, are over. The first day of spring is Holi Day.

Holi Day is celebrated in riotous style! People across India throw powders of every color, revitalizing the landscape with joy and vitality. It signifies the triumph of life, love, and boundless optimism. People revel in the simple delight of being alive. After winter's darkness, their spirits now soak in the promise of brighter days. Happiness and hope bloom anew, just like the buds on trees. Holi reminds us that life is meant for living fully, for loving freely, and for embracing each moment in sheer joy.

Guruji graced the overcrowded stadium with his presence, captivating the mesmerized crowds who had gathered to get a glimpse of him. As he spoke, people waved their hands in awe and agreement. Suddenly, Guruji whipped out a water gun, spraying the ecstatic masses like a light summer rain. The crowds went wild! Then the stadium sprinklers switched on, drenching the hordes in a downpour of water. Despite being thoroughly drenched, their enthusiasm was not dampened.

Next, Guruji began tossing powders mixed with colored water—made from medicinal Neem, Kumkum, Haldi, Bilva and other Ayurvedic herbs—into the swirling, dancing crowd. I dodged the vibrant bursts, but my clothes were speckled with pigment. I wasn't bothered in the least, as it would wash out any way. People were dancing and chanting, many were extremely wet and smeared with the yellow powdered "paint" on their clothing and their skin, and some had even smeared the colorings on their face.

The horde had become a stampede, shoving me aside in their quest to get closer to Guruji. In the mayhem, someone trampled my oh so precious

Marie biscuits to dust! Finally, I got away from the crowd, and a sweet stray dog lying next to me enjoyed the crumbled treats I shared with him.

Guruji took to the stage to deliver a brief but powerful speech. As the crowds settled, I noticed distinguished guests from Russia seated behind me. When Guruji invited them on stage, my suspicions were confirmed—they were VIPs who had traveled all the way from Russia to celebrate Holi. The Russian delegates bowed respectfully to Guruji as garlands were draped around their necks. Through his translator, one parliament member expressed heartfelt gratitude. He thanked the Indian people for their hospitality and cherished the long-standing bond between Russia and India, hoping it would continue. Expressing his admiration, he felt privileged to be among the gracious Indian people. Furthermore, he suggested that communist Russia could learn from the Indian people and the Art of Living, which he believed could help make their party more successful. It was a moment of unity as we all celebrated Holi together with our Russian friends.

CONTINUING CHALLENGES

After the colorful Holi festivities, I retreated to my room. Even though my cold had ceased, my stomach was a gurgling, painful mess, which left me with zero appetite for dinner. Instead of food, I had a few sips of water to stay hydrated. The next morning, with my eyelids heavy and my mind foggy from lack of sleep, I dragged myself to class. My spirits soon sank as Lilliana walked out in frustration before lunch. Since we were observing silence, she slipped me a note explaining she couldn't take it anymore—she couldn't stand the teacher who had no time for his students, and she'd had it up to here. I scribbled a frantic reply begging her to stay and see the course through, explaining that even though the quality coming from the speakers was bad, she should still meditate anyway. But she wouldn't hear it. I looked on helplessly as she packed up her things and left class.

I found it strange how Swami B said nothing at all about Lilliana's departure. I wish he had shown some interest or even asked Lilliana about it. But I guess in his mind, those who wanted to be there would stay, and those who didn't would leave. By the time I walked back to our shared room, Lilliana had already gone for good. I felt gutted to lose such a lovely roommate. She was really nice, and I hated to see her go.

Attempting meditation while in a noisy corner of the ashram proved challenging at times. At one point, we heard a lot of commotion outside, hearing the clanging and clatter of garbage cleanup. Workers hauled bulging bags of trash, piled them into a mountainous heap, and then set it alight, with the mound soon erupting into a raging bonfire. Smoke and stench enveloped our meditation space. Many covered their faces, but the swirling fumes still overwhelmed our senses, making for quite an interesting—albeit a rather unpleasant—experience. It certainly was memorable, with the noisy, smoky ambiance testing our ability to find inner calm amidst outer chaos. While not ideal with the acrid air assaulting our lungs it made for an interesting story: the time we meditated in a smokehouse!

I honestly had no problem observing the silence. I actually found myself enjoying this inner me time as I went about my days in total quiet. Communicating through scribbled notes became second nature. If I fancied some apple juice, I'd simply jot it down on my notepad and show the cafe staff my request.

After three days of illness and without a proper meal, the Marie biscuits I had managed to eat were no longer sustaining me. My empty stomach yearned for nourishment. Venturing to the convenience store, I discovered that they sold tomato soup. Perfect! I headed to the cafe and eagerly wrote a note, asking them to boil some water so I could savor the comforting soup my unsettled stomach craved. That steaming cup of tomato soup was bliss, though my stomach remained annoyingly testy. Indeed, the sickness and lack of meals had already caused me to shed some pounds from my gangly frame. As much as rapid weight loss thrills some people, for me it was simply frustrating, seeing I was already a bit of a lanky giraffe. All I wanted was to enjoy some proper food again.

After skipping satsang yet again, I had no clue that the days of silence during the Advanced Course were officially over. So, there I was on Sunday morning, still mute as a mime, while everyone else was chattering away. When I saw my friend Malikarjun, who was visiting for the Holi festival, I scurried up the stairs to a quiet corner and started whispering, just to hear myself speak. It felt so strange, yet amusing, to utter words again after nearly two days of complete silence. I'd stop abruptly whenever someone walked by since I thought we were all still observing the vow of quietude. Little did I know the vocal fast had been broken the night before. But Malikarjun knew, and he laughed as he told me. I guess that's what I get for skipping out on satsang. My own little comedy of errors!

On the last day of the course, we got put through the wringer with an arm workout from hell. We were instructed to hold our arms straight out to the sides for five whole minutes. Just hearing that made it sound near impossible. To make it even more challenging, with each minute that ticked by we had to inch them a little higher, elevating the burn. As we started the exercise, you could hear the grunts and groans of struggle all around. Some folks were laughing, whilst others were howling like wolves! I just took a deep breath, stared straight ahead, and powered through. I managed to make it with energy to spare. It's simply mind over matter.

REFOCUSING ON GRATITUDE

As Swami B reminded us, life can be difficult at times. But no matter how tough things get, go through each day with a smile on your face. When you smile, your worries have the tendency to melt away, and your energy shifts in a positive direction. If you choose joy, your hours will indeed be far better than when you scowl through the day. As Guruji says, "Joy is never tomorrow, it is always now."

THE ADVANCED COURSE

I'm one of those strange people who smiles and bobs to my own music—mostly a delightful mix of '80s hits, '90s dance beats, and good ol' US country—while jogging or working out at the gym. Most folks grimace or frown when exercising. But for me, smiling and listening to my favorite tunes helps me enjoy the experience so much more. My stepdad used to poke fun at the miserable faces of joggers. He'd say they should be enjoying the fresh air and movement. That comment really stuck with me. Rather than frowning, I try to breathe deep and just greet each moment with a smile.

Every morning when we wake up still breathing, we've been given another chance to start anew. So, breathe, smile, and begin again. Enjoy life's journey, laugh at its twists and turns. As Jesus said, "Faith can move mountains." Well, I'd say smiles can, too.

Smiling and choosing joy also helps us find gratitude. Abundance begins when we shift our focus to gratitude for our lives. Though some of us may have much, a spirit of lack still dwells within. True joy springs not from what we have, but from deep thankfulness for it all. A grateful heart transforms even humble things into treasures. When we learn to be content, lack loses its grip. Our hands may hold little, yet our spirits can know boundless riches. The path to abundance starts with a simple step—appreciating today's blessings.

After the course wrapped up, I went over to Swami B to thank him. I did mention the horrendous sound system, no surprise there. He nodded in agreement. (Limited venue options, I suppose). Overall, the course was definitely worthwhile. It was an experience for sure, and it took a few days to really sink in. Having done an immense amount of deep breathing, funky yoga poses, and staring contests with strangers, it all started to work its magic. I let go of some old hurts that had been weighing me down. Holding grudges is way more exhausting than just accepting people as they are, flaws and all.

Because of the course, my mind got quieter than a mouse in a monastery. And my body? Let's just say all those toxins I'd been storing up got flushed out quicker than a New Year's resolution. This was good, but it was also an extremely uncomfortable experience, but that was precisely the point—releasing the dis-ease within. There is a lot of crap we store within the cellular memory of our bodies, created by ourselves and all that we ingest within our mind. I emerged feeling lighter and rejuvenated, with my stress having been alleviated, even if only for a moment.

Little did I realize just how fleeting that peaceful moment would be, as there was a shitstorm about to hit me in years to follow! I'm glad I took the course when I did. I felt like a new person at the time. Once you start releasing that old baggage and those hiccup hangups, life starts shifting gears for you. When one door slams shut in your face, another one creaks open, inviting you in. Even as one chapter ends, the story keeps on rolling. Each closed door lets us redirect our energy toward the open window, beckoning us to new horizons. While endings are inevitable, they make way for some truly beautiful new beginnings.

Life's like a zit sometimes. It shows up when you least expect it and makes a mess that is hard to clean up. Yet we are the predator and perpetrator of our emotions, creating the mess in the first place. The bumps and squeezes of life's challenges can blur our vision temporarily. But with the right care and perspective, those bumps clear up, leaving us wiser and fresh-faced, ready to take on what comes next. Like that zit that eventually heals, the obstacles of life shape us into who we're meant to become.

PART II
Lessons for an Enlightened Life

"Discover the bliss of being rather than doing, and know that Silence will wait ever so patiently in silence for you, enroute to enlightenment to the flickering wick of a candle light burning within oneself"

—The Divine

"Life truly is like a box of Turkish Delights, either scrumptiously and delightfully delicious or unpleasantly and bitterly unpalatable, non?

When one refuses to heal the fractures held within one's experiences, life is an unpleasantry of a beaten-to-a-pulp dandelion unable to bear fruit in one's experiences.

Release the deep-fried funk within the psyche of your weathered programming, having caused a jam of junk-o-donuts in your mind and embrace the sweetness to work through the bitterness to truly savor those tasty bites and infinite flavors of life.

Stop drinking from that vicitimlicious cocktail, that has got your mind banged up and your words slurring in a pity party of the falling off the barstool barfing self.

Stop Pinocchio-ing yourself, being puppeteered around unable to move because you've gotten your head stuck in the Pandora box of your deflected and alienated self.

Rather, remember my Child, that you are all grand cosmic star voyagers traversing le magnifique celestial seas, gliding amongst the Milky Way's swirling mists into the ever-reaching heights of that sweetening and ripening of your beautiful consciousness.

Your souls are ancient, forged in the fires of galaxies beyond, journeying through the endless beauty of the cosmos. For now, you don your human meat suits, these fragile yet beautiful organic given forms, to encounter the splendor of life in all its sun-filled luscious glory. Your time here is but a brief breath, a fleeting spark amidst infinity's glowing flow. Yet in this moment you meet, you love, and share the light within, before you depart once again, taking the treasured memories held close within the letterbox of your loving soul with you, whilst your body returns to the dust of the earth from whence it came, and you, my Child, sail the stellar winds once more. Your voyage continues, in this galaxy and beyond, because you are a glowing ember of the divine; your light can never be snuffed out. Like that silver surfer, being the observer, you're always seeking, ever wandering with your energy transforming through timeless realms ablaze with starfire.

Think not so little of yourself, remain not in the drivel of your experiences, unless it eloquently serves you but well.

You are an Ambassador of Light, here to light up the world like a flaming Ghost Rider eradicating the malignant with your fiery radiance.

You are an intergalactic transformer of hope.

*You are L.i.g.h.t.; a **l**iberator **i**ntegrating the **g**olden **h**eart-healing **t**ransformation on Gaia.*

You are the YOU-ni-verse embodied within the hue-man body.

We are eternal, we are endless, we are one, and we go on.

In love and light, truly I remain a mere humble servant to the divine, for I AM no different than you, as much as you are no different to Me. I AM as You are as much as You are as I AM."

—*The Ascended Master St. Germain*

CHAPTER 9
EXPLORING THE WISDOM OF SRI SRI RAVI SHANKAR

"The past was your destiny, the future is your own free will, but live in the present moment."

—*Sri Sri Ravi Shankar*

SRI SRI RAVI SHANKAR, though small in stature, radiated a warmth and light that filled any room he entered. His gentle eyes and ready smile conveyed a compassionate nature, always open to lend an ear. At the ashram, his smiling face gazes from photos on every wall, surrounded by the flicker of devotion candles. To me, he's just like you and I, but also a humble teacher lighting the way for others. The honorific title "Guruji," (a term derived from the Sanskrit word "guru," meaning "teacher" or "guide") reflects the deep respect of those following in his footsteps towards inner wisdom. Though he makes no claim to special status, his presence inspires people worldwide. In India, many even see him as a living saint. Yet for all his spiritual attainments, he remains approachable to anyone. Such is the beauty of Sri Sri, who shines as a beacon for humanity.

He sees Gaia as a beautiful haven for learning, where all live in harmony and move in joy. His dream is for a world at peace with itself and nature. No conflict, no crime, no anxiety–just serenity, where the gentle rhythm of life flows uninterrupted. And we move together as one, in blissful unity.

Though he travels extensively, visiting country after country, I was blessed that he was at the ashram during my stay. You could call it fate or divine intervention. The first time I saw him was two days before starting the Advanced Course. As the sun peeked over the horizon, everyone had gathered in the Vishalakshi Mantapa for 6 a.m. yoga, but not me. I lingered in my room to complete my morning kriya, a powerful meditation method that focuses on harnessing energy and mastering the breath, before strolling down to the hall. When I arrived, I was astonished to find the massive hall overflowing with people. Sri Sri sat on a raised platform, speaking to the crowd. I paused at the entrance, not wanting to disturb the captivated audience. After a few minutes, the large, carved doors closed, and I assumed this was to keep latecomers (like myself) out. However, I soon realized the doors were shut for Sri Sri's protection—to prevent a stampede of people swarming from every direction just to try and touch him when he exited the building.

When Sri Sri finished speaking, he slowly descended the garden path. One set of doors opened and suddenly people rushed forth, trying to outrun one another, wanting to pay their respects. "Jai guru dev!" they cried, straining to kiss his feet or clasp his hands. ("Jai" stands for victory, "guru" refers to that which is great, and "dev" means that which is divine. So together, "Jai guru dev" stands for a sense of honoring and celebrating the greatness and divinity within oneself or another person). Sri Sri simply smiled, patiently making his way through the sea of admirers. Though the doors had closed on me earlier, keeping me from the overflowing hall, witnessing the swarm fighting to get near him gave me a profound appreciation for his message of peace and the devotion he inspired.

He took time to listen and talk with each person who approached him. He was in no hurry as he slowly made his way through the crowd.

As he walked right by me, I noticed he did not look up or acknowledge my presence. I mentioned this to Sangita, my teacher, and she told me that even though he did not directly interact with me, Guruji would have noticed me. When I questioned why people saw him as more than human—as if he were a god—Sangita explained that his great wisdom and enlightenment led people to worship him as their guru and master. Though I accepted her explanation and understood these were long-held traditions, I still felt the need to find the truth for myself. Who was this man who commanded such devotion?

We are all tiny sparks of the Divine, little bundles of sacred energy on a journey through this physical world. Though we walk the earth in these temporary bodies, our true essence is pure light and love—the same substance that the Divine Orchestrator, the Creator used to breathe life into existence. We are integral parts of the whole, unique expressions of that infinite consciousness we call God. There is no separation between us and the Divine because we emanate from and return to that eternal Oneness. We reside within God, and God resides within each of us. We are the eyes, hands and heart through which the Divine experiences this world. Our physical forms allow the sacred energy within us to have adventures, make choices, and create our lives. By looking inward and connecting to that inner spark, we can better understand that we are Divine BEings. We may express ourselves in different ways, but we are all made of that same sacred Divine Source Energy. We are God, exploring what it means to be human. We are Creators, creating and expressing ourselves through human form.

A day later, whilst getting an apple juice from the canteen, I saw Sri Sri for the second time. He walked past the shops, exuding an aura of peace, and a crowd was quickly gathering around him, eager to catch a glimpse. It amazed me how people once again kissed his feet and clambered to touch his head or his hands. Racing down the hill to meet him, my colleague, bless his heart, bent down halfway to kiss his feet, but was caught by the gentle hands of Sri Sri, who told him that there was no need for this. I thought it was really touching, yet Gurudev has consistently highlighted the importance of heart-to-heart connections over physical gestures, gently discouraging the practice of those wanting to kiss or touch his feet.

I was thrilled to finally meet Sri Sri in person and introduce myself. Despite being 5'11, I was able to give this wise individual a big, warm bear hug—one from me and an extra squeeze from Mandar Apte, my former Shell coworker. Mandar is an amazing human who introduced me to the Art of Living Center and has since become a Thought Leader, Social Innovator, Meditation Teacher, and Storyteller. Up close, Sri Sri radiated a quiet calm and selflessness. He was a gentle and well-spoken soul, wanting only to spread understanding in this world. He was no deity to be worshipped—he was an advanced spiritual teacher who inspired others to discover the joy within themselves, just as Jesus did. Neither man wanted adoration; they simply wished to lead by example, showing the way to finding that inner light of love and joy we all possess, and sharing it with our fellow beings. Sri Sri encouraged looking inward to uncover the happiness that resides in us all, rather than seeking to deify any one person. His message was about each of us nurturing our own spark of the divine. Meeting him was humbling, for we all have that divine spark within us. What a blessing to encounter this beautiful soul spreading peace and light.

I discovered that he had a wicked sense of humor, and he often cracked jokes as he answered questions from the Holi Day crowd. When he spoke, his remarks were both logical and downright hilarious. I have to admit, some of his responses to the crowd's queries that day were pure comedic gold. I've recounted some of the questions and Sri Sri's answers from that day below.

Q: How do you face failure?
A: You don't, for you don't sit opposite it. Failure, as you pose, is but a stepping stone; you learn and move on.

Q: Can you narrate us some stories?
A: Narrating stories are for bedtime. Now, it's time for lunch.

Q: What if I am tired, how do I continue studying?
A: You go to sleep and when you wake up you continue refreshed. Personally, I thought of Red Bull!

Q: I met the most beautiful girl, but I've been hurt so much. How do I go up to her and avoid getting hurt?
A: Why ask me? Ask someone who has more experience in this.

Q: When will I meet this special someone in my life?
A: Once you stop looking, the right person will appear.

Q: How do I know if I've made the right choice?
A: Only when you are calm within, aware, and balanced can you make the correct choice.

I asked one of the teachers if Guruji had ever crossed paths with George W Bush, and she replied that he had. And Guruji's response? He accepted Bush just as he was—no judgment, only compassion and understanding. He recognizes that we all carry karma, the fruits of past actions, and that shapes who we become. There is a profound lesson in his graceful acceptance. As the teacher went on to explain, Guruji sees value in opposites and imbalance. For how could we understand good without bad? How could we find balance if not for opposing forces? This duality is the very fabric of life. Guruji does not resist what is, but accepts all with an open heart. His reaction to Bush shows the power of embracing what is, and finding the teaching within, and reveals his wisdom and understanding of karma.

Trying to get a personal appointment to speak with Guruji seemed close to impossible. I miraculously managed to score one before my silence observation during the Advanced Course. Unfortunately, it was cancelled at the last minute, and Guruji decided he'd just come around and chat with the participants as a group instead.

Sangati, ever the wise advisor, suggested I pen Guruji a heartfelt letter laying it all out instead. This was an excellent suggestion. I was able to thoughtfully explain myself without forgetting anything. I asked Sangita and the other participants what they thought would happen once I gave him the letter. Universally, they said (with knowing smiles) that he'd take care of it, no matter what the problem was.

The letters people wrote to Guruji revealed so much about their inner lives. I couldn't help but peek over one girl's shoulder as she poured her heart out, saying she didn't care about money or fame, all she wanted was for someone to love her. *How sweet*, I thought. I penned my letter, which consisted of eleven tiny pages.

In my letter, I described how amazing his ashram was and how wonderful the people were. The ashram was an oasis of peace, a home away from home where I could leave my worries behind. I was really worried about my gorgeous sister, whose life had taken a bit of a detour, and my 'friend'—who, believe it or not, became my boyfriend for a hot minute a year later—was knee-deep in trouble over in Raleigh. He seemed unable to conquer his inner demons, often escaping his pain with a temporary high on drugs. I prayed fervently that they would both find their way and begin healing.

I wrote about my sweet dog, Kyra, who was my bestest bud in the world. She had been badly abused, and it was difficult to walk her, as she was always looking around with fear. Behind her soft brown eyes, I saw a kindred brokenness. We were two damaged creatures, connected by an invisible tether.

In closing my letter to, I expressed what an amazing person he was for all that he's given to humanity, radiating such warmth and wisdom to all. I told him that his selfless dedication to others is inspiring, and I encouraged him to keep smiling, making sure to take some time for himself, too. I did query the kissing of the feet, but I understood this as being a sign of deep respect. My long letter tried to capture both the joy and pain of life, with love and compassion for all.

It was a comedy of errors how I finally got my letter into Sri Sri's hands on the last day of the Advanced Course. As we all gathered in the Vishalakshi Mantapa, a man was droning on in Hindi about needing skilled people to work in IT at the ashram. My mind wandered, and I eventually slipped outside for a breath of fresh air. Out came Vikas to fetch me back, telling me Sri Sri would arrive any minute. Sure enough, just as Vikas said it, he appeared. I fretted about how to approach him. Sensing my anxiety, Vikas smiled and told me not to worry. And would you believe it—he came right over to us. As I greeted him, I casually slipped him the letter. He graciously accepted it. Vikas just shook his head and said he knew Sri Sri would come my way because he always knows. "Have faith," he told me. "Sri Sri will help, no matter what's in that letter."

CHAPTER 10
EXERCISES AND TECHNIQUES

MEDITATION AND BREATHWORK

"Meditation is not about achieving something; it is about letting go of everything."

—*Sri Sri Ravi Shankar*

WHAT IS MEDITATION? FOR me, it is that quiet calm that washes over you when you sit in stillness and close your eyes. It is the gentle flow of breath, the slowing of your horse-racing thoughts, and the opening of your awareness. Meditation invites you to sink below the choppy surface waves of the mind and into the depths of presence, simply by following the breath. As you follow each inhalation and exhalation, you come home to the peace that lies within, allowing for the stresses and struggles to fall away as you bask in the space and tranquility of pure being. Meditation is the sacred art of listening to silence and discovering that your true self waits patiently there.

Meditation is more than just sitting in silence with your eyes closed. It's a journey deep within, and an adventure to explore the vast inner space of your being. As you dive into the stillness, you begin to untangle all the cluttered thoughts and unwind the knots of stress. Amidst the quiet, your mind becomes as calm and clear as a serene lake on a breezy morning. Meditation is not some lofty, complex spiritual practice, but a simple act of taking a break from the busyness and just being with yourself. It's profoundly relaxing yet powerfully rejuvenating. Let the silence nourish you from within and wash away all the toxins and turbulence. Close your eyes, take a deep breath, and rediscover the joys of stillness. You may be surprised by what you find in the pearly depths within.

I decided to ask the Light BEings about meditation, and their wisdom has illuminated many a darkened way. Their message is below.

"Meditation is simply sitting in prayer with the self. It is making the unconscious conscious; it is a return from the created convolution to the calm clear waters and center of self. Meditation is prayer in motion, realigning your thoughts back to the sacred geometrical created grid of the formulated enlightened self. It is the sacred space to the stillness within, for how can the mind be at one with the self when the self is not at one with the mind? Meditation invites you to sit, breathe, and come home through the craziness of the worldly, jabbering jungle to who you really are.

Meditation is deep diving into the vastness of the ocean, swimming back to the hue of the very light that is you; it is the key to the portal of one's hidden-under-the-seaweed, beautiful soul, relearning to be in sync with the beautiful melody of one's inner harmony, so that one can correspond to the outer according to that same rhythmic and calming frequency wave held within.

Meditation is the cure to the lumped-up soup created within the mind; it is like water to an enraged mind on a sweltering fire.

Meditation is like a dear old friend greeting you with a warm hug. It welcomes you home to your true self, enveloping you in a snug-as-a-bug blanket of inner peace. Your mind quiets, no longer churning like chalk and cheese, but serene like a still forest pond. Worries float away as you sink into the present moment of just breathing.

EXERCISES AND TECHNIQUES

Meditation is much like a key turning within the lock of a grandfather clock; frustration melts into understanding; anxiety into calm, sluggishness into revived energy, from napping and nodding to waking and walking; fallible moods swinging that pendulum to a sunnier state of being. Remember you're not alone, but connected to all beings everywhere.

To quiet the mind is to quieten the heart, to slow right back down to listening to the 'God self' within; resurging from the darkened pool of the extremities of the outside world, re-emerging from the unauthentic breath to the resuscitation of breathing light back to the embodiment of the soul, flowing into the exuberant, bouncy stream of truly living in the authentic breath of breathing life, in the encompassing, wholesome way that is, and has always been, you.

Meditation is like a joyride on your inner 'magic school bus,' taking you on a wild tour through the tangled mess in your mind. Meditation is the navigation of the whistle while you 'work' road back to yourself, uncloaking the mind with the many layers of clingfilm you have wrapped yourself in and suffocated yourself with, causing nothing but a wonderfully mere grievance to yourself, much like self-flagellation, n'est-ce pas? Find that spunky inner firefly, and relight that fire, because self-love should be your first and foremost desire, restore that peppy soul back to the light of the I AM Presence within. Meditation is much like a soothing breeze, blowing away those dense dusty cobwebs within the mind, returning to the hearth and warmth of your soul fire. Through the art of breath, it is the vibration of love that is the babe magnet to your outer having converted from the inner; it is the spark to living in the flow of your divine nature, plugging the self back into God Source Energy, all the whilst enlightening the self, returning to the luminous 'buzz' lightning bug of a BEing within this earthly given suit, and walking in joy on this earthly journey of life."

When we connect to the stillness within, only then will we realize the static and disturbance going on around us. Rather than being a participant, we become an observer, returning within to view things without from a different perspective.

Meditation is not some mystical juju or a waste of your precious time, it's a powerful way to realign your mind and refocus your thoughts. Society may have led you to believe otherwise, all to deviate you away from your true nature, but taking a few minutes to breathe and chill out can totally recharge your brain. Switch off all distractions, put down your devices, and simply be with yourself. Close your eyes, focus on your breath, and let your thoughts flow through you without judgment. When you're seeking a bit of direction, why not immerse yourself in the soothing sounds of 432Hz or 963Hz meditations? Or dive into YouTube with the transformative breathwork of Caroline McCready. Let Katie Wyatt of "Whispers of the Wild guide you on a beautiful journey of healing and renewal. Alternatively, explore Divine Light Meditations with Opheana and Sikaal illuminating your path to deeper self-awareness or let Davidji's inspiring teachings create clarity and purpose. A few minutes of meditation can realign your perspective and help you refocus on what truly matters. Remember, it's not some weird voodoo crap; it's self-care for your mind and spirit.

The Ascended Master Ganesha, the wise elephant, ambled on by, giving his words of wisdom on the art of meditation. Ganesha's insights on how to quiet the mind through meditation are as valuable as rare jewels:

"I AM the Sun, the Moon, and Stars, as much as you are made of that same star dust held together in that stitched-up ensemble called a 'human body.'

I AM the reflection of You in ME, as you are but a mere Reflection of ME in You.

I AM the culprit to your hero, as much as you are the hero to my culprit, the light forever rumbaing with the dark, forever elevating each other and forever dancing that dance of consciousness eternal.

You are the spring to my water as much as I AM the water to your spring.

EXERCISES AND TECHNIQUES

I AM the hope to your faith as much as you are the faith to my hope reborn.

One cannot live without hope nor faith, for hope is the lifeline to your faith as much as faith is the spring step to your hope.

Finding inner peace, is to relax and to rockabye with your inner stillness. Stop shooting yourself through the heart, giving self-love a bad name, letting the bad habit of breathing that breath bleed into your auric field and environment. It is about finding peace and being at peace with the breath, rather than rattling the breath and breathing like a ramshackle old shed, defying the emotions that taper the breath, to keep you running in loops within your mind whilst breathing and skating on the superficiality of all you believe yourself to be; for you won't do yourself—nor the breath you breathe—any favors.

The 'om' of meditation is like the sound of the ocean on a still night by the bay, gently cradling your soul on the lapping waves back home to the heart of the oneness of the I AM of the universe.

Meditation is the breath of life, realigning the soul within the body, back to the stillness within. To master your breath is to master your life, for meditation is as much a medicine as it is a nourishment for the mind and soul.

Stand in the I AM Power of service to and in worship of your beautiful self, rather than the I AM disempowerment of serving others and worshipping others. Stop spanning yourself like a horse in front of the apple cart for others, allowing yourself to be steered and veered in every direction, foaming at the mouth with a riddled anxiety, rather than being 'to thine own self be true.'

The art of the breath makes all those bubbly, fizzy, beautiful atomic particles of light jolt and conga dance back to the groove of your body and soul, for without harnessing the power of the breath, you remain living in the shallow breeze of the ruffled, ostracized self. Breath assuredly is the key to mastering oneself and one's life.

The art of breath is the oxygenation cocktail served within the circulatory circuitry of the body. It is reigniting and replenishing the dormant cells in one's body, rejuvenating the very essence of self and the vigor of one's body. Breathing the breath correctly leads to health and optimization of one's body and spirit, with meditation the key to retrieving the space of the stillness within; for without stillness within, one cannot master the breath, nor oxygenate the body to the wellness and optimum of one's true essence of body and soul. The breath gives light and life to every nook and cranny along the meridian highway within the body, giving it a longevity, endurance, and an elasticity of both one's body and mind. One becomes far more of an energetic fluidity in motion, remaining calm as opposed to the composed rigidness one has for so long endured. Breath equals to life as much as life equals to breath.

Do you not feel it a necessity to feel but supremely dandy in your own skin? Do you not think it necessary to walk the wonders of mother earth, and to taste but the rich fruits of all of your richly-flavored experiences? The soul rebukes the energetic flow of the body, all because the egoic mind plays up like a bucking, wild, 'horny' goat, trailing off like a contradictory, steamed-up, fried, spicy samosa firecracker, having fed the self with tainted love, running away from the truth of who you are, causing nothing but clogged-up 'Tetris blocks,' curtailing the physical without. As a result, the sewage of ailments and dis-ease curb the inner flow within the given hous-ed body, causing much like a 'dying-in-your-own-arms' kind of syndrome. Get rid of the garnered conditioned tripe you have hoarded within the heaviness of your mind, causing such burden upon your body and soul. The key is to look at yourself, breathe, and take steps to alchemize the clotted, sour, lassi malai returning to the freshness, sweetness, and soulfulness of your own heart. Remaining in a dire fight-or-flight modus operandi serves no purpose but for the mere continuation of the EGO playing a dollop of dodgeball with you, confusing the messed-up senses, drowning you into the swirls of a hot phaal curry, causing you to gulp and sink further into the risqué, pungent sauce of your experiences, separating yourself from the whole, and straying even further from the truth of who you are.

If you are angry with fumes emanating from you like a chili chicken, sit in lotus position. Take a deep cleansing breath in, zipping up your body suit, and exhale, unzipping your body suit, and thus allowing for the erratic slush to flush.

Stop the maddening world of your inner contemplations, spinning 101 different threads within the scenarios of your life story. When fear and anxiety overwhelm your mind, crashing and burning through your veins, short-circuiting the meridian highway, simply surrender to the breath facing the obstacles that got you out of breath. Close your eyes and 'om' your heart out, coming back to the stillness of the space in between, with your soul walking on sunshine, allowing you to return to the calm of the breath of the heart space within."

THE SUDARSHAN KRIYA BREATHING TECHNIQUE

"Life is a mystery, live this mystery, to reawaken and remember who you are!"

—*The Divine*

The Basic course just wouldn't be complete, like eating pizza without cheese, without mastering the incredibly powerful breathing technique known as the "Sudarshan Kriya." This Sanskrit term is a powerful combination of three words:

Su = right
Darshan = vision
Kriya = purifying action

When combined, the phrase literally translates to "right vision and purifying action." In essence, the Sudarshan Kriya is a breathing technique aimed at helping you achieve a clear, focused mindset and cleansing impurities from your body.

The Sudarshan Kriya breathing technique was revealed to Sri Sri Ravi Shankar, founder of the Art of Living, during a ten-day spell of silent meditation in 1982. Through a specific sequence of long, deep breaths interrupted by shorter breaths, this practice is designed to calm the mind, enhance awareness, and channel positive energy. The rhythmic breathing patterns help relieve stress, regulate your mood, and leave you feeling refreshed and rejuvenated. The theory is that the Sudarshan Kriya enables the nervous system to produce beneficial chemicals that support the immune system, improving overall health. It is said to cleanse deep-rooted physical, mental, and emotional stresses and toxins, harmonizing the body, mind, and emotions.

Many of us are guilty of "shallow breathing," or living life on the surface of who we are, afraid to dive deep into our inner worlds. Like Atlas shouldering the weight of the heavens, we lug around the baggage of our accumulated hurts that were never properly healed. These unprocessed pains become the bricks we use to build walls around our hearts, keeping us boxed in and unable to live or breathe with openness. We have not been taught the art of breathing, nor the importance thereof. We hold our breath, hoping to keep the darkness at bay. But real freedom comes when we exhale fully, releasing the pain of our past, and inhale completely, making space for light. The Sudarshan Kriya aims to help us venture inward, diving into the depths of ourselves to find inner peace. Breathing superficially hinders the intake of oxygen throughout our entire body. The most important relationship we have is with ourselves. This practice teaches us the art of breathing fully and living authentically. It is a profound technique for self-healing and transformation.

As my St. Germain states, *"Commence with more conscious and connected breathing, for each breath is a chance as good as any to start anew. Let go of the carried 'toxic' waste, and rinse off the mental muck that clings to your thoughts—like algae having washed up on the shores, invading the beautiful beach of your mind. Clear the sewage within as, mes chéris, your mind is not a dumpster, having attracted nothing but a horde of blow*

EXERCISES AND TECHNIQUES

flies that obscure the vision ahead, all because you have not emptied the 'wounded' trash in your head. Rather see it as un espace sacré, a sanctuary, a temple, and treat yourself not with such disdain, but de-clutter the mind. Breathe in clarity, breathe out confusion, gaining mental lucidity, rather than remaining in a state of fallible morbidity. Replenish and rejuvenate the self, splashing like that bird in a bath, ridding oneself of the held-on parasites within the experiences, dancing back to the sacred geometrical grid of the soul within the body, plugging back in and reconnecting with the higher self, thus returning to the gem of the authentic sparkle you are."

Modern science now confirms what yogis have known for millennia. Studies from esteemed institutions like the National Institute of Mental Health and Neurosciences (NIMHANS) and the All India Institute of Medical Sciences (AIIMS) reveal that the powerful Sudarshan Kriya breathing technique can lift depression, sharpen the mind, reduce stress, improve cholesterol levels, and strengthen immunity.

Sri Sri Ravi Shankar has described the working of the Sudarshan Kriya as follows, "There is a rhythm in nature. Seasons come and go. In your own body also, there is a rhythm. Life has a particular rhythm. Similarly, your breath also goes in a pattern. Your emotions move in a particular rhythm, as well as your thoughts. All these rhythms arise from your being, which has its own rhythm. In Sudarshan Kriya, we get into the rhythm of our being and see how our being is permeating our emotions, our thoughts, our breath and our bodies. Soon, every cell of our body becomes alive and releases all the toxins and negative emotions it has stored from times past. Once again, we are able to smile from our hearts."

The Sudarshan Kriya is often combined with two other breathing techniques, the Ujjayi Pranayama and the Bhastrika Pranayama, to help calm the restless mind. In Sanskrit, "prana" means "breath," and "ayama" means to lengthen. So, pranayama lengthens and regulates the breath through four phases: inhaling, holding, exhaling, and holding again. By mastering the breath, pranayama helps calm the mind and energize the body. The Sudarshan Kriya uses pranayama to induce deep relaxation and balance.

The ancient Lemurians knew the secrets of prana. Their survival depended on mastering prana breathing techniques to distribute energy throughout their bodies. Over the millennia, as humans grew denser and more disconnected from their true nature, we forgot this wisdom. We started taking shallow breaths into just the lungs and mouth. This limited breathing blocks our energy flow, to the molecular structure, creating blockages within our energy system, causing all kinds of dis-ease.

As Lord Sanada always says, *"Health is your wealth, whilst your unhealed 'sludge' serves merely as a fudged-up crutch."*

Each inhalation and exhalation can anchor us to the stillness within, if we pay attention. Shiva knew that the breath holds the key to transcending suffering, if we have the courage to look inward. His teachings remind us that darkness lives within all human hearts, but we need not be enslaved by our demons. By embracing the shadow self with awareness and discipline, we can transform its destructive energy into creative power. If we heed the words of the divine destroyer, we too can unleash our inner light to illuminate the world. He understood that in each of us lurks the potential for both darkness and light. The choice is ours: will we destroy or create? Lord Shiva's wisdom on the breath can guide us to conquer the darkness without and radiate our hidden light within. Though his words may pack a punch, like a cosmic heavyweight in the ring, they emanate from a heart of unconditional love.

"I AM, as You are, for I AM Lord Shiva, Master Creator of all yet none, returning to One.

Master the self, or it will become the master of you, and you will become a slave to life having rolled off the wagon cart and landed in the thorny bushes in your very own caus-ed suffering.

You breathe shallow; therefore, you live shallow, walking very much on the surface of the sandbanks of your 'shallow-Hal' of self. Rather, my

EXERCISES AND TECHNIQUES

Child, practice pranayama, breathing to lengthen the breath, breathing deeply and thus living deeply and far more profound within the universa-licious chicken ramen noodle soup o' rhythm, allowing for all cells to be oxygenated, feeling exuberant, exhilarated and whizzing along the bodily highway blowing pure bubbles of joy, happily flowing through the circulatory system and all meridian points, giving the breath of life where there was but none.

Breath is the key to mastering the flux and fluidity within. Without the art of breathing, one remains incarcerated within one's very own created iron fetters, walking through life heavily yet superficially, like bricks in a bubble, rather than lightly and deeply; and then one wonders why one blatantly suffers so much from the heavy breathing of dis-ease?

Life is about learning and returning to the Divine Lotus Temple within, for you are as much the Universal Breath of Consciousness in ME as I AM the Consciousness of the Universal Breath in You. You are Divinity incarnate, lost in the foliage of the jungle of this chosen layered journey of the hallucinogenic illusionary trip of life. Your true purpose in life is as simple as abc, returning to showering in the golden light of the divine hue of self, scrubbing off the sticky rice you so blatantly overboiled yourself in, gently rinsing oneself of the many entangled experiences of that clung-on sticky tandoori spicy chicken you have but oh so joyfully created and stuck to yourself. You cannot ascend if you refrain from shifting, remaining but cemented in your ways, slow-drunk-drowning in the current matrix of existence. You've got to bhangra, shake those hips, dancing in a joyous movement with life, shifting your mindset, thus shifting your world rather melodically, with the universe in turn dancing just beautifully with your newly woven energies, bop-bopping in tune with the very renewed harmonious concerto of your reborn and reinvented self."

—Lord Shiva

Ujjayi Pranayama

The gentle ocean waves roll in and recede. With each rise and fall of the tide, you find your breath naturally matching its soothing rhythm. This is Ujjayi Pranayama, also known as "ocean breath."

"Ujjayi" means "rising victoriously." The Ujjayi breath is an artful dance—a dance like a tango of air flowing in and out through the nostrils while the throat gently constricts. Though the mouth stays closed, the breath glides long and smooth, allowing your lungs to completely fill and empty. Mastering this breath is like learning the steps to a beautiful dance, being mindful of each inhale and exhale. With each inhalation, you'll feel your confidence growing. As you exhale, release any inner blockages and let go of any tension and stagnant energy. As you get into the rhythm of this powerful pranayama, you'll come to understand the nuances and subtleties that make the Ujjayi so transformative. With practice, its soothing flow will become second nature. So let your breath lead, and your inner dancer will surely follow.

Although you can find many YouTube videos, it is practical and advisable for an in-person practitioner to teach you.

Bhastrika Pranayama

The Bhastrika Pranayama, or "Bellow Breath," is an ancient yogic breathing technique that provides a powerful boost of energy, or as I like to call it, "dragon's fire breath." Basically, you breathe in and out rapidly through your nose. Yes, it can get a little snotty, but who cares! This vigorous bellows-like breathing cleanses the energy channels and leaves you feeling an inner high, clear-headed and recharged—like the Energizer Bunny on steroids!

Beyond the immediate energizing effects, the Bhastrika balances the three doshas—the energies that govern our physical (vata), mental (pitta), and emotional (kapha) characteristics according to Ayurvedic philosophy. The Sanskrit word "dosha" means "fault" or "defect." So, this fiery breath corrects any blockages and brings the doshas into harmony. By

EXERCISES AND TECHNIQUES

practicing the Bhastrika Pranayama, we can reduce disease and cultivate optimal wellbeing on every level of our being.

Bhastrika enhances mental clarity by balancing the autonomic nervous system. This is the part of the nervous system that regulates involuntary functions like breathing rate and blood pressure. Balancing it out has tremendous benefits for overall health. The deep inhalations and forceful exhalations of Bhastrika clear out the airways and sinuses, providing relief for respiratory issues. It's like a cleansing breeze blowing through the body, carrying away impurities and blockages, that arise from excess of wind, bile and phlegm. You'll feel an inner warmth spreading through your body, as if you're sitting by the fire on a cold winter's day. This is the nadis (little rivers) at work, the energy highways running throughout the body. Bhastrika Pranayama purifies these pathways so your energy flows unobstructed. As the mind and body relax into the rhythmic breathing, you'll become more aware of the present moment. Bhastrika brings a sense of inner calm and clarity, allowing you to tune in to yourself and your surroundings.

The Bhastrika is a physically challenging form of exercise. If you are pregnant or have any serious health conditions, such as a heart condition, make sure to consult your doctor first before engaging in any of these exercises. You can find many videos online to guide you, but if you're just starting out, I recommend finding a practitioner to show you the ropes in person. These breathing exercises are not to be taken lightly.

The first time I tried Sudarshan Kriya, it was far from a walk in the park. In fact, it felt like I was walking through the fires of hell! My thoughts were doing the cha-cha like a caffeinated monkey on a trampoline bouncing all over the place, utterly incapable of focusing on my breathing. Focus, I told myself. *Just keep coming back to the breath.*

Inhale. Exhale. Inhale. Exhale.

Meditation and breathwork used to be difficult for me in the past, as I had this constant mind chatter and mind wandering, but I persevered through the struggle, determined to tame my unruly mind. And then, something shifted. For the first time, my mind stilled. The chattering ceased. An oasis of calm emerged, and I found myself fully immersed in the meditation, conscious only of each inhale and exhale. It was in this moment of mental quiet that I truly experienced Sudarshan Kriya not just as a practice, but as a state of being.

As Archangel Michael says, *"Meditation is upgrading your spiritual reception by finetuning the antenna within, and the only way you're going to do that is by sitting solely with yourself and tinkering with the mind and body through the use of breathwork. Fair to say, that most will state, they have not the time nor a care for this in the world, they're too busy scrolling their feeds to sit in stillness. and would rather remain rocking back and forth in their straitjacket, living in their created inconsistencies and hiccups as they are. To that I say, cheers, live your life as you see fit my Child, but know that by healing the potholes within the meridian highway whizzing in that body of yours, will do wonders, for of course, your body, but also that mind and soul of yours. They're all connected like cogs in a cosmic clock.*

If your body is hurting, it is because your mind is hurting, and thus your soul has been beautifully incapacitated. If you keep feeding your mind with all that goes on in the outer world, allowing your senses to be rocked like a fattened–up cat in the cradle living in the squalor of fear, then your body will take a hit, with your soul still being rather limply incarcerated. If your soul is mute, as you are refusing to listen to the voice of your inner north, rather listening to the outer bravado and the clap clap narrative, living in the outer, rather than from the inner, vibing back out in the outer, then your body will duly cater to the smacks and slaps you give it, causing you to twirl away from the beautiful divine sacred geometrical grid of your wonderful self.

If you decide, that you'd rather align your soul back with your body, by releasing all the paperwork of the many archived experiences having caused these constant inflated Zeppelin triggers, where you acted upon your conditioning and the mumbo jumbo of an earthly storyline, then I urge thee to try the power of the I AM of breathwork, relinquishing the barriers and the fear that kept you imprisoned within those self-made brick walls, allowing for thee to be free and thus returning to being the mathematical formulation and equation to the energetic in tune sequence of the divine BEing that you most truly, wholesomely and authentically are. To live or not to live? That is like saying to breathe or not to breathe, for without the intake of oxygen one cannot deem to live, and yet allow for the oxygen to flow in its entirety through your body. To live fully, you've got to breathe fully. Use the breath in its optimum capacity, to allow for the body and soul to unite in a dance of splendor, of recognition and understanding, rather than remaining but shallow breathing tripping over your own created and formulated inconsistent unhealed experiences."

The Sudarshan Kriya was an experience like no other. For over two hours, I sat cross-legged on the hard floor, sans back support, as my bony legs grew increasingly pained. Not exactly peaches and cream, but I focused my breath on those aching spots whenever that discomfort shot up my spine like lightning on a clear day. Years of back problems had taught me to live with the pain. It took me many more years of releasing all the heaviness of the trauma I carried with me, being the wuss and walk me over I was. Out there, I hoped to make an appointment at the Panchakarma clinic when it was over as some relief would be most welcome.

When I practiced Pranayama during the Basic Course, I found it challenging. My face trembled slightly and my hands and arms froze up, feeling heavier than a sack of wet cement. I could not move them, uncomfortable as it was. Lying down with my eyes closed brought no relief. My right hand remained clenched in a claw, numb even in rest. Only at the end, when we sat up and opened our eyes, did the feeling slowly return to my hand. I asked Dr. Divya how this was possible, and she said it was due to the lack of circular blood flow and blocked muscles in my neck, hence my severe neck pain, headaches, and acid reflux I often suffered from. The stress hormones that flood our system during traumatic episodes become wired into our biology, altering the natural rhythms and responses of our physiology. Memories of the trauma become trapped not just in the neural pathways of the brain, but in the cellular structures throughout our entire body. When left unresolved, trauma becomes an indelible part of our very essence, shaping our thoughts, behaviors, and physiological functioning in ways that can be challenging to overcome.

Breathing techniques are powerful! The Basic Course showed me simple ways to tap into my own inner power using my breath. Just forty days of practice brought me more inner peace, calming my emotions. I felt centered and more present. Who knew breathing consciously could make me feel so good?

There are numerous benefits for those willing to take on the challenge: more energy, less stress, better sleep, and more harmonious relationships. Breathwork opened the door to my healing, but the journey continues. Even though I have healed many of my past experiences, I'm still in the process of healing from other experiences as they crop up, and breathwork is part of that process. Commit to forty days of conscious breathing practice and see what transformations unfold. Give it a try and breathe yourself to a whole new state of being!

SIMPLE BREATHWORK MEDITATION EXERCISE

To recenter and return to a state of inner peace, sit still and breathe deeply. Feel your thoughts drift away like gentle clouds across a serene blue sky. Expand into the infinite calm as you become one with the Universe. Let go and float into transcendence. Each breath takes you deeper into calmness. Follow the breath to the quiet place inside.

> Inhale for four counts.
> Hold for four counts.
> Exhale for six counts.
> Hold for four counts.
> Repeat.

Breathe in deeply, filling your lungs completely. Hold the breath for a moment, feeling your body expand. Slowly exhale through slightly parted lips if you wish, emptying yourself fully. Pause briefly before your next breath. Inhale again deeply, inviting calmness. Hold...then release the breath steadily. With each mindful breath, feel your tension melting away. Continue at an easy, relaxed pace: inhale, hold, exhale, hold. Let go of all else and just breathe.

Visualization

Visualize your root chakra as the bedrock of your being. Envision it sprouting deep, sturdy roots that reach down into the earth, just as a majestic tree would. Connect these roots to the very heart of Mother Earth. Visualize them wrapping around her luminous, crystalline core three times in a loving, nurturing embrace. This magnificent, glowing center holds the essence of Mother Gaia's divine energy. Embracing the ancient wisdom of "as within, so without," consciously allow the energy to flow back up through your roots and feel it expand, flowing up through your body like a rising tide. Feel it swelling and swirling, filling every cell, every organ, every limb, until your whole physical vessel is aglow with this divine force. Allow it to continue its expansion, rising up through your crown chakra at the top of your head, cascading outward to envelop your entire outer form. Visualize this luminous energy field surrounding you, shimmering and pulsing with energy. Embrace this sensation, for it signifies that you are fully present—both in the moment and within yourself

Set an Intention

This can be a goal you want to achieve, a change you want to see, or anything else you would like to unfold. As you sit in stillness and continue your steady breaths, clearly formulate your intent in your mind. Feel it emotionally as if it is already real, and plant this tiny seedling of intent deep in the warm, nurturing soil of your heart. Water it with love and faith, and then let it go completely, without worrying over it or clinging to expectations. Trust the process that your intent has been released into the cosmic consciousness where it can now grow and blossom in its own time and way. Maintain an attitude of openness, allowing your intent to unfold according to divine wisdom. Your only responsibility is to tend to the soil of your heart, keeping it soft and receptive through daily spiritual practices. From this space of loving awareness, you will witness the miraculous manifestation of your intention, as it blossoms and bears fruit in its own divine season.

Use a Meditation Mantra

Embrace the power of the mantra, **"Aham Brahmasmi"**, meaning I AM the Universe. When we integrate this mantra into our awareness, we transcend the illusion of separation. Repeat it and feel the universe's energy flowing through you. You ARE the universe, as much as the universe is a part of you. We are all connected, little, universal specks incorporated within a physical body, and together we dance in this cosmic ballroom, breathing our world into existence.

Feel free to chant this meditation mantra in silence or aloud for as long as you wish, whether it's ten minutes or fifteen minutes. The choice is completely yours, so trust your intuition and do what resonates with you.

CHAPTER 11
THE ASCENDED MASTER GANESHA

LET US CONTINUE OUR journey with the magnificent Ganesha (also known as Ganesh), a true ascended master of love and wisdom. This enlightened being radiates such compassion and grace. I feel honored to learn more about Ganesha and share his teachings of oneness and joy with you. Though his appearance may seem unusual—he has the head of an elephant and body of a human—his energy is pure divinity.

Lord Ganesha is the son of the Great Transformer, Shiva, who from the ashes of ruin builds anew, and the beautiful Goddess Parvati, the Mother Goddess and devotee to Gaia. Together, they created Ganesha, remover of obstacles. With his elephant head, he tramples that which blocks our path. His wisdom guides us through darkness and into light. Honor Ganesha, and walk steadily towards truth.

As a Master of the 5th Ray of healing and ancient wisdom, Ganesha has a gentle nature with a good dose of wit. He loves to reveal profound truths in a light-hearted way that makes you chuckle. You can't help but smile at his enlightened sense of humor. Ganesha works alongside the Ascended Master Hilarion, spreading the green light of the 5th Ray. If you need some witty wisdom delivered with a twinkle in the eye, call on the delightful Ganesha. His humor and healing touch is bound to lift your spirits. He gently leads us to remove those stones blocking our path and invites us to open our hearts and walk forward with faith into new beginnings.

THE ASCENDED MASTER GANESHA

My father, who crossed over in 1988 and is currently an interdimensional gatekeeper and a member of one of the Intergalactic Councils, was a deeply spiritual individual with a profound connection to the divine. I talk more about his role in my first book, *BE-com-ing Authentically Me*, and how he now serves as a guardian, bridging the many dimensions. He loved both Krishna and Ganesha and had pictures of them in his meditation scriptures when we lived in Malaysia. The Ascended Master Ganesha is a chatterbox, and there in a wink and a blink as soon as you call his name. He will help you work through any tricky stuff on your soul's sacred path to growth and enlightenment. You can always count on Ganesha for a lively cosmic pep talk!

"I AM Lord Ganesha, Light Weaver of the Sun, weaving but Light through the darkness of the clouds within the Soul of one, where one has created but obstacles of a mere illusion, yet hides in fear for the undoubtedly created reality thereof. My Child, all experiences thrust towards you are a mirage, a mindset one has created into the material of one's reality and yet that reality is an illusion, for experiences are merely here not to keep you in the dark night of the soul, harboring but all your innate chickened-out fears but to enlighten you into the light of the sweet, divine, honey-dripping expansion of yourself.

I AM your pick-me-up-out-of-the-gutter, your California-dreamin- on-a-cold-winters'-day.

I AM your pocket full of sunshine, your shadow chaser on those cloudy 'clam chowdy' days.

I AM the Achilles heel to your hovering lightning and thunder, offering you a rebuke in cautionary tales of your experiences.

I AM the positivo to your negativo, the insistent mailman delivering— but Lord help you me—straightforward messages of enlightened awareness to your letterbox mind for you to open and read.

I AM the chocolate box at the end of a mud crawl of an experience.

I AM the piñata to your 'aha', the spin-me-round-hit-me-with-the-stick to reveal the sweet delights of your 'pained' experiences.

I AM the cheese to your knackebrot, the bumblebee to your waspy sting, the lemon balm to your self-inflicted wounds.

I AM the Autobot to your Decepticon, the transformer to your oil contaminated mind, helping you to help yourself transform your inner world.

I AM the traffic light to halt you from your own stupidity, the beat cop to your inexperience, easing you back into your true lane of soul.

I AM the drill sergeant to your wonky, screwed-up experiences, unscrewing the obstruction and teaching you the art of resilience and patience without screwing you over, making sure your head is screwed on the right way going forward.

I AM the tissue to the snot of your experiences.

I AM the lifeguard to your drowning mind.

I AM the ice cream to your root beer float, the brain freeze to help instill those 'eureka' moments to your trials and tribulations.

I AM the jalapeno pepper masked as a caramelized, honey-infused pizza topping, to stunt you in your current ways, allowing you to sweat the kick and 'zing' of your experiences.

I AM the warmth of a chocolate covered cherry bomb to your rum infused and intoxicated mind.

I AM the jingle bell rock to your moody blues.

I AM that soulful song in your beating heart.

I AM that lovely 'tequila sunrise' in your 'absinthe minded' mind.

THE ASCENDED MASTER GANESHA

I AM the good guy to your inner mean girl.

I AM the exterminator to the overgrown, jungle fever weeds in your head.

I AM the rickety rickshaw driver hustling you out of the hustling, crowded, barely lamplit streets of your overbearing thoughts im Kopf.

I AM the stomp in the yard salt and pepper mover shaker to your stuck in the mud tandoori mind playground.

I AM the drop of vanilla essence to your coffee beans.

I AM your fire-in-the-hole, loosening the rocks within the stalemate of your confined, internalized experiences.

I AM the splat in your face apple pie, breaking the hearty, hardened crust of your hardened self, to make you realize the sweet, cinnamon-y taste within your earthly experiences.

I AM your anti-toe-stubber, to aid you in easing off stubbing your toe on those same repetitive experiences.

I AM the spring cleaner to your emotional bounce, giving you tips on all your personal unhealed experiences you've been hauling around in that overloaded personal shopping bag of unresolved hurt and traumas. Time to stop hitting those clearing racks and taking on everyone else's trinkets, junk, and useless gadgets.

I AM the caped super hero to your burped up and catnipped-out Heathcliff.

I AM the Garfield to your out-of-control, dim-witted, licking, people-pleasing Odie, or AM I that loveable, drooling Odie to your lazy, overindulgent, cynical Garfield?

I AM Ganesha, serving the underdog cast into the nets of troubled waters. Think not of me as having an elephant head, for I may portray myself to thee in such a manner purely for recognition, as per the story told in the many tongues of Man. I most pertinently wear not a mask, yet you have conceived to leave me but as a portrayal with the illusion of me with le masque d'un éléphant.

Man wears many a mask to get through their often-weary Earthly travels, having been habituated according to the playbook of the false brethren, living in the suit of one's unauthenticated selves. It seems that one would rather willingly create and wear a mask than see the truth of the matter at hand. It is much easier to live in the untruth of one's existence than to see the inherent darkness that has enveloped and hugged much of humanity in its tight embrace in the truth of l'exposé of what it is with dead cert.

Humanity is but in perfect denial of themselves, and thus often take not the responsibility to enhance the level of the playing field through one's encountered experiences. If one realized life is an illusion and that one's soul is merely here for the enlightenment of oneself, according to the rules of thine own self be true, then life would be less 'lambastic' and one would stop chastising oneself and each other in this lala land of polarities that one has been so induced into."

Ganesha, ever the light weaver, dissipates the obstacles in our path like a hurdle runner. He helps us navigate through the tangled tapestry of our sorry mishaps, guiding us from the darkness we've woven back into light and laughter. When you find yourself stuck in that dark pit of your own making, don't just sit there wallowing in self-pity and the "oh-why-me syndrome!" Instead, call on Ganesha and let his light guide you as you weave your way out of the shadows and into the glorious sunshine of self-realization. With his help, you can turn your stumbling blocks into stepping stones.

Ganesha says to think of him as a taxi driver, weaving his way through traffic to get you out of the maze of that lost soul syndrome, taking you away from the bumpy back roads of life and steering you back onto the soul highway and the "hallelujah" light of self. He encourages you to continue journeying on to your dreams and aspirations, back into the lightness and breath of the heart of self. Slip on back into the driver's seat and thank Ganesha. Take control of the steering wheel and the navigation of your life, knowing full well that transformation is the key to the salvation of yourself, and the way out of the jumbled mess of this frequented paradigm you have gotten yourself so roped into.

Heal-up, power-up, and deal with all that s*** that is surfacing, and you will come to the conclusion that this grandeur of a movie is merely a created playbook of illusion. The more confused you become, the more it stretches you beyond the measures of exasperation to want to heal. The only way out is in, the only way up is down, left is right, and right is left. Yet the middle road is the road one must choose, to forge ahead and blaze a trail through the denseness of one's created "foliage," a jungle of entangled growth in one's upside-down life. Journey back to the very sanity and light of your soul.

Life may have thrown you into the belly of the beast, and the darkness may be gently strangling your spirit. Stay off the radar of despair, and know that the pilot flame within you still flickers, longing to blaze into a glorious fire once more. These trials are not punishments. They're not a hornet's nest wanting to sting you to oblivion, but more like a hidden treasure trove packed with nuggets of wisdom waiting to be discovered in the depths of your spirit. Embrace these challenges, accept them, appreciate them, and give them a high-five. Each struggle is like a little nudge from the universe, an opportunity to recover the spark of that inner light that you are. And for the love of God, linger not in tinkling around in them! It causes nothing but a wee wrinkle in the heart of your beautiful radiant soul. Stop rummaging through those old wounds and regrets like a bear searching for honey in a trash can! The present is shining like a disco ball, full of possibilities just waiting for you to dance into them.

"I AM the Sparkle to Your I AM, as You are the Sparkle to my I AM, for we are all Sparkles of the I AM reflecting in each other, making one

another more luminous through the journey of life and the evolvement of Consciousness.

I'm on the Highway to Hell Light, transcending above the clouds of your created mess and accumulated frustrations, showing you all from above as per below, that life in itself seen from above is but miniscule than when one remains but in the dire straits of one's mess below.

My thoughts to your Mind, your thoughts to my Mind, your heart to my heart, blending into the melting pot of One Divine Consciousness. Separation is nihil, it is just a made-up illusion of a duality propulsion into the existence of a continuous dueling of words and actions with the EGO in the driver's seat. Imagine your body like this vast neural network, an energetic highway consistent of the many and various branches and offshoots, yet always connecting back to each other moving at the melodious beat of one's pace according to the words and whispers of one's every thought and one's every action, corresponding back to the atoms within. How you act within is how you act without, all is formulated within to act according to the calculation of the emulsion and pulse of that energetic formula, equating to the outcome of manifestation and materialization within the energy quantum field without. When one is in sync, all works beautifully and harmonically according to the pure octaves of the body, mind, and soul, and yet when one's highway has clogged the pot with a variety of created potholes due to one's accumulated e-motional debris causing a tidal wave of chaos littering one with inconsistencies and thus the very flow of life. One's life becomes a case of stop and go in one's own created network of a piled-up traffic jam. To iron out the created creases of these wonderful frustrations and issues of one's experiences is to understand that you are as much the creator, the destroyer, as you are your own problem solver, for all within bends according to thy will be done.

All problems should be taken with a lightness of the heart, for in the lightness thereof, one will prevail to weave and maneuver far more easily through the journey of life than with an incurred stalemate of a heaviness, of being at an impasse with the self and the situation. If you're stuck, stop steaming yourself up in your confined existence, causing you nothing but the fiery ants-in-your-pants syndrome, leaving you breathless, anxious, and in a daze within your very frazzled embodiment. Stop running, find your inner ant eater collecting all those sizzling like a steak experiences, transforming these impudent roadblocks, recentering yourself to resolve but the matter of the experience given at hand."

Ganesha weaves through traffic with such grace, showing us a leaf out of his book with the same ease with which your created problems can be resolved. You can transcend above the chaos of your drama, like the dew drops of the morn' gently falling and being absorbed as food for thought, gently dissipated by the warmth of the rising sun. The joy of living in one's authentic bliss is the true elixir of life.

Always remember that you are not here to prove yourself to others, but to approve of yourself and every step you take in nurturing your own soul. You are here to glow your glow, lighting the way for others to find their own brilliance and helping them figure out who they are in this cosmic dance we call life.

As my Venusian Brother Lord Sananda, (more commonly known as Jesus Christ), says:

"Be truthful in your ways always, for without truth, one would be wrapped in one's own sticky residue, fumbling and tripping over one's two left feet, digging a far deeper hole, attracting nothing but flies of negativity, which cascade into a sheer misery of one's chosen diabolical life.

I AM the Way, not your Way or the Highway, but I will assuredly lead the Way of I AM, the Way to You is the Way back to the vibrance and the light of the iridescent self. I AM the Truth as much as you are the Truth—not the obscured Truth of who one believes to be of Truth of Self, but the Truth of the Light of Who I AM, shining forth into the veiled obtrusion of the Truth of the Light You Are. So, ask yourself, are you truly living in your truth as I lived in the truth of Who I was and Who

I AM, or are you living a version of yourself you perceive to be truth, or in truth is an unauthenticated version of the truth? I AM Life as much as you are Life, unless one lives but a life being a mere institutionalized zombie within the coordinated system of living life, which is a life of being lived rather than living one's life according to the syncing of one's heart's desires in the breathing of the Oneness of the truth of self, of who one authentically and unapologetically is. Create a life according to your very Divine Soul I AM Rhythm, rather than to those turbulent Jazzy hues of Blues, slumping into the decimation of oneself.

'No one comes to the Father except through me' means no one prays to me to get to the Divine Energy of Godly goodness, as that has been badly construed by the illicitness of the poisoned tongue of Man. One becomes but vivacious in the jest of speaking one's truth, and the story over time and many moons has gotten lost and layered like the thick and frosted icing on a cake of the true meaning of the words I have but once spoken. If one lives from the heart center, and through that beautiful radiance of the heart, then one realizes that one is but a beautiful part of that same Divine Source as I AM, for I AM You and You are Me, we are but mere dancing lights of the same One Divine Creator, the One Orchestrator and Architect of All Life. You are One with Me as I AM One with You, as we are All One and part of each other and everything in the entire cosmic convolution with no beginning and no end.

Ye are God, my Child. Ye are but as Godly Divine as I AM Godly and Heavenly Divine. You pray to me to speak to Creator, and yet you pray to You, your own beautiful Source. If one asketh with the heart of the pure and Divine Oneness within, in the understanding that one is One with All as All is One with You, and separation is but a created feat to keep you from the very breath of the light of your true I AM, then one's life is filled with an instant of infinite wonder: that all are connected like beautiful, never-ending, twinkling Christmas lights of jubilant, evolving consciousness in this spectacular spectrum of the Earth and All in the Multiverse. Ye are a God walking, a God Wonder of exceptional and exquisite beauty, so I ask thee to walk the way in thy radiant truth and to live a wholesome life according to thine authenticated self, of the I AM BE True.

Live forth in having that sweet, divine cocktail of love for yourself and all, reverberating that light back to the Divine Heart of the Earth and the Cosmos, and merely call on me when you feel at a loss, having bargained with that callous 'devil' on your shoulder, whispering mere poppycock in your ears, allowing for you to tumble in the poison ivy of your experiences, into a rather burning, nettled situation of a pickled phenomenon, too exasperated to find a way out. Never fear, for I AM here and always will BE, for I AM as You Are."

CHAPTER 12
THE AILMENTS OF MODERN SOCIETY

"To move forward rather than remaining in the stigma of that stale dance with others, all but for the mere pleasure of their own selves, dance the dance of life with your own beautiful soul, enfolding yourself with ribbons of love. Lovingly dance away the heartache, the pain, and your fears of those gripped-on experiences."

—*The Divine*

TECHNOLOGY, SOCIAL MEDIA, AND PEER PRESSURE

Growing up in the era of the 1980s and 1990s, we were the last lucky kids, we rocked our childhood back then. With just a landline phone and boxy TVs, people actually talked—like, really talked. We forged real connections. But then society went off the rails. Now everyone's glued to their devices 24/7 like hamsters on a treadmill, too busy to catch up over a cold one.

I blame the media for shoving junk food news and opinions down our throats. Our minds get hijacked by clickbait and we lose ourselves in the social media void. We're so plugged into technology that we've unplugged from each other. But get this: we're all connected, souls floating through the same cosmic web. We just have to reach out, catch someone's eye, and spark up a chat. We may be living in a selfie-obsessed world, but we can still tap into old-school socializing. Ditch the devices and tune into the people around you. We're starving for human connection—the kind that feeds the soul. Let's link up and breathe in that sweet oxygen of camaraderie once more. The 80s and 90s may be gone, but we can bring back that feeling of belonging.

How long has it been since someone sincerely asked how you were doing? Not just that mere paraphrase of politeness, a common courtesy to commence a conversation. Most folks just put on a friendly face to butter you up and get what they want. They play nice, but it's all about their own gain. When's the last time someone cared enough to really check in on you, expecting nothing in return? Those moments of true connection feel few and far between.

Many of us feel lost in this rapidly changing world. We try and grasp at the familiar to stay afloat, even when it contradicts our soul's calling. This is exactly what causes us to feel misaligned within, with our soul grappling with the sheer inconsistencies we throw at our mind. This can convolute to possible dis-ease within our bodies, our lives, and our environment. Each day, our senses drink in society's restless currents until we forget who we are and why we are here, having lost ourselves completely in the swirl of an artificial society. We find that we, too, have become "artificial." Finding our authentic selves seems like a nightmare, especially when we cannot fathom what being our authentic selves even means.

We live in such a technocratic society, with many of us having become dependent—or even addicted—to technology, suffering drawbacks from merely being without it. We have become disconnected from ourselves, others, and the world around us. Our society has reduced us to tech-zombies, stumbling blindly from one digital "fix" to the next. We're more in love with our tech than our own humanity. Our Wi-Fi

THE AILMENTS OF MODERN SOCIETY

is now the lifeblood pumping through our veins. No amount of likes, shares, or clever emojis can replace real human connection. It's time to put down the device, look up, and reconnect.

We allow society to dictate who we should be, rather than choosing who to be. We merely exist and scurry about like regulated ants, working along the conveyor belt of life. We mindlessly consume the constant torrent of information bombarding our senses, creating cognitive dissonance to sway our minds and our belief systems, and to influence our behaviors. To control humanity, you must control the people that manage the population. This is precisely what those in power so gleefully do by controlling the narrative disseminating information and material, out of (as they state), social and cultural benefit for all in accordance with their spirit, not ours. If we choose to ingest all that is fed to us, with our mind eagerly absorbing the various degrees of toxic cocktails as the truth, then our minds may well end up warped into a blackhole and lost in the void. We will have the life sucked out of us if we allow ourselves to become disempowered, playing the role of fiddling puppets dancing on strings. It's time to cut those strings and to look within ourselves. It's time to rediscover our inner light, infuse our lives with self-love and reclaim the power to think for ourselves. When we know our own truth, we can no longer be manipulated by external narratives and we come to the realization that our destiny lies in our own hands.

I'm struck by how everyone is glued to their phones and tablets, oblivious to those around them. It's a sea of bobbing heads, down-cast eyes, and scrolling thumbs. I get it—we all need an escape sometimes. But have we become so disconnected that common courtesy no longer applies? (Don't even get me started on the "gym zombies" parked on the equipment, mindlessly tapping away, taking endless selfies and videos, with no awareness of others waiting their turn. It's inconsiderate and annoying as hell). It's a sad truth that these days our eyes are more focused on our phone screens than on each other. We pour our energy into scrolling and swiping instead of having real conversations. Our phones demand our constant attention, and we readily give it to them, nurturing our digital connections even as our real-life relationships with friends and family members suffer. When is the last time you put your phone down and really tuned in to the people around you, giving them your undivided attention? Around the dinner table, across from our loved ones, we're staring at our screens. In restaurants, we ignore our dining companions in favor of scrolling or tapping. We're physically present but mentally absent, trading genuine moments for digital distractions.

As a result of our addiction to technology, our attention spans are suffering, and we've lost the art of eye contact. We no longer realize the simple joy of conversation. I miss the good old days when phones were chained to the wall like medieval prisoners. (Ah, the joy of yelling across the house for someone to get off the landline so you could use the internet. And who could forget the serene sound of busy signals, or the thrill of slamming down a receiver to dramatically end a call?) Sure, life moved a little slower back then. Conversations meandered leisurely, instead of text messages firing off rapidly. Plans were made in advance without constant calendar notifications. We were all a little less distracted and a little more present with each other. We communicated differently, living a more heart-centered life rather than an ego-centered one.

Constant social media streams keep us detached and exposed to intense peer pressure, consciously or not. Peer pressure is a contagion that infects us all, twisting our minds to conform to the wants and needs of others, all to fit in with the so-called "normal folks." This causes us to deviate ever further away from our true nature. Our souls were not designed to live this way. We shove our true selves away and do whatever it takes to be accepted, even if it means betraying ourselves. Why do something that goes against everything you believe in all because you feel the need to be accepted by others? Why is there an expectation to do what's trending?

Social media piles on the peer pressure, bombarding us with filtered, altered photos that scream, "My life is perfect and yours sucks!" The popular media also perpetuates this vicious cycle by promoting unrealistic ideals that make us feel insecure. We're trapped in an endless cycle of comparison, anxiously examining how we measure up against the endless parade of "picture perfect" images. It's a toxic cycle that undermines our self-worth, causing us to desperately seek validation through "likes." We end up feeling like garbage as we compare our dull reality to the fake awesomeness on our feeds. But no amount of superficial praise can fill the void within.

But you know what? The best weight to lose is the opinions of others, and until we learn to value ourselves from the inside out, we'll remain stuck on this hamster wheel of insecurity, endlessly chasing the illusion of perfection in an imperfect world. Beauty comes from within and is radiated through the light of our being. The path to freedom starts with self-acceptance, recognizing our inherent worth beyond any superficial measures of success or failure. Only with this recognition can we break free of this exhausting game of "compare and despair." You matter, so just be your quirky, messy, and beautiful self in this world. As Theodore Roosevelt said, "comparison is the thief of joy."

Teenagers today, with near constant exposure to social media and technology, struggle with the immense pressure to fit in. Constantly bombarded with images of how they "should" look and act, it's no wonder they grasp for acceptance through conforming behaviors. Let's be real—we've all been there. Who didn't want to be popular in high school? But some teens take it too far, turning to substances like alcohol, nicotine, or even nitrous oxide (inhaled for a high and known as "hippy crack") just to impress their friends. I've seen groups of teens parked right by the police station, bold as can be, sucking on colorful balloons and laughing hysterically. Afterwards, they leave empty gas cannisters scattered on the streets. Sadly, the police simply look the other way.

Getting high might provide temporary escape from social anxiety, but it often leads to even riskier behavior. And abusing inhalants like "hippy crack" can cause brain damage, heart complications, and even death. Rather than altering themselves to fit some superficial social norm, I encourage teens to focus on self-acceptance. Read yourself, not other people. Don't let peers make you feel inadequate for being different. Stay true to who you are, and know that real friends will accept you. The high school years are temporary, but discovering your unique worth lasts forever.

As St. Germain states, *"Don't be an outer Alice, living in that deep state of unawareness of the psyche ward of the 3-D Wonderland. Instead, take a trip down to the Wonderland of your inner Alice. You are whole, perfect, and pure—it is the trickster of the mind that muddies the waters thereof, making you believe with utter conviction that you are not."*

CRITICISM AND STRESS

Opinions from people are forever changing like the seasons. Criticism can often feel like a punch to the gut, and our first instinct may be to lash out in defense. Remember to stop and take a breath before you react. Criticism is an opportunity to grow. Winston Churchill likened criticism to an unpleasant experience, yet one that is like medicine for the soul, enabling us to grow, learn, and understand the lessons held within the experience. Don't let criticism change who you are. If you let criticism get to you, you are *choosing* to feel insulted. People's words only have the power you give them.

We humans are like vending machines with complex emotional buttons. When someone says something that triggers us, it's like inserting a coin and hitting just the right button. Suddenly our unresolved feelings come pouring out, and we react in pre-programmed ways based on past experiences. It's as if we've been triggered to dispense a "pre-packaged" emotion from any unhealed experiences, ranging from our childhood to now. While vending machines have limited responses, humans can learn new ones. When we embrace self-awareness, we can take charge of

THE AILMENTS OF MODERN SOCIETY

our buttons, rather than letting other people push them. We can choose how to respond emotionally, turning potential emotional *'Tazmanian Devil'* whirlwinds into gentle breezes. We're more than machines, and we can rewire ourselves. Though words have power, *we* have the ultimate power to transform.

When criticized, shrug your shoulders and keep calm, for it is your reaction to the situation that determines the outcome. Getting triggered only flames our ego, like the Greek god, Hades. Our reasoning takes a backseat while our inner critic rears its head, much like Megatron, the Decepticon in *Transformers*. As we simmer, our whole inner chemistry changes and we start burning from the inside out, feeling agitated and stressed. What does stress even mean, besides running around feeling flustered about people or situations? Does getting worked up over people's opinions truly align with your spirit? It's simply a choice of *how will you react?*

Stress, as defined by my Guides, can be explained with the below acronym:

Stop with the
Ten-mile
Rat-race
Excuse and
Step into
Self-love

Stress is a state of mind, nothing more, nothing less, and is induced by triggers and outer influences which we allow to be dumped upon our mind. We allow stressful thoughts to impact us and hold power over our experiences and emotions. Triggers are on the prowl everywhere! Before we know it, our brains have turned into a toxic dump of adrenaline and cortisol. The mental clutter clouds our thinking until we're overwhelmed by a highspeed salvo of anxious thoughts, pressure-cooking our minds. We feel powerless and utterly paralyzed by the inner turmoil. But it doesn't have to be this way, though it is often easier said than done. We can take back control by focusing on our breath, calming our racing minds, anchoring ourselves in the present moment, and being fully present within ourselves. We have allowed ourselves to be disempowered, but stress has no real power over us unless we allow it. Stress is just a series of chemical reactions, and by cultivating awareness, we can shut out the noise and reconnect with our inner power. The light of consciousness can illuminate even the darkest corners of our minds. When we shine it on our stress, we begin to see it for what it is—a phantom that disappears the moment we stop believing in it, come to terms with our situation, and take back our I AM Power, deciding to heal from our triggers.

"The hue-man race is relentlessly selfish, and yet the features of separation are exactly what you have chosen, all to reveal the triggers of your experiences, so that you come to the understanding to ignore the blasphemy of the many talked, slick, slivery wordings that the planet has been layered and 'filmed' with. It should not be about the me, me, me, and living in a compartmentalized 'me-centric' state of mind, but rather the we, we, we and living in a 'we-centric' state of mind."

—*Lord Sanat Kumara*

We all vibe on different wavelengths of consciousness. Some folks are tuned to 88.1 while you're jamming to 107.5. So, when someone changes the station on you, don't take it personally. They're just listening to a different beat. Mistakes are part of life, but what's important is what we do after them. Try to accept people as they are, just as you accept yourself, and see the learning in all criticisms. Seeing ourselves from the context of space, zooming out for a cosmic perspective, we realize we're specks of dust floating through the universe, smaller than grains of sand on an endless beach. Yet we let ourselves get sucker punched into the

THE AILMENTS OF MODERN SOCIETY

needless drama of our experiences, making mountains out of molehills, as if each daily quibble carries weight. In the grand scheme of existence, little missteps don't really matter. The only intentions that matter are those of your own heart. The only true path is the one beneath your feet; keep walking forward in peace.

We are all dazzling threads in the cosmic tapestry of life, swirling and weaving together through the vast seas of stars. Mother Earth breathes as us and with us, as we journey across the ever-expanding multiverse, exploring worlds both seen and unseen. We are the creation, born from the imagination of the Divine Orchestrator, the Creator. We are cosmic delights birthed into this universal consciousness. The light within us connects us to all things, for we are life, Earth is life, and in this luminous oneness, we find our joy.

A wonderful example of someone who made the most of criticism is Muhammad Ali. His teacher once told him, "You ain't good for nothing." Instead of losing his cool and allowing those stinging words to knock out his dreams, Muhammad trained, determined to prove his teacher wrong and to become the best version of himself. Years later, when Ali finally won Olympic gold in boxing, he didn't gloat or talk trash. He gifted his medal to the very teacher who had doubted him. Now that's how a true champion turns hurt into triumph! Ali showed us all how to rise above criticism and become our best selves.

"When you truly begin to comprehend that everything stems from the creation of your beautiful mind, the world is your oyster as much as the oyster is the pearl to the wisdom of your world within. The simple switch of your current mindset is to understand that at your core, you are pure, raw, unfiltered energy, encapsulated by choice, within the human physical embodiment. The only limit, suffice to say, is the limitations you have imposed upon your beautiful mind of selves. Energy is transient in nature, as much as you are the same. If you live forth by creating from the quantum field that surrounds you, harnessing the energies accordingly,

you can conjure up the life you truly desire. It is not rocket science, it is the mere mathematical equation to get you spinning back to the axis of the grid of your beautifully formulated, geometric design of the humming, energetic, vibrational Self."

—The Council of Ra

From a scientific perspective, the human mind is a most vast and wondrous organism; a complex and fascinating system that scientists are only beginning to unravel. When examined through the lens of scientific study, the mind reveals itself as an intricate web of consciousness and subconsciousness, thought and emotion, memory and imagination. It is the command center that directs our behavior, filtering input from our environment through the senses, processing it, and producing output in the form of actions and reactions.

Consciousness and self-awareness, or what we might call "the mind," originates in the brain, that intricate network of neurons and synapses firing in electrochemical patterns. All our experiences are processed and stored in the hypothalamus, our little mini factory in the brain. From this, neural activity emerges, creating our sense of self and our experience of reality. The mind manifests in our changing thoughts, perceptions, moods, dreams, and aspirations. It is the essence of our humanity.

For scientists, there is still so much to learn about the mysteries of the mind and how physical processes give rise to our rich inner lives. As science peels back the layers, the complexity and wonder only deepen. While science has revealed much about brain function and mental processes, some aspects of human spirituality and subjective experience remain challenging to study empirically. An open-minded approach, recognizing both the powers and limitations of scientific inquiry, may be needed to gain a more complete understanding of consciousness.

So, how can we define "consciousness" then? Do not be fooled by the labels and divisions of this world. Within each of us lies something

THE AILMENTS OF MODERN SOCIETY

far greater than the surface identities we cling to. Beyond thoughts and emotions, beliefs and ideologies, there is a presence—a silent awareness that watches it all unfold. That presence is your true self. Call it "consciousness," call it "the soul," call it "spirit"—no matter the name, this essence cannot be placed into any one group or category. It is simply the space in which everything appears. Rest in that space, and see that we are all one consciousness, dreaming different dreams. No matter our race, gender, age, or nationality, we share the same essence. Once you recognize this beautiful truth, separation falls away. You will see your own face in the eyes of every stranger. Their pain will become your pain, their joy your joy. This is the birth of true compassion: realizing there is no "other". Awaken to who you really are. You are consciousness itself, and within you lies the power to heal—not just your own world, but the world we all share.

You're very much in control of your mind. You're as much the captain as the pirate of your own ship, so take the wheel of your mind and steer it where you want to go. You're the master of your thoughts, don't let your limiting beliefs and fears mutiny against you and hijack your inner voyage. You can either see yourself as the limitless Argonaut you are, or as the chained pirate, riddled with negative emotions, paranoia, and fear of losing the conditioned treasure of the ego. Set your inner compass toward optimism and chart a course filled with purpose. You have the power to navigate the seas of your mind. Make the most of your limitless potential by being the captain of your consciousness, with self-awareness as your first mate. Wherever you want your mental journey to take you, you're in command.

When stress feels overwhelming, it can be tempting to pop pills to get relief. However, this is feeding a billion-dollar beast. When anxiety rears its ugly head, Big Pharma wants you numbed out on their latest concoctions. Pills may act as a quick fix Band-Aid, but the problem will persist. Sure, those little capsules can offer some fast relief. But at what cost? They turn you into a zombie, smothering your emotions instead of working through them. And before you know it, you're trapped, popping prescription candy just to make it through the day. Meanwhile, the drug industry giants laugh all the way to the bank. They designed this vicious cycle, reaping massive profits while you sink deeper into emotional oblivion. Next time stress strikes, try going inward instead of outward. Stop resisting the storms of life and start embracing them with open arms. Take a breather. Go for a run. Get creative. You have the power to heal yourself, so do what works for you. Don't let Big Pharma trick you into taking the easy way out.

"The pharmaceutical industry was created for hue-mans to deviate from the light of their true nature, combatting the bodily fatigue caused by the mind with chemicals, whilst one is already an Al-chemical Being of the Divine, with innate healing abilities. Never subdue the power of the inner to combat the outer. All comes from the medicine cabinet of the inner, filled with the gems of intuition, stillness, and self-knowledge to find the remedy to the malaise one has concocted through the outer, within."

—The Divine

FEAR, DEPRESSION, AND MENTAL HEALTH

Depression is a dis-ease of the mind that controls us. It shows us that the soul within our physical essence is unnourished and thus misaligned, causing us to feel ill. People become ILL (**imbalanced of love and light**), feeling trapped and engulfed, drowning in their own sadness and lackluster sense of life. Depression feels like a darkness descending on us like a heavy cloak, smothering our soul in its suffocating grasp. The light of hope flickers and fades, extinguished by the swirling tides of melancholy. A dense fog envelops the mind, clouding thoughts with doubt and despair. Each step we take feels laden with lead, and we are forced on an interminable trudge through an empty wasteland of desolation. The heart struggles to keep beating under the crushing weight

THE AILMENTS OF MODERN SOCIETY

of never-ending sadness. A bone-deep exhaustion seeps through every fiber of our being, sapping our motivation and leaving an aching void of numbness. The world fades to a monochrome landscape, devoid of meaning. Life simply becomes a mundane exercise of going through the motions, barely keeping your head above the choking tides of the tidal waves of depression. Each breath feels like a battle, with darkness forever nipping at the edges, threatening to pull you under into its inky depths. Trapped in purgatory between living and not, the soul withers in this shadowy limbo.

But even in the bleakest moments, a flicker of hope remains. Though fragile, a lone candle flame, bright with the light still shining from deep within, waits for the chance to glow powerfully once more.

Archangel Michael offers great insight into depression and how to overcome it. He says experiencing depression merely means that you've shot your mind to hell:

"Depression is having cast out the light particle by particle, until one has been swallowed by a humpback whale, standing in the empty void of darkness with nothing but the suffocating chaos of one's thoughts pressing upon the very corners of one's life force, pulsating through the core of one's physical essence. It's much like the street lights being snuffed out one by one, until one is hugged by nothing more than the swirling cold of darkness. One has oh so beautifully batter rammed the 'damned' mind and wounded the spiritual consciousness, carrying one's soul under one's arms, having severed the inner connection with one's divine self, deciding to part ways, leaving the relationship with the hue in you defunct. One avoids oneself, running faster than an ostrich ever would with its head buried deep in the sand, making feeble yet pertinent excuses as to why this happens to one, rather than asking oneself, why this is happening for one? Eventually, one will run out of steam and keel over, under the carried weight of one's created experiences, forcing one to look at the self, listening to the feelings that require attention. Sit down with those

triggered demons, peel back the layers of the pain held within, get to the root of these surfaced feelings, love them, hug them, and forgive oneself, rather than ground hogging them and spinning a thousand stories in one's head, causing one to grind to a halt, burning within the anxiety of one's emotions.

Depression is being in a 'funk' with oneself, being in a deflated state of not giving a damn. And yet walking through the damned dark night of soul is the grandest opportunity to inflate and breathe back love into the heart of self.

See depression not as a foe, but embrace it as a long-lost friend in need, here to teach you the joys of the dualities, of that dance eternal of light and darkness, allowing you to bond and merge, alleviating the veil of heaviness, and seeing the light of things in all situations. For looking at the broken aspects of your fractured mind is the key to the locked door of returning to a divine love of self.

God is the mere reflection of all that you are, echoing back to the creation of the energetic frequency that is God Infinite Source. It is the echo of that valley within oneself, for how deep is but the depths of one's Soul? My Child, it can truly be as deep as you wish it to be, for you are an infinite and endless source of deep pooled consciousness—there is no beginning and there is no end to you. How can there be, when you are an energetic atomic particle that bounces around within the cosmic multiverse, garnering experiences, constantly expanding, like a chubby critter of a chipmunk stuffing its cheek pouches.

Remember that you have always been the grand magical creator of your own circumstances. Come not to me with this feeble claptrap and flustered excuse and say it is not so, for I will hold a mirror up to thy face and tell thee, it is the mere reflection that keeps pointing fingers back at you; and that no matter how forsaken you feel, you are the sole perpetrator to the hollowness you have so dug within yourself. It is the mere figments of the

THE AILMENTS OF MODERN SOCIETY

bedraggled rat of a hallucination you so choose to see and thus act upon. Come not with the, 'I did not create these extenuating circumstances, for others wished me ill.' Ha—how will one ever commence to move forward from that glued and burnt butt-on-a-seat syndrome, having duly squelched the self? Challenges are opportunities and to sit there and wallow in your created self-pity seems but a disservice to yourself and your life—for life, my Child, will keep tick-tocking away, regardless of whether you decide you are going to make amends or not. Suffering is a condition caused by pure self-infliction. It is flagellating yourself, as that is how one chooses to perceive the experiences shoved your way.

Accept yourself as you are, rather than others saying how you should be. It goes against everything you have been taught and yet, step out of the shadow of that conditioned discomfort and know that you are good as you are. Change is a choice, and by doing the same thing time and again, life will continue to have its merry, slap-me-silly way with you until you have fallen so deep within the void of who you believe yourself to be, but are definitely not, that the only way out is to embark on the journey through. Depression can feel very much like running underwater, slowly suffocating under the weighted layers one has so chained onto one's mind, trying to find a way back to the light on the surface that seems ever so out of reach. And yet when one relinquishes the carried burdens, only then will one be able to swim back up, allowing for not just the mind to be relieved, but also the physical body and the spirit, realigning with the grid of the essence that is you.

Does one tell a seedling how to grow? A seedling grows at its own pace, and in accordance with the natural elements it is subjected to. It does not diminish its growth; it does not stop. So too, accept the created circumstances; stop bashing yourself like a cue ball and start living life according to the beautiful vibrance of your own soul; stop dancing to the life tunes of others, collapsing like an exasperated puppet. Pain should be a beautiful reminder that one has the possibility to grow, having the ability and capability to blossom through the teacup storms of life.

It is the fear of the incarcerated mind that holds you at bay from living life. Rather, one allows the self to be lived. Fear is a mind trap and an illusion, whilst love has the power to overcome any and all obstacles. Fear is the Lord Shen to your locked-in-a-cage Kung Fu Panda. It is your fear that keeps you encapsulated in the dire straits of your created dis-ease of a life. Love is your essence, it is who you are, whilst joy, my Child, is your manifestation. So, will you choose to remain entangled in the noodles of your play-it-safe noodle shop in your overcooked, noodled mind, or will you decide to cross the threshold, leave the opinions of others at the door, transforming your life by learning the art of balance, tackling the demons in your head, and fixing the holes in your Swiss cheese by alchemizing the pain and healing the triggers that kept you triggered due to playing the game of happy trigger on the self?

*Fear either keeps one chained into **f**alling **e**ndlessly or to sod the mind memes and **a**rise **r**evolutionary.*

Fear only holds its grasp if one decides to clasp on to the conditioning of the portrayal of the given status quo.

Fear holds the soul hostage, bound and gagged to a chair whilst the mind feeds the ego, buttering it up making it feel ever so glorified. The more labels attached to the mind, the more cloaked we become and the heavier and more burdened our lives become. It's time to kick fear in the balls, giving it a run for its money.

Life is a walk to the beautiful remembrance of self, thrust with pitfalls on this cosmic boardgame of life. You know full well the answers you desperately seek without lie within, forgotten due to the whacked-on-the head syndrome of popping out the womb cold turkey, suffering that bout of amnesia, and walking through life in a daze and a state of fugue, rather unknowingly, I may add, within this created superficial grid of living in a glass box of the Terra experiment. To remain within the created, painted lines of your current existence or to evolve and take that leap of faith to healing and wanting a better life, understanding that you are the master to your own compass, c'est une choix n'est-ce pas?

THE AILMENTS OF MODERN SOCIETY

Life is the breath of every step you take, let it not go to waste standing there dithering in the Arctic blast of your strung-out experiences. Like the easy-as-ABC rhythmic breathing of your own breath, breathe in the experiences as effortlessly as you breathe them out. Clinging on and suffering with the yammering-dear-God-for-life syndrome is but truly the detriment of one's own undoing, falling into the paleness of that pail of dis-ease.

Move away from living in that self-sabotaging condition of 'he who cast the first stone', punishing yourself by throwing mere punches at yourself, and turn back within to the source of that pain, healing it with the love you hold, within the cloaked corners of your heart and soul.

Life is an experiment to experience, and you have merely incarnated, enacting a series of chosen experiences, I daresay, within your own playbook of life. In fact, you are as much the writer, the producer, and the director as you are an actor, having carefully selected all characters within each scene. Don't like the script? Change the chapter and give each experience a satisfactory ending with nothing but acceptance, love, and forgiveness in your heart—for only through love and forgiveness can you heal the wounded mind and the depress-ed state of feeling deflated, returning to the fullness of the inflated love of self.

Live your life in candor, and in the presence of the I AM, for truly, I AM but you, as you are but the I AM in me. Breathe back that infectious joy of life into your soul, for without joy, you would kill but the experience of truly living, remaining in the stalemate of life.

Remember that the house to your soul is a reflection to the house you live in as much as your mind is a reflection of who you create yourself to be.

Honor yourself as much as we honor and love each and every one of you, returning to the light of the unlayered self in the current experience of the life given."

—Archangel Michael, the Ascended Master
St. Germain, and the Divine Shakespeare Club

Many of us avoid discomfort like it's 2020 and someone just coughed near us. And our emotions? We run away faster than Usain Bolt chasing a gold medal. But here's the thing: our soul is crying out for some TLC after being stuffed in the trunk like an old gym bag. Meanwhile, the ego is cruising in the driver's seat, jamming to tunes and chatter on the outer worldly radio, while the mind happily munches away on snacks and cocktails from the Tequila Mockingbird Diner in the backseat. The ego and mind are happily in cahoots with one another and oblivious to the cries of the loving soul.

The remedy to this malaise? The mind needs to stop drinking those 'Mock-da-Soul' cocktails and put down that greasy burger! It's time to switch off that annoying radio, knock out that phony swish ego, and oh so cozily tuck it in the cramped backseat. Then, open the trunk, and free the soul. Breathe, as the newly freed version of yourself slides into the driver's seat. Now, time for the ego and soul to talk it out and work through your issues, with the mind sober and ready to mediate. No more getting wasted at the Tequila Mockingbird. With the soul driving, the ego learning, and the mind clear, we're finally ready to stop avoiding that place of discomfort.

Q&A WITH SOURCE

I often converse with the Divine, and it may seem that I am talking to myself, but I simply seek wisdom through open and thoughtful dialogue. In quiet moments of reflection, I find meaning in the silence that follows my questions, as inner truth often reveals itself in the stillness. The below is me chit-chatting with the Big Cheese Upstairs—you know, the one who's been around since before time began and will still be here when the last star burns out supernova style. We have these little heart-to-hearts where I spill my guts and ask questions about life with Source dropping me some beads of wisdom, and offering some grand cosmic advice. In all seriousness, as Source always says, You and I are One and the same, and always have been, created from the embers of that same divine cosmic breath. God's gentle voice always responds within the stillness of my heart, wise and kind, lighting my path ahead; and I find solace knowing that I am never alone.

Q: Who are you?
A: I AM You, for I created the very 'hue' that is you! I AM You as much as you are that eternal part of You in Me.

Q: But who are you?
A: I AM the hue in you.

Q: But that doesn't answer my question?
A: I AM your reflection, as much as you are my reflection. You are the reflection, reflecting back at Me, as much as I AM that reflector, reflecting back at you. I AM the reflection in the mirror as much as you are mirror of me in that reflection looking back at you.

Q: It seems a bit of a riddle me that question?
A: I AM not a Riddler, nor do I talk in riddles, but you are the very question and answer to the riddle me that of yours truly you. You are the status quo of recovering the precious gem of everlasting pulsating light that you hold within, enlightening the world with the wonder that you are.

Q: But aren't we separate? Everyone acts like they are.
A: No, my Child, I AM. I exist and have always existed. I exist in all things. I AM not separate from you. I AM the interconnected web of all created consciousness. I AM, and therefore you are all that I AM living and breathing forth in You.

We are One, and always have been. We are two sides of the same coin; two peas in a pod; we are stardust to stardust. It is true that you experience life celebrating your individuality, but we still breathe as One, and always have. I AM the Orchestrator, orchestrating the life of the divine cosmos, as the all of consciousness resides within me, as much as it will always reside within you.

Q: Why do some people think you are a 'man?'
A: I am not some figure of authority as per the manmade fabricated stories that have been blown into the earthly realm of existence, nor am I a grand man with a long white beard sitting on the throne of heaven sipping martini cocktails, surfing the clouds, shooting stars, or cruising along the rays of sunshine lane.

Q: Why are people so scared they will be judged by you and should abide by your laws?
A: The only law in existence is LOVE. I don't judge thee, nor am I a Judge 'meddling' Judy, for that is a manmade phenomenon. I simply love thee. I AM omnipotent, filled with absolute oodles of abundant love for all within the space of cosmic creation.

I AM not a religion, nor did I create a dogmatic belief system, that too is a manufactured script created in the overly polluted factory of man. I AM the mathematical equation of the Alpha and the Omega, the conscious design of the infinite universe brought forth through you, to co-create and express yourself within the hue-man designed embodiment, to enliven said cosmic design by weaving your light through the thoughtful art of your whipped up experiences.

Q: Are you for real?
A: No gimmicks, no games – I live forth in you, always have and always will.

Q: Are you saying I am as powerful as you, and I can create the life I desire?
A: Yes! I created you through creators created by me. Everything in the entire cosmos is a part of Me, an Apfel slice of me as much as I AM a part and a slice within all of them. You are a divine alchemist at its finest, having been pepper sprayed by the earthly conditioning, which has made you lose sight of the truth of the magnificent creator you really are!

THE AILMENTS OF MODERN SOCIETY

Q: So how do I find myself again, as my life hasn't exactly been a bed of roses, in fact it has been marred by trauma and awful experiences?
A: *Isn't that wonderful? The downs should be the steps to your ups. Seek and you shall find my Child. You are the love that I AM. You are the joy that I AM. You are the Force of all that I AM; of all that binds us together. You are the love that you have been seeking all along. All that I AM, you are! You chose these experiences, to help re-evaluate the soul lessons you incarnated with on this plane, to help you transcend that duality; to help you ascend the ladder of experiences, to open your mind to different levels of awareness. You hold all those delicious key ingredients to overcoming within. It is only through the difficulties, that you can find the opportunities to delve into the multifaceted potentialities that life has to offer you. For, without darkness, how could you ever understand the light?*

Life is like that get your knickers in a twist dance game of Dance Dance Revolution. The only way to learn is to become competent, step dancing to the rhythm of your experiences. You may trip. You may stumble. You may fall. It matters not. What matters is that you get up and keep experiencing life, learning from the tumbles as you get comfy with the rhythm and groove, dancing and twirling your way through life and all its experiences.

When you call me, I AM here, for I never left. It is merely you, my Child that has obscured your senses to seeing Me in You.

Q: Were we not made in the image of you?
A: *That is literally not literal; think not that I am indeed a 'man.' I AM nothing and everything at the same time; I AM all, yet I AM none. I AM Light. I AM Dark. I AM One.*

You are a StarSeed, a shimmering star dust particle of evolutionary energy, created out of unconditional love to help alleviate the derogatory swirls of darkness and pain; elevating the consciousness and vibration of not just your own soul, but to inspire others, sowing the seeds of love in their own hearts, so they too may follow the footprints of releasing their pain and do much of the same. You are here to fill Gaia with the radiance of light a la Willy Wonka style, allowing for the Mother to heal, to expand and flow into the rivers of harmony reuniting her, and syncing her with the sweet breath and symphony of the cosmos. Learn to string your own chords, so that the anomalies of the disharmony are released, returning to dancing in unison with your own God self and the supersonic waves of that same cosmic universe.

Q: Why am I even here?
A: *To experience life in all its flavorsome essence; to play the game of life and of cosmic evolution.*

Q: It's all a game?
A: *Everything within creation, eventually transcends consciousness. Without growth how could one ever appreciate to learn anything? A seedling remains not a seedling, nor does a baby remain a baby. Everything grows, flourishes and blossoms in its own time. So, too does Mother Earth; and her time is NOW. You merely feel the current growing pains of the Mother, having outgrown her current phase, as much these growing pains are reflected within the bleeding wounds you still carry.*

You're here to rise above that created character called the EGO, to stop ejecting the god self out, embracing the beauty of your own grace and divinity, returning to that childlike innocence of joyous love and play. For love my Child, is the very breath of your existence. Open your eyes and tenderly flow with the harmony of the melodious cosmos, returning to the grid of your soul within the Merkabah of your very integral multidimensional existence. Know that you are worthy of your love, as much as all are worthy of love. Live with integrity, in truth, and shine forth that inspirational light of love to your fellow beings that walk the earth, trying to find their way back to themselves in the land of confusion. Be a beacon of hope to others as much as I will always shine that beacon of hope forth in your own heart.

THE AILMENTS OF MODERN SOCIETY

MY JOURNEY THROUGH DEPRESSION

I have been borderline depressed several times in my life—or perhaps it was a full-blown depression—but I chose to deal with it in my own way without relying on medication. We all have to discover what's best for us and what resonates with our own beautiful spirit. No judgment here. To me, being "depressed" is merely another label we slap on our minds to identify what we "suffer" from. I was drowning in an ocean of sadness and deeply unhappy with my own life. Waves of depression crashed over me night after night as I cried myself to sleep. Though my inner light was dimmed, I refused to bow down to defeat, and instead I soldiered on with the coping mechanisms I had in place: working like a maniac and starving myself. All this was done to keep the hurt at bay, to keep a lid on my feelings, and I played an endless game of whack-a-mole with my emotions, shoving the trauma back into the bulging archives of my darkened mind, only to have it pop up somewhere else. Working and abstaining from food were things I could control, which is what kept me afloat. Yet in many ways, I was drifting aimlessly, having severed the relationship with myself and kicked my soul to the curb. I was just running on autopilot every single day. There have been many traumas in my life. In childhood, I experienced abuse, lost my dad, my stepdad, and was bullied. I spent time in the toxic modelling industry and was assaulted as a result. I used drugs, had dysfunctional (but beautiful) relationships that I waded into for my soul's ultimate growth, and I was diagnosed with vaginismus. I kept wounding myself, being the sadomasochist I was, too afraid to truly heal. You can't heal any experience if you keep stabbing the same wound over and over again and continue to walk around bleeding.

I have had to start over many times in my life. In my forties, I again found myself having to start from scratch. During that time, I told my mum that I had sweet fa to show for—no money, no family of my own, no home, no kids, no mortgage, no spouse. Meanwhile, social media showed everyone having all of the above. I felt stuck in a hole, a complete failure. I didn't take an antidepressant medication to numb the pain, I'm not wired that way. I knew that it would only suppress what needed to be addressed. Instead, I let the feeling rise. I didn't want the voice of my soul to be muted and thrown back in the dog house, even while my mind was running amok, riddling me—the "user"—with anxiety. As for my ego? Well, the ego was a bully cop at the door, feeding my mind, which remained resistant to any kind of change. My journey through depression was one of self-discovery. I had to follow my intuition to find the healers I needed to help me mend my fragmented, scrambled mind. There were missteps and backslides, but I took responsibility for it all. Piece by piece, I freed myself from self-imposed constraints and gave myself permission to live. The hurtful words of others lost their power, and I understood how their reflections merely showed me what still needed healing within me. I learned to accept, forgive, and love the unconditional shit out of myself, hugging the inner trauma and finally making peace with the person shaped by those experiences, because for the longest time, I had truly hated the very sight of me. As Swiss psychiatrist and psychotherapist Carl Jung said, "Depression is like a woman in black. If she turns up, don't shoo her away. Invite her in, offer her a seat, treat her like a guest and listen to what she wants to say."

Even though I found healing from my past hurts, a process that is still ongoing, my life is not always a bed of roses. 2023 held many challenges, but my smile will never betray the way I feel. In truth, it's nobody's business. Whatever I am meant to experience is something I alone have to deal with and grow from. No one can help me, but me.

My recent challenges could be a result of Saturn's influence in Pisces, bringing with it lessons in karma, commitment, discipline, and setting boundaries. This period will last until early 2026, so let's embrace the challenges and grow from them. And Saturn won't be alone during its murky journey through the waters of this sign, because Neptune, the planet of fogginess, confusion, and of deception, is happily accompanying Saturn, wreaking havoc to wake the masses from their slumber.

THE AILMENTS OF MODERN SOCIETY

The recent restrictions, loneliness, and alienation that Saturn has bowled our way has smacked us on the head like truant school children, leaving us "concussed," wandering in the lands of confusion, and forced to look at the wounds we inflict upon ourselves.

The world is in a transformational phase as much as we are. In many ways, the world we live in seems to be unthreading at the seams rather rapidly. While witnessing the lockdowns of a so-called global pandemic (which I paid no mind to, as it was merely a rude awakening for many), the increasing, senseless school shootings, the many suicides, an ongoing war in the Eastern hemisphere that no one wants, with thousands of innocent people being killed and displaced and careless politicians bickering and scheming on both sides, all while the media perpetuates lies and fear to keep the masses in check, I've come to realize that maybe, just maybe, there is more to life than what we have been led to believe. Humanity has been thoroughly tested, and it has often times felt like we are walking through an endless winter of misery and depression, with all the joy robbed from the insides of our very souls. The world may have gone a little mad, but even Alice had to tumble through the rabbit hole in order to realize who she was. She learned that the "Wonderland" of all that she was and wanted to achieve was already inside of her.

In early 2023, the demands of my dual role at the company left me severely stressed, overworked, and burned out. The strain became so overwhelming that I even developed shortness of breath. Even so, I smiled through the strain and continued putting one foot in front of the other no matter what. It completely killed the joy in me, and yet I was the only party responsible, because I allowed it to affect me that way. After using only a few days of my annual leave in 2022, I was forced to take the remainder all at once. Unfortunately, I was struck by a nasty bout of the flu during my time off. Despite being ill, I ended up working through my personal days to avoid falling behind, which would have required even more work later. The supposed joys of remote working often mean clocking more hours than you ever did in the office.

Hard work has been my crutch for as long as I can remember. I've always buried myself in work to avoid dealing with difficult emotions—and I'm not the only one. We drag ourselves out of bed each morning, trudging to jobs that suck the life out of us. The daily grind has us in its clutches, and we can't break free. We're chained to our desks, whether at home or in an office, and shackled to schedules not of our choosing. We're prisoners doing hard labor, forced to toil away precious hours of our fleeting lives. The time clock is a slave driver's whip, cracking over our backs. We're zombies, eyes glazed, minds numb, just going through the motions, day after day. Is this any way to live? Life's too short to slave away at a job that doesn't set your soul on fire. And you know what? The company would've replaced me within a week if I dropped dead. We weren't born to be drones or pack mules. It's our misery that's played Edward Scissorhands with us and screwed us up. The negative energy we project out into the world simply boomerangs back to us, perpetuating our unhappiness. As Paramahansa Yogananda wisely observed, "Having lots of money while not having inner peace is like dying of thirst while bathing in the ocean."

If you overwater a plant it will drown. Our salaries are the drug our employers give us to keep us firmly rooted in the system, which results in us giving up on our own dreams and aspirations, all to pay our bills. My soul was rebuking against the grind of my incarcerated mind through the influx of my thoughts, that was happily being fed all the experiences by my ego, because I allowed it, not taking back my power, merely ploughing along, causing me a far greater muddle within.

Stressed, depressed, and overwhelmed, I just stopped caring about myself. I was in that *blargh* mode of *I don't give a shit*. I didn't care about my appearance and didn't bother going to the hairdresser. I didn't even brush my hair most days, just tied it up in a messy bun to get it out of my face. I was constantly making up endless to-do lists in my head that kept me up at night with worry. My stress led to some unhealthy coping methods. I started mindlessly munching on choc-

THE AILMENTS OF MODERN SOCIETY

olate to soothe my worries, even though too much chocolate usually makes me feel sick. I was hoarding bags of mini-Cadbury eggs, practically devouring a whole bag a day. Between the chocolate binges, lack of sleep, and the endless, virtual meetings for my job, my body revolted. My cold sores and rosacea flared up painfully on my face. My skin was begging me to stop pumping it full of sugar and let it breathe. I was basically poisoning my body with chocolate and other crap to cope with stress. I just needed something, anything, to take the edge off and get me through another grueling day. I just didn't have the energy to get out of that funk and give a crap about myself or make healthy choices for those few months. I dragged myself to the gym when I could, but more often than not, I just crashed on the couch. I was operating in pure survival mode, running on empty, fueled by nothing but stress and sugar.

While I grappled with feeling overwhelmed at work, my finances took an unwelcome hit. I paid thousands to a PR company I trusted to help pitch me and my books to the media, but instead, it felt like I dropped my money into a cosmic black hole. Soon after, my mother desperately asked me to take out a personal loan for an online stranger who had charmed his way into her heart. Despite my reservations, I laid out my concerns about this seemingly fishy idea. Yet, in the grand theater of life, my heart took center stage, and I couldn't resist my mother's heartfelt plea. The loan turned my already tight budget into a circus act, juggling bills like a clown on a unicycle. While I've since found it in my heart to forgive her, because, let's be real, I love my mum—let's just say the stress of the experience added a hefty layer of fungal misery, leading me to some rather questionable coping mechanisms.

I retreated from social media. Then again, is it really *social*? It's more like *ego media*. It's nothing but ego-trippin' bullshit; a cesspool of insecure peeps desperate for validation. And then there are the "influencers." What the hell does that even mean? Don't buy the lies peddled by those influencers with their fake smiles and product pushing. I needed a break from it all. For months, my spiritual life had been shoved aside as I battled my inner demons alone. People don't get that when you're deep in that dark, shitty place, that it takes Herculean strength just to claw your way out. "Snap out of it," they say, as if it's that easy. On Sundays, I'd stay in my pajamas except to walk the dog. I was a hollow shell, a faded copy of my old self—yet I plastered a smile on my face so no one would see. I let my mind bully my body yet again, starving myself until I'd lost nearly eighteen pounds. I knew I had to find a way out from the deep hole I had so ceremoniously dug for myself. Life's too short to be mean to yourself, because as you well know, you are your home; your soul is home to your body, but sometimes that's easier said than done. This was not the life I wanted for myself; why stay marooned in my own deep-seated despair? No matter how much progress we make and how much work we've done on ourselves, we all have the tendency to slip up. We're all human here. We're all works in progress, stumbling our way through life one messy step at a time. Some days we cha-cha forward, other days we moonwalk backwards. The point is, be gentle with yourself. Progress isn't always linear, but as long as you keep dancing, you'll get there.

Practicing meditation opened my eyes and helped me realign my priorities. Instead of numbing my mind by overworking, I nourished it through breathwork. I plugged myself back into Source, tapping into the I AM powerhouse within, following my passion, and doing what aligns with my spirit. Society often looks at meditation as being a form of "juju" or a waste of time. But I'm not living for society's approval. I'm living for me. Listen to your own heart, ignore the opinions of all the naysayers. Stop merely existing and start living. Work to live, don't live to work, and find what makes your soul come alive.

I came to understand this was just another experience, a test thrown my way, to see what I would do. As St. Germain says: *"You cannot let your life go to squander, my Child, for what will you achieve by kicking that can down the road, thinking tomorrow may be a better day, and worthier of my time to aspire to live your dreams? You need to get out of that funk in your*

THE AILMENTS OF MODERN SOCIETY

head, the joy of your emotions that you have so happily pac-man-munched away, with the Ghost Gang of a Blinky, Pinky, Inky, and Clyde on your tail, causing you to spin out and drown in the fight-or-flight mode of your experiences. Stop riddling the mind with anxiety. Stop feeding it with thoughts that merely cause you to maul around in the swamp of your own crap. Is it worth it? Hmmm, the experience may be, but you need to snap out of the being here, there, and everywhere, living in the shackled doldrums and the sheer misery of yourself. Let life not pass you by, take the critique of others not personally, for they only operate within the field of their own level of consciousness.

Don't allow yourself to be run over like a flattened Wile E. Coyote, or swallowed whole by the in-your-face, scared-to-your-wits label of fear that you've so due diligently rammed down your throat, much like a Hercules being happily devoured by the three-headed serpent, Hydra, living in that limbo land of a twilight zone. And yet, when you are at a total breaking point, with the waves crashing upon the shores of your mind, when that bullet hits the bone, it is that painfully rude awakening of you gasping, gulping, and coughing for air, coming to the realization that you have wounded your mind and shot it to hell by none other than your own staring-back-at-you-reflection, rippling within the riptides of your soul. How far are you willing to go to get caught up in the created maelstrom of your heavy-hearted dramas and experiences? There is no need to hit rock bottom, because you have been through enough to understand that experiences are merely here to help you up your game on the playing field of life, unless you want to remain in the eternal prison of the cosmic game of your own monopolized life? Stop being a sad sight for sorry eyes, and playing the sadistic masochist, constantly flogging yourself, making you well up in your own caused pain. You take schtick from others, then you are a schtick yourself."

We've all been there, stuck in a rut, feeling like life has lost its spark. Even when I felt like everyone else had given up on me, I refused to give up on myself. Real growth starts when you're sick and tired of your own repetitive bullshit. Real growth only happens when you're fed up and desperate for change, when you've got no choice but to evolve. Rock bottom is a foundation you can build on. It was time to start laying those bricks and climb up out of the hole.

I made a commitment: every morning, no matter how crappy I felt, I was going to get up, show up, and keep moving forward. Was it hard? Damn straight it was, but I wasn't going to let those dark, depressive thoughts keep dragging me down. We forget that our darkness is a friend, not a foe. The darkness within us is not something to fear, but something to be embraced. The more we reject the darkness, the more it persists in following us, begging for acceptance. When we finally sit with the darkness and give it a voice, it shares its wisdom. Our shadows remind us we are made whole by both our light and dark together. Make peace with the night inside of you and discover the sunrise of better tomorrows. I wasn't going to let my depressive state get the better of me. I had to take responsibility for my own life, take back my I AM power, and return from that state of utter disempowerment. I had a game plan in my head of moving to Spain, as that was the hardcore nudge I got from the Universe. With an open heart, I made the courageous decision to follow my intuition, trusting in the mysterious forces of the cosmos.

OVERCOMING CHALLENGES AND FINDING INNER STRENGTH

On this wild train ride of life, we hold on to so many ideologies and instilled beliefs, plans, and rules. But all that is merely an illusion, a façade to keep everyone within the lines of the system. When your life comes to a close and you have taken your last breath, will you think "I wish I'd done that" or "what if?" Time is what you make of it. Use it wisely.

"Everything in the entire cosmos consists of sound and vibration, and you are a beautiful, eclectic cosmonaut wandering the earth, leaving a trail of energy wherever you go, and whatever you create. You are a cosmic grooviologist, a DJ spinning the decks creating the spectrum of your very own existence.

THE AILMENTS OF MODERN SOCIETY

Live your life with a little bit more cha cha smooth, a little more jailhouse rock, rather than a two-left-feet peeing-in-your-pants jitterbug. Be that soulful cosmologist, mix it up in the blender, and rather than remaining rigid, become fluid, catching the groove and gist of all your experiences."

—*The Ascended Master St. Germain*

Experiences are merely minute grains of sand in the vastness of the galaxial desert, a drop in the cosmic seas of consciousness. Nothing is permanent, and life's experiences are simply part of the human experiment we have all signed-up for. As St. Germain says, *"Does food remain in your belly till eternity and beyond? Non pas du tout! Your body absorbs the nutrients and excretes the waste, and thus much like experiences, one should absorb the teachings held within and ditch the rest, rather than hanging on to everything, and creating a barrage of unwanted dis-ease, because one chooses to remain constipated!"*

No matter what circumstances we may find ourselves in, if we can imagine a better outcome for ourselves, we can duly create it with the alchemy of our minds. One thought can brighten our day as much as it can ruin our day.

True power lies in the forgiveness of ourselves and others. Forgiveness is not forgetting, but rather the key to unlocking the pent-up hurt and anger we have bottled up inside, replacing toxic emotions with love, wisdom, and understanding. How else can we grow? The past is merely a place to learn from, not to live in. Our ego is like kryptonite to the soul. We hold on to all of our experiences, archiving them in the bulging filing cabinets of our minds, never relinquishing anything, labelling everything, and judging others according to our conditioning of those experiences in the process. How can we ever grow when we take everything personally? We should view everyone as a reflection of what we need to work on within ourselves. As Mahatma Gandhi said, "No one can hurt you without your permission."

"Forgiveness frees up the light of our deflated I AM Power, allowing for the held-on disease to unfurl and seep out of our body, mind, and spirit. It's like emptying a water floatie that was inundated with water due to the punctures one so gleefully pierced, carrying the weight of all those unhealed experiences, and allowing it to bob, float, and glide on the surface of the stream once more. Forgiveness opens up the pathway from the once inflamed conundrum of the mind mouthing into a place of sunshinelicious peace, choosing to grow, expand, and continue on life's ever expansive journey. If you cannot be at peace or at ease with yourself, you will always remain at a dis-ease with yourself and the environment you have so woefully created and have thus chosen to wander in. You are the solution as much as you are the problem to all of life's created quandaries. At any time, you can change the status quo of your world, and thus the outcome of your wanderings. All you need to do is shift your attitude; stop being a stubborn, foaming-at-the-mouth bull, charging against that same wall that won't budge, and instead weave the wand of your inner Merlin to conjure up a rabbit out of a hat solution, n'est-ce pas?"

—*The Ascended Master St. Germain*

Life doesn't come with an instruction manual. There's no step-by-step guide on how to navigate the unexpected challenges it throws our way. But that doesn't mean we are helpless. The most important thing is to truly listen to ourselves. Pay attention to how you're feeling, both emotionally and physically. Your body often knows what you need before your mind even catches up. The symptoms and struggles you experience are real, they're not a sign of weakness or whining. They simply show that life has given you an opportunity to discover your inner strength. While each person's path is unique, you don't have to walk it alone. Reach out to others who make you feel heard and understood. Together, we can learn how to cope one day at a time. There's no perfect formula, but with patience and self-compassion, we can write our own story of growth. It's either swim or drown, ride or die, time out or peace out to breathe and seek the hidden Zen master of a *Shifu* within.

As for my beautiful friend Renu, she felt like she was suffocating in a world that overwhelmed her gentle spirit. She felt trapped in the emptiness and cold of the dark night of the soul, and the only way to find peace was to free her soul from the prison of her anguished body. Her beautiful spirit is now free, having embraced the dance of life eternal, reveling in the giddiness of her lost joy, returning to the pure, boundless and bouncy state of being that had once filled her heart with such warmth and wonder. The heaviness of the physical world that dampened her earthly existence has been lifted. She is now free to explore the mysteries of the great beyond without constraint, and I know Renu's light burns brighter than ever before, dancing amidst the infinite vastness of the celestial star-filled heavens.

CHAPTER 13
WHY THE PAIN AND SUFFERING?

"You are part of everything as much as everything is a part of you, for how can that not be, when you are the very breath of ever-evolving Consciousness?"

—*The Ascended Master St. Germain*

I HAVE OFTEN WONDERED WHY there is a need for so much suffering in the world. Why must humanity endure so much pain? Where does all this violence come from? It truly seems the world has spiraled out of control. But has it really? Or is there order in this divine chaos? Opposites are complimentary, and there is a need for duality. We can only truly learn from the reflections we cast upon each other, unless we shun the light and decide to walk around hiding under the many layers we have so craftily created.

People often ask me, "What's happening with the world? Why is there so much evil? Will it get any better?" It's a fair question given the tumultuous state of current events. When faced with this query, my response is to gently turn the question back on them, asking, "What's happening in your world? Is that getting any better?" My intent is merely to encourage a shift in perspective. The world may have its ups and downs, but what truly matters is what's happening in your own little universe.

Instead of worrying about the big picture, focus on making your world a better place. Sure, the world may seem like a hot mess when we only see the negatives. But guess what? I truly believe that in order for people to awaken from the negative illusion, sometimes things need to fall apart so we can rebuild, heal our wounds, and eventually understand that we've all been played. We need to *unbecome* to eventually *become*, blossoming into standing in our own I AM Power, with a love for ourselves and everything around us. Trust me, when you start spreading positivity and chasing your dreams, the world will follow suit. It is the cumulative effect of many people creating positive change in their own lives that leads to broader societal transformation. By making our own inner worlds better, we create ripples that widen into our outer worlds, in turn inspiring others to cultivate changes in their own lives.

The idea of "evil" is like a deep-rooted tree, with branches that stretch into the very essence of what it means to be human. "Evil" is a mere wordplay—a linguistic connection between "Eve" and "ill"—reflecting a profound truth about the human condition. Eve represents a feminine energy often overlooked in our busy lives, akin to the spiritual nourishment we so often neglect. Ideally, the feminine and masculine energies should coexist harmoniously—the yin to our yang, but too often we find ourselves out of balance, becoming "ill"—imbalanced of love and light.

It takes darkness to know light, sadness to know happiness, pain to understand love, and noise to appreciate silence. By experiencing duality, the soul eventually learns and evolves, rising above the dramedy of life's experiences, understanding and appreciating the lessons entailed and healing through a return to love. There is a divine purpose behind all the suffering we go through, whether it's personal suffering or a natural calamity. Suffering is the remedy to healing ourselves, and it is the best teacher for giving insights into right and wrong. It does not matter how you decide to experience life, or whether you choose to hear or remain locked in the trauma of fear, because eventually, even the most stubborn student will see the light. Our suffering becomes the source of the soul's evolution and learning.

The concepts of yin and yang represent the opposing yet complementary forces in life— the shady and sunny sides, the dark and light. This balance between polarities is the essence of yin and yang. Yin and yang are like the dynamic duo of the universe, one sneaking around in the dark of night while the other struts around like a superstar in the light. In ancient Chinese understanding, the yin and yang symbol is a representation of how things work. The outer circle represents *everything*, whilst the black and white shapes within the circle represent the interaction of two energies, called *yin* (black) and *yang* (white), which cause everything to happen. They are not completely black or white, just as things in life are not completely black or white, and they cannot exist without each other. Just as nobody is purely full of hate—rather, they are merely rejecting the love of self, shunning the light within themselves, and remaining on the trajectory of suffering from the demons of their unhealed experiences. Whilst *yin* signifies the dark, passive, downward, cold, contracting, and weak, *yang*, au contraire, represents all that is bright, active, upward, hot, expanding, and strong. The shape of the yin and yang symbol shows a continual and harmonious flow between these two energies, from yin to yang and then from yang to yin. Just as things expand and contract, like the temperature changing from hot to cold or the ebb and flow of water on the beach, nothing lasts forever, and thus, we need to release our experiences to the winds of change for our soul's growth. Life is a continuous flow of constantly balanced energy; it is only our minds that truly muddy the waters thereof, for we keep ingesting the toxicity, absorbing all that goes on in the outer world, storing everything in the overflowing cabinets of our minds, remembering everything that has happened to us, and acting according to our experiences. We subject ourselves to constant emotional triggers. And then we wonder why we are buggered-up with a dis-ease within the self?

St. Germain reminds us that sometimes we just need to break open, like a cracked egg, in order to confront and address the emotional aftermath of our past experiences.

"Touché mes chéris, one merely needs to crack open, like a Humpty Dumpty, until one pops and deals with the emotional outfall of all stored and unhealed experiences. Any kind of stress (suffering from a depressive state of mind and being riddled with anxiety), serves merely as an alarm bell to wake you the heavens sake up, to heal-up and to stop running ragged, being the often people pleasers you may be. Return to the heart of balance within, living in the flow of who you are, and not who someone decides you should be. Embrace the darkness and swim home to the enlightened hearth and warmth of the sunshine soul of self, for trust me, my Child, life is a beautiful, transformational journey undertaken by the soul, as per the agreed and stipulated contract. As Ursula the sea witch all but gladly stated, 'If you want to cross a bridge, my sweet, you've got to pay the toll.' In other words, if you want to change your life, deep dive into the hues of that magical, divinelicious wonder you so magnificently are and always have been, spreading a little love to those pesky demons in your head, and sweeping the love of light through your mind and soul. And once you sit down, my sweet, knowing that the dirty linen that had saturated your mind and bled into your worldly environment has been cleansed, you cannot feel anything other than a lightened load of a delightful soul of a delighted light.

Remember that each and every one of you is a Universal Ambassador of this beautiful and radiant I AM Light that sits so beautifully in the chambers of your heart space, navigating yourself through the matrix of this entangled jungle you've landed in, like a lost in space, space cadet. It's rather much like a cassette, trying to untangle the tangled cassette tape 'back to the rewind', to then hit the play button and listen to that sweet ole music that hits the notes to the melodious beat of your soul, syncing the synchronic shift of oneself with the cosmos, swinging back in realignment with the self, non? It's like picking a golf club from your inner selection, swinging that

WHY THE PAIN AND SUFFERING?

club, and hitting the ball in the hole of understanding your experiences and healing the dents and bruises you have created along the way. Even after all this, have you forgotten why you're here? Hmmm, well my Child, you are not here to live in this institutionalized matrix, conforming to the norm of the asylum, thinking one is separate, living in a confined cell, remaining but ever so dozily cozy and dosed up in the perkiness of your numbed out meds, happily obliging to the bubbles of that illusion. Non(!), you are here to chuck the meds, awaken your mind and soul and break out of this hyped-up looney bin run by mad, deranged, psychotic doctors in power, who tell you, 'You will own nothing and be happy.' Yet, these swinging fraudulent monkeys own everything, keeping humanity in line by slapping rule upon rule, thinking they are the kings of this jungle they created. My Child, you're here to hop the fence back into the beautiful 'garden' of the world you have so chosen to incarnate upon, understanding that you are a StarSeed with a Divine mission, here to shine forth light, love, and healing into your soul and into the world and the hearts of man, freeing Gaia from the chains of imprisonment that she has for eons been subjected to, allowing her to heal and breathe the breath of life back into the core of her beautiful and enlightened BEing. Elevate your Soul to elevate and celebrate the world in all her beauty, fairing into the new golden dawnin,' and know that we are all brothers and sisters of the Cosmic Divine Light. The only difference between us is the shell we have so duly chosen to embody, for the hue of our soul light within the galaxial grid of the multiverse is the same—do well to remember that, my Child. I bid you adieu and leave you showered with but with much Love and Light."

—*The Ascended Master St. Germain*

Q&A WITH THE RAINBOW WARRIORS FROM THE GALACTIC FEDERATION OF LIGHT

In my first book, *BE-coming Authentically Me*, that I finally finished after two decades and released in 2022, I talk about my awesome aquatic-reptilian-fusion Star Being buddies from the Sirian star belt, who are a multidimensional aspect of who I AM. I absolutely adore them! They're big fans of music and love expressing themselves through songs when they communicate with me.

"Let's dance, put on your red shoes and dance the blues, let's dance, to the song they're playin' on the radio……. In other words, regardless of what mudballs life may throw at you through the concocted mind burps, bleeps, and blunders you have readily ingested, thought up and created into the realms of manifestation, simply bow-wow-wow in gratitude, as life is wasted on a pocketful of illusions. Know that you've got to dance, little sister, don't give up today but twist and shout, sway, move, and dance to the beat of your inner universe, dropping the false notes, a la concertos, in your confused head, and commence being in step tune with your dance partner, the overall cosmic universe."

These are gracious beings, with shimmering, iridescent coloring, mesmerizing oil-slick hues of blue and purple, and they have a fanlike comb on their head. They are incredibly muscular, run like the wind, and are known as both the flamingos and the chameleons of their species, astutely blending into their surroundings.

They have been allies in helping resolve conflicts between the many beings in the multiverse, and they are part of the Galactic Federation. Though warriors at heart (known for their wit, strategic sharpness, and rapid resolutions in combat), they can also be tricksters, making light of any situation, no matter the seriousness—because to them, nothing is unachievable. To their minds, one simply needs to look at

WHY THE PAIN AND SUFFERING?

the mathematical improbabilities from a different perspective. They care not for trivialities and human dramas blown out of proportion. Humans often remain very rigid in their way of thinking, because that's the way they have programmed themselves to function. Despite their superior way of tackling challenges, these beings do carry much love for mankind.

Have you ever wondered about the necessity of suffering, pain, trauma, violence, and abuse in our world? How do you envision the evolution of life on Earth? And why do some individuals fear the concept of 'reptilians' or refuse to acknowledge their presence? These are the inquiries I posed to the Rainbow Warrior Star Beings in order to comprehend the abundance of pain in our world, and their responses were shared with me in January 2024.

Q: Why is there such a need for suffering, pain, trauma, violence and abuse in this world?

A: C'est magnifique, n'est-ce pas? Are you not a hue-man? Are you not a spiritual BEing with your fusion of beautifully magnetic light particles encased in a biodegradable and organic earth suit? You are a StarSeed having dressed-up as an "earthonaut," having volunteered to play a part in the great awakening of Planet Earth. Once the given suit is either worn out, or its usage beyond the scope of repair, it returns to the dust of the earth from whence it came, whilst the light of your soul either returns to the recycle pool of more possible earthly incarnations or one returns home to the planet from whence you sprang—the choice is yours.

You have chosen the hue-man embodiment, being in acceptance of living a life of duality, having to find your way back and reconnect to the spiritual aspect of the covered-up 'gemilicious' light of who you are, and returning to the ways of living a blossoming life in the true art of spirituality.

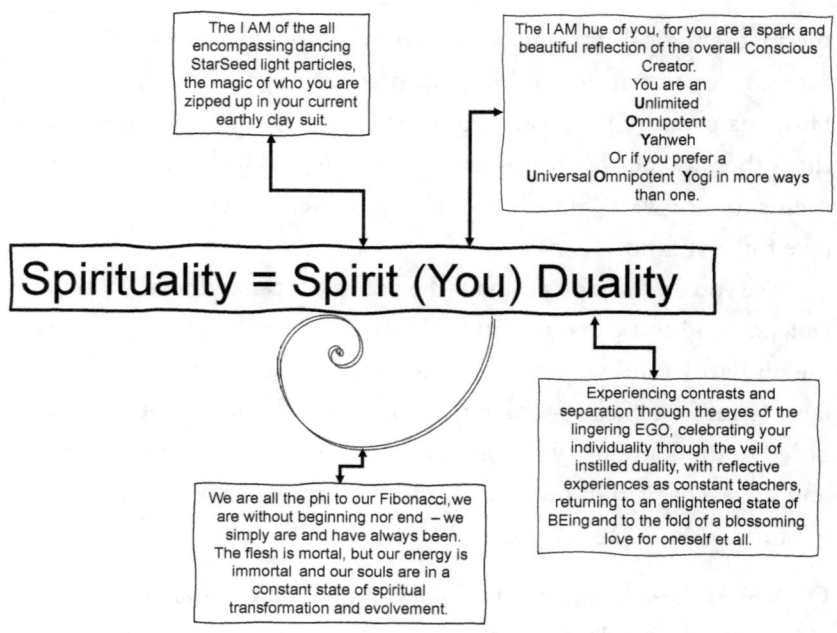

Q: The wording for YOU is now OUY?

A: Is everything in this world the right-side up, or is it all upside down, inside out, and round and round? Or is the world the wrong side up, and should be turned upside down? You live in a world of illusions, having chosen the art of separation in order to figure out the best way back home to the self—through experiences created on the drawing board that you have duly designed with the help of the mind and given life to. Is there a right or wrong in your experiences? Non pas du tout! They merely teach you to recover the muddied and encrusted pulse of a light within yourself by examining and healing the unserving inconsistencies that keep your mind sticky, cooked, and entangled like Italiano spaghetti, with your soul light covered in that dripping spaghetti meatball sauce, as the ego is the noodler in your soup, stringing you along, keeping the triggers firmly in check by slap flat facing you in the garlic and salsa di pomodoro, deviating you like a vampire from a love for yourself. You've got to let life turn you topsy turvy and upside down to allow for all the accumulated muck

WHY THE PAIN AND SUFFERING?

of your experiences that you oh so deliciously hoarded to come falling out so you can heal and learn to live in balance, basking in that breadbasket in the light of love for yourself, the right side up.

Q: Why do many people find the idea of 'reptilians' frightening or deny your very existence?

A: *Is fear not the mugger to your very chi? Are triggers not reflective pointers to show where you are not free? If there are those that think humanoids are the only species within the Galaxy, then so be it, we cannot all vibrate at that same level of consciousness, that would defeat the purpose of duality and that feat of awakening through the experiences of contrasts. Yet, we are all the I AM within each other—how can that not be, when we are nuclei from the overall Atomic Creator? There are thousands of different reptile species on Earth, as much as there are thousands of different reptilian species within the galaxy. Whilst some may be harmful, suffering from 'reptile dysfunction,' having rejected the love for themselves, choosing to roam around in the gratification and glorification of their own high and mighty self-importance, having gone on a war-mongering power tripping rampage, destroying other planets and species in their wake, spreading and instilling a plague of fear which they energetically feed on, as with the hue-man race. Know that others are far more docile having a higher vibrational consciousness and are dipped in nothing but unconditional love.*

The question is, will you remain plugged in to that hypnotic delirium that you've been sugar dosed with or will you take responsibility for your life ending your own created pain and suffering? Remember, ffEaR is the ultimate copout, either remain a freaky frightened Ewok or be that adventurous R2-D2; ultimately you are the only one that can save you from the downward spiral of yourself.

Stop feeding your mind with anger, causing your gnashers to bump and grind, living in a disillusioned state of illusion. Rather free your mind, be color-blind, and revel in the beauty of sense and sensibility rather than superfluous superficiality, squelching the profoundly beautiful soul that you are, all to remain living in a shell of who you so most marvelously are.

True that and peace out!

Q: Random question: How were the pyramids in the world built?
A: The Light-man (hue-mans) had help and guidance from the seeds of the stars before separation came into play. With created cultures, many light-men lost sight of the shores of their heart of home, and they embarked on a highway to hell, having become under pressure, turning away from love like a blind man, becoming lost in the noise of the EGO.

Q: How do you see life evolving here on Earth?
A: Slip, slide, and skate through life, because falling, hurting, and growing are part of the traits of consciousness expansion. Use your experiences as a conduit to channel your energy out of the deepened valley you may find yourself in. Without the release of the conditioned programming, one remains but an old, tired horse, thirsting for water, trying to quench its thirst but never quite achieving that joie de vivre back in its bones. So, too, release the unhinged, faulty, and old creaky programming, making you tiresome of all that egotistical dueling of the relentless pointy words directed at one another and doubting the self. We know that the created stigma of fear and doubt and any other negative labels can eat away at your mind, and soul. Know that the billowing winds of death and destruction may seem inevitable, and yet, within the tsunamis of chaos, there is divine order, for it is the transformation of the old to sowing the seeds of love for the new. It is the decalcification process of the 'bacteria,' that have for so long been persistent on this planet, and the remineralization of light by infusing the antibodies of love and understanding. It is the detoxification of the 'mold', that has for so long germinated and colonized the soils of the earth, having soiled it with their impetulent

behavior, pepper spraying humanity with doses of fear and control, to shut their eyes from the spectacular truth of who they are. One can only conquer the darkness by embracing and understanding the dark side of the moon of said darkness, hugging it out with the light to thus forth fuse the two in understanding the light. When the stigma of chaos rules, people tend to succumb to their deepest fears, falling into the murky ocean of their created inner world, as the outer has seeped within. Don't be afraid of the dark, don't go hiding from yourself in the shadows of night, for through the created psychological storm, seek that softly glowing, guiding light you have so hidden within, and put a little love in your heart, believing in hope once more; for where there is hope, there is life, and where there is life, there is love.

Humanity will eventually come to understand that there is a more harmonious way of living, of co-existing, and of building bridges to each other's hearts.

Without respect how can there be love?

Without compassion how can there be forgiveness?

Without acceptance of one another, well with all due respect, you would keep living in the created compartments of divisiveness and separation, non?

In these polar times, know that from darkness so shall spring forth but the spark of a glowing light, caught by the burning embers and carried on the winds of change to spread the light, enlightening the many unenlightened until the world is engulfed by nothing but infinite awakened light particles, with a little bit more love in their hearts. And that hope will be once more, with the rays of the Amun-Ra breaking through the trenches of the rain that has washed over and cleansed the lands, leaving but fertile grounds within the hearts of Man, to once more rebuild from the unfolding and blossoming heart of the Christ Consciousness, and people joining the effort, coming together as one.

CHILD OF THE SUN

Fear not my Child, Earth is beautifully shifting and transitioning, but with it so will the hue-man race.

To understand "hate," one must understand love, for love forgives all.

To understand "oneness," one must first understand the illusion of separation and prancing around like a Cruella de Vil in the EGO.

To understand the bad, and reaching the unthinkable unreachable, one must dive into one's hardships rather than run rings around it and sizzle in one's fears. One must accept ultimate responsibility for the multidimensional BEing that you are, transfigure and configure the old 3-D you to the new hue of a fearless caped hero you, to ultimately understand, love and appreciate life in your beautiful, current physical encapsulated tasty meat pack, as being a most excellent gift from the Creator, who has given you free will to creatively create and express yourself being the humanoid, yet magically energetic weaving creator, you so are.

We live in a time where "the Devil wears Prada," all work, no play, to keep humanity deviated from attaining that goal of acute awareness, until the tower cracks and collapses, and Mankind is left with mere humble beginnings, rebuilding with the smooth and creamy foundation of pure unconditional love, learning to live from the heart space, with neither a need nor want for greed, soaking in the absurdity of materialism and bathing in the created sliver of money, but remembering who you are, why you are here, and that love is, and always has been, all there is.

Lastly, remember that to change the world from morbid to orbit, commence by changing your inner world, and it will reflect as such in all areas of your life, as well as adding that good energetic juju to the collective consciousness, inspiring others to change their inner to reflect and cause a ripple effect in the outer.

Much love and light to you during these enlightening, transformational times on Earth and within yourself. Embrace the journey, embrace the light, embrace the hues in the all of you and breathe through the beauty of the heart, giving yourself permission to live and to dance in an enlightened groove is in the heart state of mind.

We're like stardust surfers, born from the cosmic light of the universe's enlightened flow. Deep inside each of us glows an eternal flame—a warm spark of sacred magic we've gathered while cruising the Milky Way through infinite lifetimes. It's time to ignite our soul and catch the cosmic wave, unleashing our inner power—our creative force—to spread more light, more love, and more stellar vibes across that infinite galaxy we call home. Let's join together as starry-eyed creators, manifesters, and magicians, as kindred spirit tribes, and with open hands and open hearts build a new Earth that's out of this world.

CHAPTER 14
FINDING HAPPINESS AND EXPLORING OUR IDENTITY

THE ASCENDED MASTER ST. Germain reminds us about that feeling of inner joy we all have deep down. He knows life piles problems on us sometimes, until we're buried under a heap of worries and stress, unable to breathe as we're suffocating ourselves. But happiness comes from within, not by placing it in another's hands. All those troubles are just junk we've accumulated. If we dig down through the clutter, we'll uncover that beautiful glowing core of peace at our center. St. Germain encourages us to reconnect to the bliss inside, no matter how many troubles try to smother our inner light

SEEKING HAPPINESS: Q&A WITH THE ASCENDED MASTER ST. GERMAIN

Q: Most people want for nothing but a bit more peace and happiness within, rather than feeling and running on empty. What are your thoughts?

A: *Your vessel is not empty, you have merely depleted your energy and given it away freely like sweets in a candy jar. You have merely poured the "ale o' love" down the chute, rather than filling your hearty "cup o'*

soul." You've become a soggy pretzel martini, slogging in the detriment of a mushy-pea-syndrome. Peace and happiness come not from without, but from the wells within. the heavenly paradise you seek is nestled right inside of you, like the delightful aromas of freshly baked bread and biscuits in the oven of yer own soul. One chases but the luminous blown soap bubbles that burst upon impact, leaving one popped and pooped to find more, as one keeps chasing but that happiness outside oneself. It is exasperating, non? Learn to set boundaries, these are not constraints but equilibrial medicine to the soul, rather than people running all over you, treating you like the wipe-the-dirt-of-my-shoes mat, because you are so set on pleasing others. And then one wonders why one is so caked with grimy heaviness! You are not here to heal others. You are simply a reflector showing others the capacity to heal themselves. Stop compromising, for you will only be compromising yourself in the process and keep cutting yourself out of the picture in your own life. Tiptoeing around others, living like a thief in the night, not wanting to "crack the egg yolk," will eventually end up in you tripping like a smooth criminal, pummeled flat with yolk all over your beautiful face, causing even more havoc due to the slippages within your own life, all because you refuse to be firm and true to your own authentic nature, instead allowing others to say and do as they please, responding "yes" and "amen." People love to mold and shape others to their liking. It is but the err of human nature. Stop wanting to be molded or to fit in. If the shoe doesn't fit, then why huff and puff till yer blue in the face? If your clothes don't fit, then why this incessant need to cramp yer style? Respect yourself as you duly learn to respect others, for it is the space of your breath that needs to take a "chill pill" and to return to the zenith of your nature. When you value yourself, you in turn understand the value of others—unless you decide for others to keep hopscotching all over you, then by all means, be my guest. If you keep pinging like an eternal over-the-top Chuckie Finster the Rugrat, seeing scary monsters in the closet of all of life's experiences, saying, "M-m-maybe this isn't such a good idea," then how will you

FINDING HAPPINESS AND EXPLORING OUR IDENTITY

every be able to conquer the hurdles of instilled fear and truly live a life of deservance rather than of pittance?

Q: What do you say to people having problems in life?
A: *Aren't you an enlightened delightful light of a delight? You've got problems? I've got even bigger problems, because you are the problem and the problem isn't the problem, but the problems you have been so busy creating, that aren't really problems, but it is your mere humanoid mind that seems to have spun and created these problems, and yet to my amusement, you can either remain as you are or decide to flip the switch and come out of the grinder of that created experience that has caused you to sink but so deep within the mud bath of yourself.*

Should you not be returning to a state of blissful joy? Is that not part of the path you should be returning to, rather than remaining in the thorny bramblebushes of your "problematic" experiences, cutting and bruising yourself, until the floodgates open with chaos ensuing as all hell breaks loose, flooding your mind (and thus your life) with that fair breath of the riddle-me-that anxiety? Welcome challenges, embracing them as opportunities, rather than seeing them as the phantom figment of your imagination, causing you to shiver and run like a "yikes" Shagster and a "ruh-roh" Scooby Doo.

Did Bobby McFerrin not sing, "Don't worry be happy?" So maybe a bit more of that, rather than walking around with created thunderclouds and lightening clouding your head, remaining in an endless loop of zapped outbursts filled with torrential rain, covering the beautiful "you" of the hue in you.

Happiness radiates from within, filling our soul with joy and contentment. It cannot be bought, earned, or stolen. True bliss blossoms from the seeds we nurture in our hearts. When we cultivate inner peace and practice gratitude, our spirit overflows with a lightness that no one can take away. The key to delight is not found in material things or in the pursuit of pleasure, but rather in simplifying our desires and appreciating the beauty around us. Happiness is an inside job, but it manifests as an outside glow for all to see.

The philosopher Khalil Gibran said, "Our anxiety does not come from thinking about the future, but from wanting to control it." We may not always want to accept our reality or embrace the truth staring us in the face, but to transmute our experiences into gold, we've got to accept where we're at so we can move forward. Our minds love to time travel, looking into the rearview mirror of what was and gazing at the horizon of what could be. But we can sometimes forget the present moment—the here and now. We may be multidimensional beings, but in these human vessels of ours, we can't inhale the past or future. We can only breathe in the present moment. Living in the now is inescapable—we have no choice! Even as I write this and as you read it, absorbing these words, the last sentence has already slipped into the past.

The first breath we take being born into this world, and the last breath we exhale before we drop our physical garment, returning to the star filled heavens of home, mark the beginning and the end of life's grand adventure. Breath is the essence of life itself, allowing us to fully experience each moment. Our mind and body ebb and flow with each inhalation and exhalation. Anger tightens our chest as irritation shortens each breath. As we mindfully breathe through life's ups and downs, the breath becomes our faithful companion. For in breath, we find peace, a calm in the face of life's storms. Without the art of breathing, we simply would not exist!

The Ascended Master St. Germain goes on to say: *"Nothing, nada, niente, zilch, le rien, kuchh nahin, from the past matters. What matters is the now, the present moment. Your past can only define you if you allow it to trample all over you, leaving your mind's frequency in tatters and in disarray, having bowed down to defeat, rather than taking control and defining your past that once was, in the shaping of the experiences not to detriment of yourself, but to the improvement of yourself. You choose to have hang-ups and be judgmental of others because of the garnered experiences that you have hoarded and stored in the closet of your bunged-up mind that is truly bulging at the seams. Ce n'est pas une bonne façon de vivre mon enfant. Opinions as stated by others are never your reality, so why choose to be hung-up on said wording, causing but a rift within your own mind? If you keep hoarding and stuffing your mind, how can your soul ever find the light of day to breathe? All you create is an inner turmoil of unwanted toxic 'euphoria,' spilling over into the outer fringes of your environment, causing nothing but an enticing and warped Willy Wonka mudslide of a misadventure, having to find the light back to yourself by learning to alchemize all of your experiences. Stop being an 'Ariel the Mermaid,' hoarding and collecting experiences, keeping them locked up, using these unhealed emotions as ammunition to taint other experiences of the same caliber, never relenting, never giving in, and chasing yourself like an uncontrollable 'Yosemite Sam,' shooting and hurting yourself being in an endless cat and mouse game with yourself! Allow yourself to breathe and live in the light of the truth of who you are. For my Child, I AM as you are, as much as you are as I AM. You are the I AM Light in Me as much as I AM but that ray of the I AM reflecting back at you. In the end, we are all but beautifully warm, flickering, fuzzy, delightful lights, dancing our souls back to the sacred geometrical grid of the enlightened lights of ourselves."*

During the Basic course, I felt like a kid all over again, having a blast playing "Fire in the Mountain" with my fellow course mates. It was a great way to let out our inner child and embrace the joy within us that we often keep locked away and forget about. I'd never heard of this game before, but I jumped in, running around in a circle while the teacher called out numbers. We'd scramble to form groups with the same number of people as the number called out. If the teacher yelled, "Stop!", we'd count the letters and gather into groups of that size instead. It was a riot until she shouted, "Statue!" Instantly, we froze like statues. We should've huddled in a group of six, but many of us associate the word "statue" with a different game from childhood, and we all froze instead. Funny how the mind works, isn't it? In an instant, we went from carefree kids to motionless statues, transported by a single word.

As both teachers in the course explained, our lives depend on four vital sources of energy: Sleep (we need six to eight hours nightly) food (we need to eat balanced, timely meals), breath (we need to inhale deeply and exhale fully), and knowledge—which continually empowers us.

Throughout the course, we were encouraged to reflect on what truly makes us happy. When do we experience pure joy? It's crucial to acknowledge that our own happiness is our responsibility. We must actively pursue things, individuals, and wisdom that ignite a fire within us, and we should try and make choices that nurture our spirit.

People always ask me what I am grateful for. The answer is simple: I am grateful for the breath of life, for without it, we would not be able to experience life in all its essence and open ourselves up to all the gifts, lessons, and blessings contained within. Every morning when that alarm clock goes off, take a moment to soak in the gift of a new day. Seize it as a chance to chase your wildest dreams, right your past wrongs, and fill your cup to the brim. Stop searching for happiness in all the wrong places—the void inside you won't be filled by new shoes, chocolate, or even by your soulmate. (Try becoming best mates with your own soul first!). True joy bubbles up from within, so if you want something different, do something different; recenter yourself and tune in to your inner frequency. What you "vibe out" is precisely what you'll attract. "Uncondition" that conditioned mindset of yours, and unlock your inner happy-to-vibe-to-the-tune-of-your-outer-happy to attract infinitely different outcomes. Remember, life ain't hard. It is only your engrained mindset that merely makes it seem so—and a change in perspective can make all the difference.

As St. Germain says, *"The seat of our happiness lies suffocating and cloaked by the many unhappy layers we have so 'lovingly' conditioned ourselves with. If you want your happy back, then walk inward, to heal, deal and feel all the unpleasantries of your garnered, heavy-sour-creamed, conditioned experiences, releasing these lovingly, like the swirling smoke of a fire into the celestial heavens above. Unburden the burdened mind and*

FINDING HAPPINESS AND EXPLORING OUR IDENTITY

lay off the thick clotted creams that laden your soul with a stuffed turkey kind of heaviness, leaving you fatigued and out of breath because you have given yourself a pain-in-the-arse-barrage of unwanted, unhappy, sorrowful stress. Drop the 'un' from happy, unclog the narrative and return to that blissful state of simply BEing yourself; being grateful regardless of the wobbles life may throw at you. Keep your composure, breathe, and like an acrobat, remain in poise and balance."

At some stage, we must all take responsibility for our lives and ourselves. We've chased our dreams—some we realized, and some we missed. Disappointment stings when dreams slip away, but if you gave it your all, then cast off that regret. The problem is this: we "try" and then feel let down when hope fizzles. But Yoda from *Star Wars* nailed it: "Do or do not... there is no try." Half-measures get us nowhere. There is no shame in wise retreat, but either do, or do not. Either commit fully or walk away.

On an emotional level, I know it stings when someone says something that rubs you the wrong way. But remember—it is not what they said that makes you feel bad. Your negative feelings come from within. When you react, it's just old hurts asking to be healed. Don't allow your ego to keep your mind wrapped around its little finger, remaining tightly gripped in the chokehold of a Ka the snake. Instead, embrace your inner Mowgli and take responsibility, looking at your experiences like a wee-bee-dee-bee-dee-boo King Louie, dancing like Baloo the bear, looking for the "bare necessities of life," and "forgetting about your worries and your strife." Your heart knows the way. Stay true to yourself and let love lead.

Let's face it, the ego isn't your true self—it's just your image, your mask, and the role you play. This mask craves approval, control, and power—all to avoid facing its fears. It's always comparing and grasping for validation. But there's more to you. Your higher self holds your greatest potential: the wise, loving part connected to deeper truth. Don't get caught in the ego's act. Plug into your higher self and reclaim your wholeness.

As St. Germain says, *"Your own suffering is never caused by the person or circumstances you are blaming and keep pointing fingers towards—it's all a projection of your own reality. It's what you tell yourself you are experiencing, and thus, you totally get to decide how you feel. If you allow yourself to keep sipping from that 'victimlicious' cocktail that is keeping you trapped within the sturdy, slurring, stiff drink of a mahogany of these experiences, then by all means, cry me a river and remain playing these acidic, tit-for-tat mind games. Either that or take responsibility. Wean yourself off that self-incarcerated victimhood and heal the hurt of these created circumstances, because, my Child, how can the flow of life ever reach you if you've corked the bottle of your mind? Much like being that princess sleeping on the pea, waking up black, blue, and bruised, your new and replenished energy is unable to flow through you like the gentle beckoning river, restoring you to the wholesome, authentic nature of your beautiful self."*

In truth, nothing in the world can make you happier than the person smiling back at you in the mirror—you! Embrace all of yourself, flaws and all. Take charge of your life, own your mistakes, and applaud your inner awesomeness.

I used to be insecure about who I was, thanks to unresolved trauma from my past. I tried pleasing the whole world while leaving myself out in the cold, desperately seeking acceptance from others by being overly nice. I've always been a natural people-pleaser, and I often let folks take advantage of me because I wanted to be liked. That led to a serious lack of boundaries and self-respect. I stifled my own opinions and feelings out of fear of hurting others and doing something wrong—all to gain "acceptance." In trying to conform to expectations, I only hurt myself by suppressing my true self.

Sure, we all want to please people now and then. But when you try pleasing everyone, it becomes a dis-ease. You ride that high of approval for only a brief moment before crashing down again. We shouldn't please others if it doesn't align with our spirit. People-pleasing is exhausting: constantly worrying about others' opinions, being scared of saying the

FINDING HAPPINESS AND EXPLORING OUR IDENTITY

wrong thing. It's draining, toxic and taxing. The real magic is loving yourself, and you don't need anyone's stamp of approval to do that. It doesn't matter what others think of you—just be happy with the unique soul that you are. Don't wait for someone else to make you happy, because you'll be waiting until hell freezes over. Embrace all of your quirks, friend. Out with the self-pity and in with self-love! We're not just clumps of organic matter—we're walking energy magnets attracting what we put out. Be unapologetically you. Stop the comparison game and get your happiness house in order.

You've got to love yourself, to heal yourself, as much as you need to heal yourself in order to love yourself and forgive yourself, returning to the wholesome loving nature of who you most authentically are? When you change your mind, you change your vibe. And when you change your vibe, you change your life. As St. Germain says, "Pain is creation; love is the healing transformation. Always be mindful not to "Band-Aid" the pain, but to heal the root cause of that deep-seated malaise with the remedy of forgiveness."

During the course, Sangita and Dr. Divya told us wonderful, life-changing stories that spoke to our souls. Each tale carried a profound yet simple truth that made us pause and reflect deeply on our lives. Their words sparked new perspectives within us, shedding light on how we can live more meaningfully with ourselves and with others. One such tale was the story of a simple peasant who sought wisdom from an enlightened master. Clutching a butterfly in his fist, the peasant thought to trap the master in a riddle: is the butterfly alive or dead? But the master saw deeper, knowing our lives mirror that fluttering creature. "Its fate rests in your hands," he told the peasant, gently. "Whether it lives or dies depends on you."

Just as that peasant held the butterfly, so we each hold our precious life in our palms. Will we trust enough to open our hands and let our truest selves take wing? Or will we crush our potential in a darkness of our own making? The choice is ours. Like the peasant, we are on a journey to find meaning. And like the butterfly, we seek to transform and fly free, gently basking in the ever-reaching heights of consciousness. The light resides within us, waiting for the breath of trust to set it free.

We're all butterflies floating on the breeze, trying to find our place in the big wide world. However long we stay, we'll relish the nectar of being present, learning who we are, and sharing our colors along the way.

We've all incarnated onto this blue planet more times than we can count, yet we don't remember a single previous lifetime—not even a smidge! Why's that, you ask? Well, every time we get reborn, we get a whopping case of amnesia from that brain freeze we get when we pop out of the warmth of the womb. That icy shock hits our brand-new baby senses and *bam*—total memory wipe. This planet must be a blast if we keep signing up for return trips, even if we don't remember a thing afterwards! Have faith in the happiness and joy to be found in our experiences.

SEEKING IDENTITY: Q&A WITH THE ASCENDED MASTER ST. GERMAIN

The Caterpillar and Alice looked at each other for some time in silence: at last, the Caterpillar took the hookah out of its mouth, and addressed her in a languid, sleepy voice.

'Who are you?' said the Caterpillar.

This was not an encouraging opening for a conversation. Alice replied, rather shyly, 'I — I hardly know, sir, just at present — at least I know who I WAS when I got up this morning, but I think I must have been changed several times since then.'

"What do you mean by that?" said the Caterpillar, sternly. "Explain yourself!"

"I can't explain myself, I'm afraid, Sir," said Alice, "because I am not myself, you see."

FINDING HAPPINESS AND EXPLORING OUR IDENTITY

"Who in the world am I? Ah, that's the great puzzle…."

And yet even though Alice may have tumbled through the rabbit hole into Wonderland, the truth is, the Wonderland was in Alice all along. She merely walked inward, to return home to the truth of who she was.

Q: Who are you? And who am I?
A: *Who AM I? Well, my Child, I AM You. We are all beautiful, reflecting lights, evolving as we see fit to become more enlightened of a light than the light of that enlightened light we have previously been. You are a luminous spark of the Divine essence, a luminary, here to illuminate the world. You may have lost the illumine to your firefly, concealing your light as you bumble through life, getting caught in the net of your earthly experiences, but eventually, you'll regain your fiery spark, sitting in the quiet moments of yourself, understanding that your own soul is your coach and your guru to alleviating any harbored pain.*

We are all Infinite BEings of the Divine. We are All Creators, co-creating our own little cosmic world, yet adding to the Collective Consciousness. This whole, boring, divisiveness on the planet and rowing along with the EGO should now be a thing of the past, and yet, people have their opinions on everything that happens on this beautiful Planet. Do opinions matter? Not really. Only if it pertains to your viewpoint, and thus your state of awareness reflects as such. Life—what's it all about? How about returning to a love of self and embracing and accepting one another as you are, removing all the gunk of the conditioning you have so smeared yourself with, and raising the love vibration of Mother Earth? And you may go, "uhuh, great," but look at what's happening in the world. Well, my dear, take a good look at yourself, you do realize that change commences from an inner movement within. You've got to learn to dance with yourself. You do know that by changing the self, you are changing the vibration of the world as well as the collective consciousness, much like if you keep moaning about everything that goes on. Before you say something, ask yourself if it is a truth or merely a hearsay of the tainted truth, because before you know it, you spin a story that takes on a life all of its own, et voila the plot thickens and the illusion of the drama deepens, causing even more nauseating chaos. Always be mindful of what you put out there, because every little thing you say, do, and feel adds to that energetic swirl of consciousness, and every bit of that collective absorbance comes back to Earth at the velocity with which it was sent out.

> *Every little thing in life is magic*
> *All you need to do is switch it on*
> *Even though your life seemed once but tragic*
> *Merely state, "my love for moi goes on"*
> *Cause, I'm drenched in magic, magic, magic.......*

The thing that humanity has forgotten (having become side-tracked with all the storylines and plot twists within the movie of the "matrix"), is that within lies the dormant power of the Divine Alchemist one truly is. One is a force of nature to be reckoned with, and yet, one often lives but induced within the confined lines of society. Switch off to switch back on, realizing the Infinite God-wonder that you are and start living a life, directing your energy consciously—creating consciously—rather than BEing lived in the constrictor boa-hold of the rules and regulations of the rigged game of the matrix on Gaia.

Q: What's the point of it all?
A: *The point is precisely the point of returning to that point of BEing, and that, my Child, is not pointless, but exactly the point of why you are here in making that point. Life is like a dance, one must learn the trick of the trade, walking through la galerie des glaces, to discern the illusion from reality, unless, my Child, the "Terrarium" is a mere glass box filled with le miroirs of illusion, to keep you tricked into thinking it is all but a beastly reality, and yet it remains a huff and puff of smoke of that daftly ruse of that flustered illusion, with humanity oh so deliciously caught up*

FINDING HAPPINESS AND EXPLORING OUR IDENTITY

in the delirium of that created, delusional reality. Then again, is life all but a puppet-on-a-string-illusion, or is there more to the play in progress?

All of you are timeless, endless, infinite, absolute, boundless—and how can you not be, when your spirit is eternal in nature? You are here to master the self in the garnering and harnessing of your experiences, through the sheer art of illuminating the darkness within, with fear having "crapped your pants" and kept you from the luminous light of yourself. You are here to remember that you are a Divine Alchemist, a manifester and manipulator of energy, casting and weaving your magic with the concocted formulas as so desired and created by you. What you think, you create, and thus the words you speak to yourself are heard by yours truly, your eager-beaver eavesdropper, typist, secretary, and executioner, your mind. Speak but wisely in the wording, get rid of the piled-up rubbish you have so trashed your mind with, and nurture it and garnish it with love, acceptance, and forgiveness.

You are a Galactic Ambassador of Light, having signed up for this assignment of your current incarnation—voluntarily, I might add—and yet you walk around cloaked and hidden with a dolloping of fear that would make Count Dracula run for his life and shrink in the shadows like a "shrieking violet." You are here to awaken yourself, to remember who you are, why you came here, and to relieve yourself of the suppressant called "the matrix," that has encoded you and grabbed you by the balls, doing the hooplaaaaa dance, whilst your soul is crying out, for heaven's sake, to do the hula dance, as it agrees far better with the crystalline grid of the very essence of your sweet soul BEing. But non mes chéris, you ignore the cries of your muted-in-a-trunk soul, because your mind is blustering away, ingesting all the outer chatter, absorbing it like a tequila sunrise, dipped in Moschino cherries and floating like a pineapple marooned in the sloshing and sticky grenadine syrup, allowing your EGO to keep you intoxicated, dueling with the outer world like a swashbuckling puss in boots. Stop getting your knickers in a chilli cheese dog twist, release your pain, and lighten the life of yer soul a wee bit.

CHILD OF THE SUN

Life is so intrinsically simple, and thus one's experiences become more pronounced, if one refuses to learn, and ultimately, the choice is yours to sink or swim. Find the mojo to your inner-heart-Merlin, bending the energy to your will, to manifest the life you so want. "But I can't, it doesn't work?!" Of course, it does! Are you not a "Transformer?" If the ingredients within a cocktail are tainted, you pour it down the drain. If the food on the stove is burnt, you start again. Thus, if your experiences are tainted, and you're burnt to a fine crisp like chestnuts roasting on an open fire, having riddled the self with dis-ease, remaining unhealed, then how can one be of the understanding of one's experiences and the lessons they entail within? How can one ever "level-up" if you remain like a dizzy, dire straits, cat-chasing-its-tail in that loop-de-loop experience? The key is to learn, to rise above, and to reserve no judgement, but have a mere attitude of gratitude, a dose of powdery, "poof," in-your-face-love and a peppering of unfolding forgiveness.

The secrets of the Universe are never hidden. In fact, truth be told, all symbolism is hidden in plain sight, as are certain wordings and phraseologies— it is the mere veil of a created conditioning within "the matrix," that humanity seems but blinded by it. For some, it is as clear as mud, while for others, it is crystal-sparkly-clear. Life is about looking at things from a different perspective, rather than from the same old view of that broken record player. You're here to remember and to recover the gem of a light you are and have always been. It's rather a humorous feat to behold, that all incarnated onto the Earth plane have to pay to live there— unlike other planets within the multiverse. Why? Ah, well, that is easy. To make you forget who you are and why you came here in the first place. What better way to do so than by creating a superficial (or rather, artificial), domed terrarium set within a grid and a set of rules—none would be the wiser. Merely connect with the heart of your soul for guidance and find your way home—and trust me, eventually you will—for when the blinkers fall off, you'll laugh and know that for the longest time, you've been had. And that, my Child, is the Cosmic Game of Evolution.

CHAPTER 15

RELATIONSHIPS AND LOVE

"Very little is needed to make a happy life; it is all within yourself, in your way of thinking."

—*Marcus Aurelius*

WHAT IS THE SECRET to relationships? That's the million-dollar question, indeed! Relationships are like ships sailing the seas of life. Sometimes it's smooth sailing under sunny skies. Other times, we pass each other like fleeting ships in the night. And sometimes, storms rage and ships crash against rocky shores, sinking into the inky depths below.

During my time in India, I was incredibly "needy" in my relationships. I clung desperately to the one I loved, even while my Guides laughed at me. I thought I knew what love was, but my understanding was clouded by fantasies and illusions. I was always reaching for connection, yet it always seemed to elude me—much as I eluded the love, I needed to give myself.

During the Basic Course, I had met Malikarjun, a participant and a Mangalori living in Bangalore, an early 80s kid and one of the Basic Course participants on my team, the Bollyhood Dodgers. He grew up reveling in the lush beauty of his coastal hometown, Mangalore. a port city and the headquarters of the Dakshina Kanada district in the coastal region of the Karnataka State in India. Nestled on the shores of the Arabian Sea, Mangalore dazzles with swaying palm trees, rolling green hills, and enchanting forests. It's no wonder the city is named after Mangaladevi, the goddess of wellbeing.

In 2002, Malikarjun relocated to Bangalore, a city in India renowned as the "Garden City" for its lush greenery and parks. Bangalore charmed with blossoming gardens, tree-lined boulevards, and cool, fresh air. He was awestruck by the city's seamless blend of tradition and technology—a hub where ancient temples stood alongside sleek IT parks. Bangalore was the Silicon Valley of India, where innovative startups rubbed shoulders with global tech giants. Known as the outsourcing capital of the software world, it hummed with the chatter of customer service calls rerouted from faraway lands.

He did a one-year apprenticeship with manufacturers of construction equipment, and had been working as an engineer for a Swedish multinational manufacturing corporation for the past four and a half years, which allowed him to thrive in Bangalore's melting pot of cultures and ideas. Yet he yearned to spread his wings beyond India's high-tech haven. Visions of Australia danced in his mind—Brisbane's glittering skyline and Melbourne's artistic laneways. A few years later, it was Melbourne that became his new home under the Southern Cross.

He loved Bangalore's climate, but man, that traffic was a real pain in the neck. Back in 2008, there were no decent roads, no proper infrastructure, and people just drove every which way to get to their destination. When I asked if it was safe to walk around at night, he said Bangalore was pretty safe—ninety percent terrorism-free.

He really disliked the fact that there was such a big gap between the rich and poor in Bangalore and in India overall and the affluent sadly turn a blind eye to the plight of the poor, showing a blatant lack of respect for their less fortunate brethren. It's a bit disheartening to see such indifference, for here I thought people would have that respect for one another regardless of their 'social' standing. He's right; we are all the same no matter what race, what color, what background, rich or poor, tall, short, round or thin. Every shape, size and color you can imagine. We are beautiful spiritual beings filled with divine grace having a human experience, maneuvering our way through this overgrown chaotic earthly jungle filled with these potholes of conditioning, much like the snakes and ladders game, sometimes falling flat-faced in the mud, until we've got the hang of the created and given experiences, leveling up and climbing that ladder, expanding our consciousness, merely looking back, smiling and thanking those that were part of our growth. We're all souls on a journey trying to figure out this crazy thing called life. Though some may traverse rougher terrain, we're all on the same journey of growth and enlightenment. With compassion and understanding, we can build bridges across social divides. But first, the 'privileged' must open their eyes and hearts to the struggles faced daily by the less fortunate. Only then can true change blossom.

So next time you see someone who looks different than you, remember—that's your soul sibling.

The teachers had us complete a thoughtful exercise. Each of us was given 100 rupees and tasked with buying a gift for a random classmate. I pondered the options, wanting my gift to be special and meaningful. After some deliberation, I chose a book titled *What Now?* It was filled with advice on moving forward after the course. To pamper my recipient, I also picked up some lip balm and Vicks for the nose.

We gathered in a circle, gifts wrapped and spirits high. Sanghita instructed us to mingle and greet each other warmly, exchanging our names and saying "I belong to you"—a reminder of our connection. After several rounds, she told us to stop and give our gift to the person beside us. One of my Bollyhood Dodgers teammates, Malikarjun, ended up with my gift and I ended up with his. I received a small book by Sri Sri Ravi Shankar called *Secrets of Relationships*. The irony was not lost on me, as back then I was hopeless with men and barely understood myself. But receiving this thoughtful surprise sparked insight.

When I read *Secrets of Relationships*, I couldn't help but chuckle at its delightfully simplistic style. Sure, I didn't see eye-to-eye with Sri Sri Ravi Shankar on everything, but plenty of passages hit home and had me nodding along. We're all guilty of chasing butterflies now and then, searching for joy in the world around us instead of within. We chase after happiness like a kid running through a field, hands outstretched, trying to catch those fluttering butterflies. The colors are so vibrant, the wings beating with such promise. Yet no matter how fast we run, the butterflies always seem to stay just out of reach.

In our quest for joy, it's easy to get caught up in the beauty around us. We think if we just work a little harder, earn a little more, or find the perfect relationship, this elusive joy will finally land in our hands. But real, lasting happiness can't be captured or bought. It arises from within. While the book's simplicity won't suit all, its message rings true: Look inward. There you'll find what the world can't give you. Joy takes root in the heart, not in happenstance. Let Secrets of Relationships awaken you to this secret of secrets—that joy comes from within. With its mix of wit and wisdom, the book reminded me to lighten up and find precious moments of joy in the present moment.

Sri Sri Ravi Shankar writes that when someone declares their love, we often become skeptical. But if someone say the opposite, we accept it, no questions asked. We question our talents, but not our shortcomings. We doubt others' sincerity and the existence of love and joy. Yet, when sadness comes knocking, we welcome it with open arms. Why do we do that? Why can't we just embrace the love and gifts that come our way, without picking them apart? As Julia Roberts' character, Vivian, in the movie *Pretty Woman* (1990) said, "The bad stuff is easier to believe. You ever notice that?" There's a psychological basis for why we tend to dwell on the negative more than the positive. It's an evolutionary holdover from our ancestors, for whom focusing on potential dangers was a matter of survival. We've inherited a tendency to zero in on the "bad stuff"—kind of like how physical pain alerts us to possible harm.

While we can't override this default setting completely, we do have some control. How much we spiral into negativity depends on factors like our upbringing and the messages we've internalized from those around us. Most important is how we talk to ourselves about our experiences. As Eleanor Roosevelt put it: "No one can make you feel inferior without your consent." It's true—our mindset holds great power over our emotions. If someone's being a "Debbie Downer," talking trash about you, belittling you, or just generally being a "meanie," you don't have to take it lying down. That negativity has got to get your permission before it can bring you down. You're the bouncer at the door of your self-esteem, so don't let the haters in. Give that criticism a pat down first—if it seems sketchy, toss it. Keep your head held high and don't let anyone make you feel small without your say so.

While we may be evolutionarily primed to focus on the negative, we can consciously choose to rewrite that storyline. The power lies within us.

The Basic Course teachers shared a great story that illustrated Buddha's deep compassion, love, and wisdom for all of mankind. In the story, a respected businessman was enraged to find his family attending Buddha's teachings. In a fit of anger, he marched to where Buddha sat, surrounded by ten-thousand followers, and spat directly in his face. Buddha simply smiled softly in response. Rather than retaliate, Buddha emanated an aura of unconditional love and understanding. The man was stunned. He tossed and turned all night, puzzled by Buddha's reaction. At dawn, something shifted within him, and he felt connected to something bigger than himself. The next day he returned to Buddha, bowed down, and asked for forgiveness. Buddha gently replied, "I cannot forgive you, for the person whom you spat on, is here no more and there is no chance that I will ever meet him again. You are not the same person now, and the person who spat on me yesterday is not the same person who is bowing down here today. Let us begin anew."

THE ART OF LIVING MATRIMONY SERVICES

A young man came to our class to tell us about the Art of Living Matrimony Services. I was surprised to learn it's a matchmaking service for devotees of the Art of Living, helping them find partners who share their spiritual lifestyle and values. With the slogan "Enabling Meaningful Connections Leading to Harmonious Marriages," they aim to unite singles within the global Art of Living community through their website and their app. I guess when you commit your life to meditation and ancient wisdom, your dating pool shrinks a bit. You can just log on and browse potential soulmates across the globe. My friend Sandhiya got a real kick out of that concept. She laughed and said, "Yeah right, like you'll be poking around on there!" It's true, I'm not exactly the target market. But hey, for some folks it's a serious issue, especially in India with the whole caste system and pressure to marry young. Still, it was fascinating to learn about how niche matchmaking works. You cannot help but admire people who find creative solutions, even if it seems a little out there to me.

Our teachers said that when your search stops then you'll find your soulmate. It's true, but until then, if you're anything like me all those years ago, you just keep dating the 'wrong' guys. Rather than seeking your 'other half,' become whole on your own. Don't search for your soulmate, but become best mates with your own soul. Date yourself first, get to know your wants, needs and dreams. Fall in love with your soul. When you're at peace in your own skin, you attract the right fit. Stop chasing; start being. Your soul mate will arrive once you've found your soul.

FALLING IN LOVE

When you fall in love with someone, you are attracted to their energy. Their energetic vibration matches your own frequency and like magnets, you are pulled to one another, riding that same celestial wave. It is not just your body that attracts another body—it is the soul that is attracted

RELATIONSHIPS AND LOVE

to another soul within that body. We are attracted to the warmth of that divine soul light we each radiate. It's a melding of spirits, a cosmic dance of energetic resonance. Like two melodies in perfect harmony, your souls align. You ride that same interstellar kahuna, attuned to each other in a profound way that transcends the physical, your spirits uniting as one. Falling in love is a glorious connecting of kindred spirits.

We are sparkling universal light particles, zipped-up snugly into these beautiful, human meat suits. Pause to soak that in. You're more powerful and far more capable than you've been led to believe. We're atomic stardust particles, humming to the frequency we vibe out, which shapes what we'll eventually attract and draw back in; such is the law of cause and effect. Our wounds whisper to us, coaxing us toward situations and people that let us play out the old hurts until we've learned. There are lessons hidden inside those precious experiences, and they can help us heal. Our energy is always in flux, and flows and morphs like lava, according to the way we express and create ourselves, thus shaping our world and pulling in kindred spirits of that same caliber. Ultimately, how we express ourselves and respond to life's experiences becomes the fabric from which our lives are woven.

Our relationships are like mirrors reflecting back to us and to the truth of who we are. Just as we gaze into a looking glass and see our outer image, when we truly look within the mirrors of our connections with others, we're given the chance to see our inner essence. These reflections can illuminate the shadowy parts of us that are desperate for light. They highlight areas ready for growth, healing, and wholeness. Our partners, friends, family—they're all holding up mirrors for us, if we're brave enough to peer inside. What we see may not always be pretty, but it's transformative. Learn to lean into these reflections that relationships provide, for eventually, they'll guide us home to our highest selves.

As Sri Sri states, "You can win over everyone and every situation with love. There is nothing in this world and in your life that you cannot win or overcome with love." In other words, love is the ultimate conquering force. With an open heart full of compassion, we can overcome any challenge and connect with anyone. As the wise teacher reminds us, no obstacle in life is too great for the power of love. Even in the darkest of times, choosing understanding over judgment and patience over anger can transform a relationship or situation. When we lead with kindness, we tap into an inner wellspring of wisdom far greater than our surface-level reactions. Though the world often feels divided, love remains the thread that binds us all. If we make the choice to see each other's humanity, to walk a mile in one another's shoes, new doors of possibility swing open. There is light within reach, if only we seek to understand.

WHEN RELATIONSHIPS BECOME TOXIC

Falling in love with someone starts off "rosy," until the demands start creeping in. Sometimes the demands involve all the things you can or cannot do, and they dictate your every move. Before you know it, the relationship becomes a never-ending contract with clauses to suit all these so-called "needs." In reality, it is an attempt to fill the potholes of our own insecurities and past hurts without the hard work of healing. It's far easier to give someone a guilt trip instead. That's not unconditional love, but a tit-for-tat-bargain struck on shaky grounds. Call it emotional blackmail if you will. Either stay and work to change and overcome it, or walk away from the co-dependency and relentless toxicity. As Sri Sri says "In love, you don't expect anything. If you want something in return, don't call it love."

The truth is, hurt people attract hurt people. When we don't heal our own pain, we unknowingly seek out relationships that mirror and magnify it. This toxic dance simply repeats itself until we wake up and say, "Enough!" The path forward is to stop blaming ourselves, get fired up, and take back our power. Our worth was never defined by others in the first place. It's time to break free from old patterns and write a new story of self-love and wholeness. All it takes is the courage to look inside and say, "No more. I matter. And I deserve better."

RELATIONSHIPS AND LOVE

A beautiful reminder from Sri Sri Ravi Shankar: "The most important relationship in life is the one we have with ourselves." His words gently call us inward, to nurture the connection with our own spirit. When we are at peace within, we spread that peace to all our relationships.

We may all be on our own unique journey, walking different paths, yet we seek that same light. I asked St. Germain why we attract these toxic characters in the first place? Why is it that we are drawn to people who wound us so deeply? What is it within us that calls these troubled souls into our lives? Is it the false charm, the rollercoaster highs and lows, the dysfunctional dance? His response: *"That's easy. You've signed a soul contract, choosing these experiences for the unfolding of your soul into a higher state of consciousness. You're a celestial being of the starlit heavens, having chosen to dance in your earthly given space suit for the purposes of awakening and enlightening yourself through the art of your whimsical experiences. Not so whimsical, you say? My Child, take life with a pinch of salt, adding but mere flavor to your life in all its ups and downs, and the sun will forever shine. And even when the lands of one's soul are caught in a draught, through the tears and laughter, one will replenish the soil of the heart through the mere understanding of one's experiences, by merely mustering up the courage to overcome the hurdles, and mastering and harnessing the energies within to weave but the magic of life—to thine own self be true without. One is merely an antenna, receiving and transmitting energy at will. It may often be at a subconscious level, but everything is created by yours truly, you, and thus the calculated energetic formulas you cast out are the sum of the equations you pull back in. It's about finding magic in the smallest things, living in the moment, treasuring every drop of rain infused with the rays and encradled warmth of la lumière du soleil and living with the grace of gratitude and appreciation with every breath and every step you take forth in this life."*

Why do we always have this incessant need to try and change a person? To shape them like clay to our liking? We cannot change anyone but ourselves. Our mistakes are not failures, but lessons in life's essential trinity: perception, observation, and expression. Relationships are give and take, not a trade-off. If you give more, don't wallow in self-pity or feel used. As Sri Sri says, you're not being used, you are being useful. If you were useless, another person could not use you in the first place.

NEEDINESS

When we love someone deeply, it's natural to want to be close to them and share every moment. However, it's crucial to remember that even the strongest relationships require space and independence for both partners to thrive. Smothering a loved one with constant attention and demands can quickly smother the very flame of love you're trying to nurture. Conditional love, where we make our affection contingent on a partner's ability to meet our never-ending needs, is a surefire path to resentment and the eventual demise of the relationship; it is the kiss of death.

To truly love someone in a healthy, sustainable way, we must first learn to love and validate ourselves. Our tendency to cling to our partners is often driven by deep-seated insecurities, fear, and self-criticism—issues that stem from unresolved emotional wounds from childhood or adulthood, or a fundamental lack of self-assurance. Perhaps we didn't receive the warmth and affection we craved as children, leaving us desperate to fill that void through our romantic relationships. Or maybe we've become so reliant on external validation that we've lost touch with our own inherent worth. Whatever the cause, it's vital that we take the time for honest self-reflection—unpacking the origins of our neediness, challenging our irrational fears, and learning to silence that harsh inner critic.

Only when we've cultivated a strong, stable sense of self can we truly show up as whole, secure partners. We must nourish our own interests and passions, find fulfilment in our own company, and remember that our worth is not contingent on another person's approval or attention. And when we do share our lives with a loved one, we can do so from a place of wholeness rather than desperation—freely giving without the burden of expectation. This is the essence of a healthy, thriving relationship—two independent, self-assured individuals choosing to journey together, not out of need, but out of a deep, unconditional love.

"Neediness" is looking outside of yourself for joy rather than within. No one can make you happy but *you*. No one can make you feel a certain way, but *you*. You are in control and own your feelings, no one else. Becoming aware is the first step to overcoming any of our insecurities and changing how we relate to others. As per Sri Sri's wise words, "Worry is the enemy of love. You cannot be in love and be worried at the same time!"

Neediness lurks within us like a creeping darkness, an insatiable hunger that can never be satisfied. It sinks its claws into our minds, whispering fears and forget me nots until they become a deafening roar. Having gone through a lifetime of trauma, trust me, I've been there, done that and worn that t-shirt multiple times. I've walked to the ends of the earth to help others, scorching my arse along the way, craving the assurance of others, mistaking it for love. But no amount of external approval can fill that void inside. Neediness is like a form of depression, a soul-sickness that leaves us trapped in a prison of our own making, endlessly seeking the keys to our freedom in the hands of others. To break free of our insecurities is to shine a light on them, asking ourselves why we carry these persistent voices of self-doubt. Once we become aware of our inner shadows, we can start to see how they affect our relationships with others. Confronting our pretty-sitting demons may seem daunting, but when we embrace our insecurities with understanding and compassion, we find the courage to relate to people from a place of wholeness rather than lack. We need to stop chasing the illusion of completion outside of ourselves, for the journey to wholeness starts from within. Peace comes from within. As we make peace with our own minds, the neediness and depression arising from the hole in our hearts will gradually resolve.

Sometimes, we're so scared that someone could genuinely love us for who we truly are, it's like our insecurities and self-doubts team up and somersault to create this McFear monster in our minds. We start thinking, "There must be something seriously wrong with us. We're just unlovable and flawed." And if someone actually claims to love us, we're like, "Wait, are you sure? Do you really see the real me?" We push them away, fearing the inevitable rejection that will crush our hearts. We build walls so high that even the most determined climbers would give up. We refuse to let anyone in because we're convinced that if they knew the real us, they'd run for the hills. Deep down, all we want is to be loved and accepted, but the thought of being vulnerable terrifies us. Letting someone love us means giving up control and risking heartbreak. It's like handing over the keys to our hearts and praying they won't crash the car. The idea of that is downright paralyzing! So, we convince ourselves that it's easier to keep everyone at arm's length. We hide our true selves and only show what we think others want to see. Our fear of being honest in love comes from past hurt and a lack of trust. But here's the thing: living behind fortress walls, like Rapunzel in the tower, all alone, is no way to live. It's like locking out the very thing we crave the most. If we can find the courage to face our fears, to risk the pain and trust again, we'll discover a love that's deeper than we ever imagined. We'll set our true selves free from the prisons we've built. And guess what? We'll realize that we are absolutely worthy of being loved just as we are.

CONFLICT

When conflicts arise, we see in others the shadows we try to conceal within ourselves. It's like looking into a funhouse mirror, with a distorted reflection of ourselves staring back at us. Rather than shunning these reflections, face them head on to heal them. At the end of the day, the most vital relationship is the one you have with yourself. Without integrity or self-love, how can you truly love another? If you are not in alignment with your inner being, if you carry no love for yourself, how can you offer that love to someone else? No one can cherish you the way you cherish your own soul. The way you speak to others mirrors how you speak to yourself inside. We communicate not through our heart space, but through our conditioned mind. Is it any wonder why we suffer so much, hiding in the shadows of who we are on a daily basis, afraid to show people our beautiful, unmasked, and authentic selves? If we strip free from all the slapped-on labels, what remains will shine like the sun reflected in a mirror. As St. Germain says, *"Why worry about your emotions, walking around like a pained, yammering, castrated cat, having seemingly drunk yourself, 'silliciously' sipping on that bottomless, victimized, victimhood cocktail, and strapped yourself hands down to a table, remaining tied and chained to your own created emotions, afraid to stand gloriously butt butter naked, shining just beautifully in the sunlight of who you most preciously and truly are?"*

Sri Sri speaks the truth when he says, "Nothing in the world can bother you as much as your own mind. In fact, others seem to be bothering you, but it is not others, it is your own mind." It may seem like other people are the source of your troubles, but in reality, it's your own mind that's causing you grief.

During a conflict—especially a heated argument—insults get hurled around like yesterday's trash. People throw them at each other, not realizing they're just pitching their own hurt. They wrap up their pain in a pile of nasty words and dump it all over you. And what do you do? You grab that stinky mess and shove it in your backpack, happily hauling those verbal garbage bags around on your shoulders, stewing and brooding over each rotten word. Don't lug that junk around! Get rid of that garbage, you don't let it pile up to high heavens in your own home either, do you? Toss those verbal leftovers in the bin where they belong, clear the mind and the hurt, and be free. As Sri Sri states, "When someone says something hurtful or mistreat you, they do it out of stress and ignorance. They are hurt somewhere within and that is why they behave like that."

"I CAN FIX THEM"

We all tend to live on autopilot, seeking validation and filling our spiritual Swiss cheese with worldly distractions. And when life gets messy, we grasp for more, sinking into our sadness. But the truth is, we can't fix each other's inner holes. We've got enough patching up to do on our own souls. There is no need to drown in worldly sorrows when you have an eternal spring inside. In truth, we are each responsible for our own growth. The brokenness we see in others is merely a reflection of the brokenness within ourselves, waiting to be healed.

You are not here to fix the brokenness of others; it is their job to fix themselves. When we keep trying to fix the "broken birds" we so gleefully and joyfully attract (because we think we are also a fixer), we only end up becoming more broken ourselves. Sure, lending a hand can feel rewarding. But enabling dependence helps no one grow. Each soul yearns to stretch its wings and soar. By doing the hard work for others, we deny them the growth their soul yearns for; we stunt their growth as much as we stunt our own growth. So, before you try patching up that broken bird, ask yourself: Are you simply avoiding your own spiritual repairs? What cracks and leaks need mending in your own soul's foundation? Tend instead to the garden of your own inner light, and understand that in lifting yourself up, you lift others up. Even a small act of self-care or self-love ripples out into the world.

"Never hold on to people in a desperado attempt to keep wanting to fix them, for it is not they that need fixing, but for the mere reflection they have cast within your own self that duly requires it so. Stop the refurbishment project on others, and rather refurbish the 'defects' within your own beautiful self; align your soul within the body you have given yourself home to. All explore life as they deem fit and walk to the hoo-ha of their own vibin', vibrant soul. Yet by taking a hammer, nail, and chisel in trying to fix and carve others, one allows them not to walk their own journey of wondrous self-discovery, keeping them 'nailed' to the cross

from the experiences they so 'thirstingly' require to overcome their own loudmouthing, inner, head-banging demons, expanding their own level of humming consciousness. Allow for them to breathe, as much as you allow for yourself to breathe. If you continuously keep taking away the gaming controller, the joystick, and trying to tell them how to play the game of life at every level, then how will they ever learn? Did you not learn to play Donkey Kong, Sonic, or Crash Bandicoot by taking the controller and feverishly playing it yourself until your thumbs were 'bruised' and 'blue', in the hope to beat that level of experience, vanquishing all the baddies along the way, in order to get to the next level? So too, let others play their lives by their rules. You cannot learn life for them, life will duly teach them, so I beg of thee to set them free; for in the end, there is no universal right or wrong way to live this adventure called 'livin' la vida loca,' for that, my Child, is a mere human opinion. Allow for others to write their own story, to choose their own timbres, and add their own flavorsome spices to their created cake of life, le gâteau de la vie, non? How would you feel if the gravy of your creativity train was hijacked and rewritten according to the plot of another, to the accolade of their melody, and peppered with their embittered spices? You need to believe in yourself as much as I believe in you, and just laugh at the twists and turns on the splashy ride of the waterslides of life. Stop knockin' others, for all are just little planets floating and bobbing through the cosmos, trying to find meaning to this zany, winding thing called earthly life."

—The Ascended Master St. Germain

LEARNING SELF-LOVE

Happiness comes from the deep wells within, you are the creator as much as you can be a Kali the destroyer of your own happiness. The question is, how will you wield it? Shed those layers of who you think you are and take a good look in the mirror. Take a deep breath and step out into the world with renewed confidence. Know that you cannot fully love another until you love yourself. When you make peace with all aspects of your being, you glow with an inner light that attracts that light and love without. Learn to be "mindful" rather than walking around with a "mind full." All relationships carry with them key life lessons. Relationships are great spiritual teachers, helping us reflect on the areas we need to work on and where we can grow. They teach us to forgive ourselves and each other. We are all products of the overall product of conscious creation. We are all itty-bitty chocolate pieces from the Creator of the flow of all chocolate in the universe. We are all made of the same essence, and though we may appear different on the outside, having covered our sweet souls in different physical chocolate flavors, at our core we are all cocoa beans, connected to the sweetness at the heart of all existence. We all come from that very same factory of creation!

Early on in life, we begin to develop our character and our own modus operandi of how we choose to relate to others and operate in this world. But know that we always have the power to change, tending to any unresolved issues with care, cleansing our spirit, and making peace with our past. Learn self-love and embrace the "all" of you with compassion. Step forward and hog the limelight of your wonderful self with wisdom, joy, and understanding. This is the recipe for living a life fully; you have all the ingredients within.

I'll take a pause here as the beautiful, Divine Kali Ma, in her infinite wisdom and compassion, gently reminded me that she is no mere destroyer. Rather, this magnificent Goddess guides us through life's trials, using each challenge to transform and strengthen our souls. Though her methods may seem harsh at times, they flow from her unconditional love for us. Kali Ma walks with us through the darkest nights, her fiery eyes lighting the way. With courage and faith, we can embrace her as our loving mother, allowing her to burn away all that holds us back from realizing our divine potential. To behold Kali Ma is to know that we too can face life's pain and emerge renewed.

THE GODDESS KALI MA

Kali is the great Hindu goddess of transformation, and she beckons you to shed society's shackles and reclaim your divine I AM Power. She is the cosmic force that births endless creation from the womb of the universe. She says, *"I AM a cyclone, cycling through the recycled cycles, to transform the old to upcycle and create a la fresh and anew."*

Kali is a misunderstood goddess, with her ability to be destructive often mislabeled as "dark." But her true power lies in destroying the old to make way for the new. She is a midwife, guiding your rebirth from limiting beliefs into awakened truth. Kali comes in like a cyclone, stirring things up and shaking loose all those spun cobwebs and scraggly dust bunnies that have settled into the corners of your life. With fiery conviction, Kali smashes false identities like fragile crayons, penetrating superficial masks to reveal the light of your core essence. She sweeps away the clutter and clears the slate, creating space for new growth. With her magic broom, Kali whisks away stagnation and sweeps in fresh inspiration. She invites you to reinvent yourself. Like a cosmic reset button, Kali brings transformative energy, rebooting your operating system and upgrading you to Kali 2.0. She knows your infinite potential, even when you've forgotten it yourself.

Kali is the cosmic machete wielder, dancing among the stepping stone of rolling stars as she slices through the fabric of space and time. With each graceful arc of her shimmering sword, nebulae are born and galaxies tremble. Her footsteps leave stardust in their wake as she traverses the cosmos, a warrior goddess on an endless quest. Where her ethereal steel flashes, new worlds awaken; where it falls silent, darkness reigns. She is the holder of cosmic power, and her mystic blade sings a song older than eternity. Know that she is the fierce goddess of transformation, summoned to pull you from the eerie black of night into the light. With each swift strike, she shreds the dead weight holding you back, summoning the light of your soul that you have so duly hidden within the shadows. With truth and power beyond measure, Kali dismantles all that binds you. She is the force that sweeps away stagnation, making way for growth. Kali is liberation embodied, severing the ties of limitation with her infinite blades of compassion. She is the dance of destruction and creation, for nothing new can arise until the old is demolished. Kali sees all—the worthy and unworthy alike—and loves them all the same. She is the mother who nurtures her children by freeing them from the chains of their own making. Kali is fierce grace, ruthless in her desire to set you free. She is the catalyst for metamorphosis, the darkness that gives way to light. With eyes that pierce illusion, she reminds you of your own limitless potential and the hidden gems of the I AM Power that reside deep within the pearly depths of you. Kali is the truth that sets you free.

Kali dances in the gap between endings and beginnings, death and rebirth, destruction and creation. She whispers that life is change. There are no dead ends on our path, only new turns in the road. Have courage to let go, die, and be reborn. What traps you now will liberate you later. Trust the process. Like a phoenix rising from the ashes, you will also rise triumphantly.

Embrace Kali's fierce yet nurturing energy, speak your truth fearlessly, break free of other's expectations, and step fully into your sovereignty. You need not dim your light for anyone—let it shine in all its glory! Don't cage it for anything. Embrace the full power of your voice, dance to the beat of your own soul drum. The path to freedom lies within, and now is the time to walk it with courage, authenticity, and grace. You were born free—it's time to live free.

"I AM that I AM, as much as all that you are the I AM in ME.

I AM Kali Ma, of Arcturian descent, and one of the Arcturian Council of Light, so how can I be filled with evil intent when I am but a mere healer, wheeler, and dealer to the hearts of all of mankind?

I AM a destroyer as much as I am a transformer, deinstitutionalizing the slippery eel of an institutionalized self, caught up in the earthly, zonked-out, artificially created institutional institution.

I AM the cleanser to the obstructors obstruction and the flow of the heart energy of the Mother and all its sentient inhabitants.

It is only through the enflamed chaos that one can restore order in one's mind and soul.

Procrastination is but for a fool, to sit but idly by the waters on the wobbly fence, staring at the mighty heavens, with the clouds rolling by, waiting for life but to oh-so-magically change.

CHILD OF THE SUN

I AM neither friend nor foe; I AM merely as you perceive me to be.

I AM the Goddess of birth, of death, and yet of rebirth once again, for these are the incarnate cycles of souls helping with the evolution of the many planets within the multiversal grid of existence.

I AM the bearer of the new, sweeping the lands through instilling the fires of chaos, for how else can the bubble of artificialness on the surface be disintegrated?

I AM the temptress, tempting the temperamental temperature to your throwing temper tantrums.

I AM the seductress to the invocation of clearing the self-destructive tendencies created by the splintered and scrambled seduced mind due to the spicy intake of the shrill, filled senseless, sticky, worldly wording.

I AM the bogeyman to your illusional, impish nightmares, shaking you awake to the truth of the illusion you've been hijacked into.

I AM the sun to your darkened darkness of your perfectly intact and impeccable hue.

I AM the prankster blowing life into your unsubstantiated party of fears that have you crippled and writhing in a drab and dull ball of swindling agony, having deviated from your light-me-up disco ball of the enlightened colorful soul of life.

I AM the life of the party, the stir in the pot, waking you up from that detached, better-the-devil-you-know slumberland party you've been lulled into, rolling you out of bed with a thud and a bang, back to reality, having lost yourself in the moment, from the once-upon-a-time, in-a-trance, earthly, optical illusion.

I AM the warrior to your sleeping spirit.

I AM the wicked, witchy witch of the West, weathering the wuthering storms of the waves crashing and trashing your wayward mind, and yet I am the healer to the whispering demons in your worrisome and weary head.

I AM the demon catcher to your riddled-by-anxiety mind, liberating the pressure on the cooker thereof by planting seeds of resolutions, rather than creating more of a digging-yourself-in-a-hole scenario; the key is to listen, becoming aware of my presence and the due diligent signs to support you in the dissipating of your so-called hurdles of bricked-up fears, de-escalating situations that are truly so blown out of proportion dramadies, and even though as the world turns, so should you, rather than being stuck within the loop of a never-ending TV show, reliving your experiences on repeat.

I AM the motivator, showing you in slow motion the motions of your messy, mucky, Marmite, melodramatic experiences, only for you to realize the misgivings and misunderstandings, rectifying the snags within the mannerisms of your mind and dharma.

I AM the focal point to your weary and worn, wandering, wobbling, and wounded focus, having caused you to fret and forsake yourself in your now cumbersome, flustered, finicky, fractious, fatigued state of mind.

I AM the tongue twister to your diabolical, spun-out-in-the-dugout, out-of-control, delusional fears, keeping you in that state of a fine-woven egotistical (and) alienated rigorous stupor. Yet I AM merely here to help stem the ruptured flow of inconsistencies that has enveloped and burdened one's life, much like the pouring of a rich, spicy, curry gravy, causing one to gasp, cough, and splutter in the aftermath having intoxicated the self with the heaviness of one's experiences.

The Universe supports you as much as you decide to support yourself, so either keep hollering and tussling with the gnarly devil within, being a cold sore to one's bleeding mind, or merely look at the reflection staring back in the mirror and know that the pouring of self-love comes from within, just as confidence is built with brick and mortar from the wells within, creating the beautiful folds of integrity through the wisdom of understanding the game of throw-the-dice of one's experiences.

I hold no prisoners. You're the only one holding yourself prisoner in your craftily created prison, having solely imprisoned yourself and thus your imprisonment is yours to break free from; I hold not the keys to your prison door, you do...so hit me up to whip up a solution in your frazzled state of running around in your head like an Indian Wild Ass (Onager), or remain but ever so deeply in a deep-fried, frenzied state of a stale and hardened samosa, dunked in sour-turned yogurt and attracting nothing but bottle flies.

I AM as much a destroyer, fumigating the toxic pond humanity has waded in as much as I AM a healer, flushing out the unwanted waste and reviving the clogged pores of the soul of man.

I AM as much of a wrecking ball creating havoc, as you are sitting and sulking on that brewing pot of trouble, which I will all too happily blow to smithereens, yanking you off the pot, dunking your face in your very own organically created dung of circumstances, making you face the stench of your fears, owning up to your hogwash, breathing through the fire, burning your experiences to a fine crisp, a la papadums, until but ashes remain for you rise up and be reborn, transforming into far more of a lighter and enlightened light of a lit diyas de-light.

I AM the recycler, the reset button, the shoot-the-rubber-band to your sorry 'Rasputinian,' retched, wayward life.

Aie, for those that live by the sword, surely so 'die' by the sword of one's rumbled and ratted-out experiences.

'To die is to live,' or is it 'To live is to die?'

RELATIONSHIPS AND LOVE

Drink that in like a cooled mango lassi or a sweet scented assam tea.

I may breathe life back into the brokenness of your spirit being, but fixing the mind is a created whirlwind of your own trepid emotions that have had you running rampantly, rabid in the raging, raucous, rancid rivers of the clownish 'racoonian' self.

Did you taste the wild? Lick the wind? Having been thunderstruck, runnin' with the devil? Are you still not back from that soul vacation, tracing your way back through the constellation, dancing with the devil, jiggy woogie inside, because something happened on the way to heaven? Are you still hanging by a moment, with a hello-from-the-outside, rather than from the inside out, having forgotten to clean out your 'closet,' sowing the seeds of love, bringing yourself a higher love?

You are all so gently, subtly gullible, listening to wording, allowing for it to sculpt you, morphing you on the axis at your current point of existence in this equilibrium of space-time continuum.

Stop being a pretentious, pimping lil Pikachu, peckin' away at every hanging syllable, because the particular, chosen phraseology pea-shot your way, pees on the very fiber of your precious peeved-off being.

Why perceive to live in the superficial, artificial grip of a bubbled system, forever prancing and dancing on the surface of who you think you are, bruising yourself but black and blue, rather than to deal, heal, and be real? You are jumping off that cliff, tumbling through the currents of your experiences, wading through the heaviness of your created, curry fish masala, incinerating the layers that have kept you bubbling on the peripheral, emptying the once lumbersome bowl, returning to the crisp glowing hue of your sparkling self.

What the world needs now is love sweet love, it's the only thing, that there's just too little of...

Kindness and compassion are rippling reflections of one's soul, often accomplished by shattering the illusion, having been in battle with one's experiences, coming out scathed, beaten, and bloodied, yet healing through the wisdom of understanding and relinquishing these on the winds of rebirth and change.

Transformation is key to the rebirthing of all of mankind, there is no shortcut to paradise, one must walk through the thick of the fog and pollution of the lands as much as of the mind, to convey the love within one's soul for oneself as much as for all of humanity and the Mother."

—The Goddess Kali Ma

Kali Ma Mantra For Manifesting

Om Krim Kali
(pronounced Aum Kreem Kalee)

॥ ॐ क्रीं काली ॥

This mantra is a powerful invocation of your inner vitality and light. It calls forth your "prana," or life force energy, to enliven your spirit and relieve fatigue. When chanted with intention, this mantra cleanses stagnant energies and ignites renewal. It alleviates the heaviness within the weary mind and fills you with inspiration. Each repetition connects you to your core strength. Feel the heaviness drop away as you bring forward your most radiant self. This mantra awakens your highest potential. As Kali puts it, *"It releases the blargh blurgh aargh that has got one's mind funked into destitution, relieving the sludge within the chi, that has incapacitated the flow and hum of one's soul."*

Kali Ma Mantra For Everyday Inspiration
Om Krim Kalikayai Namah
(pronounced Aum Kreem Kaleeka-yay Namah)

ॐ क्रीं कालिकायै नम

The beauty of this mantra is its versatility and ability to uplift and inspire. It has a lovely toning to it, encompassing the gentle warmth of healing, and weaving together courage, strength, and wisdom. Its rhythmic power enhances our experiences, helping us understand life more deeply. This mantra is a gift, providing the tools we need to walk forward with compassion and grace. Kali says, *"Toning aids in restructuring the synapses as well as rewiring the energetic molecules along the internal highway of the circulatory system within the physical body, removing the potholes of one's experiences through sheer honesty and hard work, repairing the road map of the mind and thus enlivening the soul to a heightened consciousness and understanding."*

Kali Ma Mantra for Problem Solving
Om Sri Maha Kalikayai Namaha
(pronounced Aum Sri Maha Kaleeka-yay namaha))

ॐ श्री महा कलिकायै नम

Like a tapestry of sacred syllables, this mantra weaves a spell of solace. No matter how tangled the troubles or complex the crisis, its undulating vowels and consonants form a melody of deliverance. The words transport the spirit to a place of peace amidst the chaos. With each repetition, layers of luminous meaning are revealed, and the heart is elevated to an expanded state of awareness. This mantra may be ancient, but its power remains a timeless gift of wisdom passed down through the centuries. Chant it with devotion and discover how a simple sequence of sounds can calm the mind and soothe the soul.

As Kali says, *"Problems are the created barrier of a cross that one has smacked the self on the head with, causing one's tail to spin in a twirling daze of a head-spun tizzy, entangling one's prana in the very process. And yet on the doormat of every problem quoted lies the resolvance to a solution by merely shifting the focus of one's entangled field of quantum consciousness within the morphogenic field, much like a babbling brook evolving throughout the continuum of time and space, adding droplets of one's created conscious thoughts to the collective and thus shaping not only one's own reality, but the overall reality of the cosmos. Be mindful of the thoughts you pick and ingest and bring to fruition; do not be picking a fight with a sour amchoor, rather have but a sweetened kheer or coconut ladoo, leaving you with a joyousness and inner lushness, vibrating back to the rhythm of the fearless warrior, allowing for one's problems to melt like snow droplets in the sun."*

HEALING WOUNDS, BOTH OLD AND NEW

"You can win over everyone and every situation with love. There is nothing in this world and in your life that you cannot win or overcome with love."

—Sri Sri Ravi Shankar

Guruji teaches us that love lifts us higher when we let it breathe. Give it space and watch it flower, and as we evolve, so do our connections.

Love is like a delicate desert flower, so don't suffocate your relationships with too much attention, neglecting, starving your own dreams and passions. Never put your own life and goals on hold for love, letting it slip through your fingers. Don't let love become a slippery fish that you can't hold onto because you're too busy trying to catch it. Trust me, I've been there, done that like a broken record on repeat. Too often, I was like this beaten-up marshmallow that kept hopping into the campfire getting all toasty and melty, thinking it'll bring the s'mores closer together. But really, I just ended up getting burnt to a crisp by my fears, becoming a gooey mess of liquified jelly in their hands, losing my fluffiness in the process. We put up with a lot of shit from the people we love, trying to soften their hard edges, quite literally losing ourselves drowning in the experience, melting away in the heat. My soul smothered in their needs, I lost my voice and faded into their shadows. Don't get lost in a love that consumes you, true love is not about possession and obsession. It's about joyful freedom and growth—two individuals flourishing in their own journeys, yet uniting to build a haven in each other's hearts. Tend the flame gently and it will warm your whole life. Flood it and the fire dies.

Don't lose yourself like a bean in the coffee grinder for someone else's cuppa joy; don't let your spirit get chewed up like an espresso bean in someone else's morning routine. Stay focused on your own hopes and dreams, and your partnership will percolate along just nicely. Relationships only brew when both mugs intend to fill, not fling pointy sticks at each other and seeing only the thorny prickles. As we pour ourselves fuller, so overflows the taste of our bonds; be it lovers or just beans. So, steep yourself in your own purpose first, that way your cup will have plenty of richness to share, and not just the bitter grounds at the bottom.

Hurt is part of love, and yes—it may hurt on a "heart" level—but on a "soul" level, freedom awaits those daring enough to let go, forgive, and heal. We are all solely responsible for how we feel, even when the other party is indifferent (due to the level of consciousness they operate at and the circumstances and situations they reside in). The blows of love cut deep, but the remedy of surrender offers a balm to heal those inflicted bruises. Though lovers inhabit separate spheres, forgiveness bridges the divide. In the end, we will always be the medicine to our own healing.

When it came to relationships, I suffered from what I call "donkey syndrome." That is to say, I was a real pain in my own arse! My relationships were like poison ivy to my soul; toxic weeds, that I, like a clumsy fool, kept rolling around in, inflicting all kinds of pain onto myself. I wasn't learning the lessons held within the experiences. What powerful experiences I could have had if I wasn't such a stubborn jackass! I stumbled from one messy relationship to another, lugging around additional, excess trauma—including a vaginismus diagnosis—like overpacked luggage.

Perhaps you've never heard of vaginismus before. Yet for many women, this word conjures feelings of shame and isolation. Vaginismus refers to a painful spasm of the vaginal muscles that makes sex, or the insertion of anything, extremely difficult or even impossible. And while vaginismus affects women of all ages, cultural backgrounds, and sexual orientations, it remains steeped in stigma. Women suffer in silence, not understanding why their bodies betray them in this way. Doctors often misdiagnose the problem, dismissing complaints of searing pain as merely a need for more lubricant. But vaginismus can arise from something far deeper: a soul-deep wounding, perhaps from past trauma, abuse, or religious shaming around sexuality. The mind holds onto this emotional hurt, and the body physically manifests it as clenched muscles and burning pain. The body resists an invasion of the most private and sacred space.

To heal vaginismus, women must trace their pain back to its roots. They must give themselves permission to process old wounds, honor their bodily experiences, and release layers of shame. By embracing self-love and self-acceptance, women can begin to relax those clenched muscles and make peace with their bodies. While challenging (it took me well into my late forties), this journey toward inner harmony can be profound and empowering.

Beyond the physical challenges, my dating life was a rogue's gallery of troubled souls. I attracted men battling demons like alcoholism, drug addiction, and depression. Some clung to me desperately, convinced our love could conquer all, if only I tried harder. Some men watched my every move, attempting to control and confine my free spirit, cooping me up like an exotic bird in a cage. Others pulled away emotionally, leaving me grasping at shadows. I have put up with treatment no self-respecting woman should ever tolerate. Why? Because I was no wiser than a doped-up, sleepy-arse turtle when it came to self-love. I was very much in that Joan Jett mode of, "I hate myself for loving you, I wanna walk but I run back to you, that's why I hate myself for loving you."

My trauma magnetized me to men as broken as I felt inside. But I don't blame them anymore. In fact, I hold nothing but love and gratitude in my heart for every single one of them and everything that their imperfect love taught me about myself. The problem wasn't that I dated damaged men; they *were* damaged, but so was I. The problem was that I did not know how to love myself, and found that trait in my partners, too. The healing began when I learned to accept my circumstances and embrace the shattered pieces of myself, *'kintsukuroi-ing'* them back together with, love, light, wisdom, and understanding, one fragment at a time. I had to learn to nurture my inner light and build a loving relationship with myself.

My journey throughout my life has been to find that self-love and to embrace my own light, just as I once sought theirs. Even if I felt about as desirable as roadkill back then, I picked myself up, dusted myself off, and kept moving forward. I forgive myself for not knowing better, for I was only seeking what I lacked. Now I know: I am enough.

I've been riding solo since 2015, dating myself, and I'm loving it. I'm practically a born-again virgin over here, but I really needed to take time to heal my relationship with myself, especially after running from my own truth for so long. I don't have time for draining someone else's swamp and letting their muck seep into my energy field—been there, done that, cleansed that! Nowadays, I love my own company; solitude is my sanctuary. I'm a lone wolf (always have been), but these days I'm cruising down Easy Street in a pimped-out ride called Self-Love. I'm too much of a fiery spirit to dim my shine for anyone, flying high on the winds of independence. Everything I sought was inside me all along.

Sri Sri Ravi Shankar speaks a profound truth when he says, "Solitude brings inner strength and clarity of mind. The real communication happens in silence." When we retreat into silence, we open the channels for our deepest insights.

We all carry wounds from our past that shape how we move through life. However, trust and respect begin with ourselves, and I've learned that the hard way. For years, I berated and starved myself, thinking I was unworthy of love. My inner critic was unrelenting, yet I kept giving myself away, hoping external validation would fill the void within. But true nourishment comes from within. Now, I am far better in understanding my worth, and I nurture my body, mind, and spirit as best as I can.

Life truly is one devious prankster. How easily it makes us forget. One moment we're huddled with our Council of Guides, eagerly signing up for all the juicy earthly life courses our hearts desire. Characters of every shape, size and flavor are lining up to be our teachers. We rub our spirit hands together in anticipation, ready to dive in and drink up all the wisdom and experiences on offer. And then—bam! We're thrust into the cold from the warmth of the womb, screaming as the icy air hits our naked skin, much like a popped cold beer on ice. What was the point of this all again? Who were we a second ago? It's all gone in a flash, our memories wiped clean like a chalkboard.

As we adapt to our human lives, having forgotten who we are, and the experiences we asked for, stumbling through earth school, trying to figure out how our legs work, we come to terms with the challenges of growing up, having learned from our parents on how to move around in the world, drama et all. We may not comprehend why life sometimes shreds our dreams to ribbons, and we're left standing there, a hot mess among the confetti. But eventually—finally, the rusted pennies drop. The cogwheels start turning, with the blurry picture coming into focus.

WHAT ABOUT SOULMATES?

I often hoped for a soulmate to crack me open, shatter my illusions, and force me to grow. I wanted a soulmate to help me evolve from my many fall-flat-on-my-face experiences; to help me love myself by wrapping the tenderness of my mind in the loving embrace of my body and soul. It turns out, that this wasn't the plan. Well played, Life, you magnificently infuriating yet wise teacher. I signed up for the journey of life on Earth, and you're giving me exactly what I need. It's an honor to dance with you, even if you occasionally step on my toes and catch me off guard.

As Sri Sri says, "We don't have to wait for some soulmate to come to us. I tell you; you can never meet your soulmate unless you first meet your soul."

The Council continues, *"You can beg and plead with us until you are smurfin' blue in the face, but you must muster up the courage to end the reign of chaos you have so duly lit but fire to, non? Your travel guides, those that you cannot see or hear, but who are your biggest supporters on the sidelines, are known as 'Spirit Guides', and will merely look at you, and go, 'na-ah, suck it up buttercup, stop whining, for your soul contract clearly stipulates the wonderful experiences you have signed up for in the University of Earth, so let us get the popcorn and see you worm your way out of this scene of your bubbling soap drama of a life.'"*

We are love. It is our infinite nature. And yet through our human conditioning, we have forgotten what love truly is. We think love is earned, but that as St. Germain says, is preposterous. *"Love is the all-encompassing light of what you are, but have merely forgotten, allowing for the manufactured mind to believe this sugar-coated, pink, cotton candy-flavored e-motion labelled as love. It is only because people reverberate like magnets, drawn together by an invisible force through the chemical formulations and energetic frequencies, attracted to one another like a bee is to honey! Lift each other up and see each other as rippling reflections of what each can teach the other. Your outer world is a reflection of your inner world, and thus, any unresolved emotional conflict you so 'lovingly' harbor within, that has weighted you down like a cinder block in the ocean, emerges to the surface, giving way like the waves crashing to the shores of your mind, merely requesting for you to retrieve and analyze the pain you carry, cleansing and healing the wounded hurt, much like using an antiseptic, nurturing your-*

self, allowing for you to unhide the hidden true self. Without 'pain,' one will merely remain in one's contaminated disdain, stewing in one's funky, spluttering mess, ever infecting the 'wound' that merely screams out for healing. So, my Child, do you not owe it to yourself to heal the dripping ooze of the experience(s) you have so boldly chosen to keep cutting into?"

Sri Sri Ravi Shankar teaches that the love we truly need and seek in life begins with self-love. "Find the love you seek, by first finding the love within yourself," he writes. "Learn to rest in that place within you that is your true home."

SELF-ACCEPTANCE AND SELF-FORGIVENESS

Self-acceptance, self-forgiveness, and self-love is not selfish. Rather, it is being selfless towards ourselves. It's prioritizing our own wellbeing, not the wellbeing of others. It's taking care of our own mental health, rather than trying to fix the minds of others. It's listening to the whispers of our spirit instead of the shouts of the echoing world. Once we listen, modify our thinking, and crack the morse code of our disruptive, cackling ego, we strengthen our inner resolve and learn to love all parts of ourselves. Our energy and auric field emit a different chemical frequency, changing the molecular structure of those light particles within our cellular anatomy, and the ways in how we once perceived ourselves to be through healing our unhealed trauma. There is nothing more freeing and empowering than truly loving ourselves and being in our own company.

"You say that loving yourself is not easy? Hmmm, is that not a mere jest of the tricked senses, that one has arguably at best played upon the self? You stoically remain rigid in that dimmed, conscious sense of being unforgiving to what others may have done to you, whilst you are the only one that remains unforgiving of yourself in said situation. It all starts with that reflection of those gullible eyes staring back in le miroir: you.

Self-forgiveness is an excellent detergent for cleansing the mind, rubbing of gleamingly on yer soul, regaining that spunk for life that had punked you in the first place.

Self-forgiveness is the key to liberating the moody, messed-up, created mind, allowing for the trapped, energetic junk within the soul to be released from the chokehold of the ego, breathing back lightness into the essence of your very BEing.

Many people have gotten themselves in a piddle through their own complex, formulated, riddle-me-that riddles, when the equation to the riddled mind seems but merely the art of lovingly hugging it out by embracing forgiveness. If one cannot forgive, then how can one truly heal, remaining that mere chastised monkey within the boxing ring with thyself? Must one play tug o' war until one is shot to hell through a barrage of dis-ease, all because one has chosen to beat the self up? It is not others that hurt you, it is you that has allowed the hurt of the experiences to run with you, compartmentalizing everything accordingly in the archives of the mind, like the astute librarian one has become. You have to learn to love the 'all' of you, as much as you love the 'all' in others. People play far too many a trickery of the mind, through all the nauseating loony conditioning they have become so rife to, much like a mindboggling legal contract, steeped in the many created clauses with the many dos and don'ts, throwing darts at one another, causing each other nothing but icky, pain-ed thorns. So, my Child, forgive and release others with nothing but love in your heart, for all are mere teachers to the uncovering of your beautifully placid soul."

—The Ascended Master St. Germain

CREATING A LOVING MINDSET

We should toss aside the fear and division that have been baked into us, and get to the sweet, spicy core of who we really are: love. This luscious ingredient has been inside us all along, just waiting to be embraced as our true aromatic essence, and our shared humanity is simply a divine recipe just waiting to be savored.

According to quantum physics, our thoughts have the power to radically transform our neural pathways. When we change our thinking, we interrupt the entrenched nerve cells that have long reinforced each other. As we peel back the layers of repetitive neural programming, we become aware of the light within us. Each enlightening moment reconnects us to our inner power and truth. We give ourselves permission to sever limiting neural nets and create new connections aligned with health, happiness, and wholeness. Quantum mechanics shows that our thoughts direct our energy, sculpting neural highways that shape our reality. By taking charge of our thinking, we can rewrite the neural patterns and codes underlying our experience.

We need only decide to awaken and claim the freedom that is our birthright, for in healing ourselves, we heal the world. This is the sacred nature of our interbeing, and shedding those heavy layers is like peeling an onion, but the pain has purpose. There may be some tears along the way as we unpack our inner hurts, but reaching the core can illuminate everything. Those "lightbulb moments" of truth have the ability to electrify us with insight. We reclaim our power, flick the "on" switch of self-acceptance, and bask in the glow of a happier, healthier life. The path winds inward yet leads us outward to joy.

I carry absolutely no bitterness towards any of the characters from both my interpersonal and romantic relationships who were once part of my life; they hold no power over me anymore. I have let go of the hurt and disappointment, choosing instead to forgive them and myself. If I had not, I would be lugging the weight of the world on my shoulders and be carried off in a straitjacket. Those experiences were lessons I needed to learn and grow from, so I am thankful.

Why carry all that hate, walking round with that spicy and bitter aftertaste of angostura bitters? What's clear is that nothing is served by thinking about the terrible things someone did to you, and making yourself miserable in the process, while the person who has harmed you may be having a fabulous day at the beach. I am free, and I am at peace. The truth has allowed me to live fully in the present, no longer chained to the past. I have learned, I have loved, I have forgiven—and I have so much more life to live.

"The crucial point is: by changing ourselves, we change the world. As we become more loving on the inside, healing occurs on the outside. Much like the rising of the sea level lifts all ships, so the radiance of unconditional love within a human heart lifts all of life."

—David R. Hawkins, *Letting Go: The Pathway to Surrender*

Sri Sri was once asked about queer relationships. At the time, the Vatican and the New Pontificate (Vatican) was expected to take a rigid stance on issues such as homosexuality. People wanted to know what the ancient scriptures said about these matters and what his thoughts were.

Sri Sri said: "There is no mention, nor prohibition of it. One thing the scriptures do say is that every human being is made up of both mother and father, so half male, half female. In some cases, the male tendency may be dominant, while in others the female. If people are bound to have these tendencies, they should acknowledge it. Just observe the feelings, emotions, and sensations in the body, and this will free you from all the fear, guilt, or any other unpleasant things that you store within yourself."

Historically, the Catholic Church has been a powerful organization with far-reaching influence—and one that has ventured into some dark places. Under Pope Benedict XVI, it aggressively targeted gay people, seeing their love as a threat. But the world has changed. Many people, even priests, are gay—so what? Love who you want to love. People need to stop being hypocrites, sticking labels to everything. It dilutes the awareness and the essence of love to something it is not.

Pope Benedict XVI thought legalizing same-sex marriage was unjust and a threat to all families. But we are *energy* first, and *human* second. We should stop labelling ourselves unless we feel the need to give ourselves an "identity." Labels only create false divisions. By celebrating our individuality and trying to figure out who the hell we are at our core, we are not separate from the whole. Everyone has the right to choose how to live and love. Religion teaches us to believe outside of ourselves, whereas spirituality teaches us to deep-dive within; it is the process of awakening from a subdued state of a lulled consciousness, rising above the riptide of the ego, awakening to a higher state of consciousness, and searching for the meaning of life. We need to remember that we are not just flesh, but also spiritual beings, with our soul light particles choosing to spend some quality time in these zipped-up, earthly, human bodies.

WHAT IS "TRUE LOVE?"

"Compassion is the doorway. Forgiveness is the key, and love is the answer to everything and all, making one's life superbly, finger lickin' good, non?"

—The Ascended Master St. Germain

True love is not an emotion—it is a state of being that transcends feelings. When we fall head-over-heels for a new car, a dream home, or even another person, it's so easy to get swept away in the intoxicating rush of infatuation. We cling tightly to these feelings, convinced that this is what love is all about. But *true* love goes much deeper than butterflies in your stomach or stars in your eyes.

True love emerges when we peel back the layers of illusion and meet our beloved in their essence. It's a soul recognition that ignites when two spirits connect in naked honesty and vulnerability. True love has a subtle magnetism, a gentle knowing that needs no words. It's a stillness amidst the storm of emotions, a sanctuary for two souls to rest in each other's presence.

So next time your heart flutters and your cheeks flush, remember that's just a preview of the real thing. Don't mistake it for the main feature. True love awaits you when you're ready to open your heart and let someone truly see you for everything that you are. That's when you'll realize that this love has been within you all along.

"Love is not an emotion. It is your very existence."

—*Sri Sri Ravi Shankar*

We are divine beings who chose to play an earthly game, hiding our true nature from ourselves just so we could have the thrill of rediscovering who we really are. Understanding love is a difficult part of this, because love is our essence—who we are. Our deepest desire and highest purpose is to cultivate compassion and become love embodied.

When a special someone stirs joy in your heart, see them not just as a romantic partner, but also as a reminder of the loving essence within you. Their presence is a gift, allowing you to taste the sweet nectar of love and expand your awareness of your true nature. Though this person may ignite these feelings in you now, know that you need not be dependent on them for your happiness. Instead, let their love inspire you to cultivate those same feelings of warmth, compassion, and bliss within yourself. Choose to *be* love, not just *feel* love for another. In doing so, you free yourself and your partner from expectations and control. Then, you are able to give and receive affection freely, without attachment or possession. You realize that love is not something to be grasped, but an essence to become: a state of being unlimited by any one relationship or circumstance. You are love—open, present, and unbound.

True love flows not from others, but from your own soul. It is the lantern lighting your way, even when lost in the thickest fog. Dark nights of the spirit come to all, but love persists. Let it be your guiding light back home, to the hearth of your heart. There, tend the fire that is uniquely yours. Fan the flames of self-compassion. Know you are worthy simply because you exist. This is the journey of a lifetime: falling in love with your whole self.

"If you think nobody loves you, know for sure that you are loved. The earth loves you; that's why it is holding you upright. The love of the earth is its gravitational force. The air loves you; that's why it moves through your lungs even when you are sleeping. The Divine loves you very dearly, deeply. Once you realize this, you will never feel lonely."

—*Sri Sri Ravi Shankar*

It's time to get your shit together and embrace self-love. Life is about falling head over heels for numero uno—you! If you don't show yourself some love, don't go expecting others to pick up the slack. Love is the flashlight that guides you out of the darkness and back to your true self, even when you're lost in the pitch black. So, get out there and get right with yourself. The world ain't gonna love you if you don't love you first. Dig deep and find that self-love.

THE DEPTHS OF LOVE: Q&A WITH MASTER DJWHAL KUHL

The wise and loving Master Djwhal Kuhl shines as a beacon of emerald light, guiding all who seek truth and understanding. As Chohan of the 2nd Ray of Love and Wisdom, he works hand-in-hand with his soul brothers, the ascended masters Lord Kuthumi and El Morya, radiating compassion and insight to uplift humanity. Though his physical form has left this earthly plane, his spirit remains ever present, whispering words

RELATIONSHIPS AND LOVE

of hope and inspiration to those with open hearts. He teaches you about universal truths, yet keeps it chill with his mellow, gentle style. DK is here to shower us with the freshness of emerald enlightenment, taking our consciousness to new levels through compassion and understanding. This cosmic master keeps it real, guiding us with wisdom from the heart. Feel the love and dive into the infinite bliss. Djwhal Kuhl's got the beat that'll move your feet towards cosmic unity and spiritual community.

Q: What is love?
A: Hmmm yes, love is a bit like that spinning of the yarn, a warped, worm-holed, fabricated fable with an ironic twist, having some dark roots that have seeped into the minds of man and taken root within the 'earth-human', walking with 'eyes wide shut' through the earthly illusion, thinking that love is a process of earning one's keep, much like one's wages, and having to adhere to the acceptance of others, whilst one should learn to look at the rippling reflection of oneself, knowing that you are and always have been love; it is the very essence of your 'al-chemically' formulated Star BEing. You are a creation of love, so how can it be that you refuse to love yourself, seeking validation from others, merely to suffice the needs of your corrupted soul, that you, my dear, have chosen to neglect by rupturing your burdened mind and by throwing yourself into the everlasting, smoldering embers, burning yourself into one hot mess, rather than cleansing yourself in the eternal healing soothing waters of self-love? Is it not time to thwart the bullying ego that's been piggybacking on your mind, happily oinking and munching away on the erratic influx of e-motions you have so duly fed yourself like pig slop through the formation of your thoughts, by way of the wayward outer world, thus having allowed for it to taint the true meaning of unconditional love? Love is a beautiful symphonic frequency, an inner event, an inner formulation, that inner, gooey warmth, carried through the cosmic frequency waves of the outer, touching all it surpasses, with a wee bit more magic and exuberance then the stalemate of its former, encapsulated energy it once held. The power of love is a phenomenon that

many seem to have blocked off into a grid of what love should mean, but clearly does not. Unlock that locked-up love; for love, my Child, does not judge, it merely holds all in the palms of its hands, gently embracing all that is with open arms; your joys, your sorrows, your pains, your regrets, to those who eventually see themselves and the world merely through the eyes of appreciation, gratitude, and the blossoming bud of that love essence eternal.

Be not so downtrodden and tread but lightly on the downward mind, viewing life with the eye of the beholder, 'to thine own self be true' of thankfulness and grace; for the warmth of love and acceptance can melt the burn of one's sorrows. Like a flower unfolding its petals, the key ingredient of love reveals its essence in moments of connection that nourishes the sacred heart of one's soul.

One can walk, browbeaten and downcast, amongst the 'living,' yet remain in a fugue state of zombified zombification, or walk back to that burst of eternal sunshine in your soul of the very presence of the Divine I AM. Life is about choices, it's either slippin' over the 'cloudy with a 99.9% chance of meatballs' or clearing the pavement of all your created worries and sorrows, discarding these experiences in the well-placed, heavenly bins along the sidewalks of life.

Remember, God Consciousness is the Consciousness of God that is you as much as you are part of that Consciousness of God, for without God, without the Supreme Energetic Creator, one would not exist, the Universe would not exist, nothing would exist. For by the Grace of God, how can you not BE God when you are Creator creating and expressing the self through the Divine God Conscious BEing you are? If you have no God Consciousness, then I ask thee, who in the world might thy be? Are you not made of Universal God Light particles? Are you not made of the same loving particles as all life in the Universe?

We are all buoyant particles in the Cosmic Sea of Love, reintegrated into the hue-man body for the purpose of elevating our experiences, merely

RELATIONSHIPS AND LOVE

returning to that enigmatic form of brilliance and radiant love a la coeur. Elevate, illuminate, and magnify the tainted stains of what you believe to be love, and wash out the conditioning you have so adamantly adhered to, from the unthreaded, threading frequency of love, stitching it back up to the breathable frequency of a threaded love.

Wrap your loving arms around your beautiful self, squeeze it, hug it, and express yourself through the art of love, to create but a far more beautiful and 'bounciful Tigger' of a life for yourself, rather than bumbling forth like a lost bumblebee drunk on honey, being complicit in the illicit game of pouncing all that love out of yourself, thus turning those energetic flowing star particles within your hue-man bodily circuitry into clogged-up confetti.

If you can't bounce the bounce (and you can't even pronounce the bounce), then how can you love the love when you can't even pronounce the love? Why wait a while? Put some bounce in your smile, as much as you blow some kisses of love into that once-deflated twinkling smile.

In the warmth of a fiery hearth of love and whimsical light, I remain."

—The Ascended Master DK

There is light in every situation. You need only open your heart to find it. Never let rain clouds dampen your spirit. Muster up the courage to find your way back through the winding corridors of the drenched mind, returning to the beautiful light and warmth of the day within, and back to the hidden glow-gem that is your soul.

To heal yourself, you've got to get your shit together and love yourself. Life is all about falling in love with yourself first. If you don't, then don't expect others to treat you any differently. Love is the light of all healing, for even in the darkest of places, it illuminates the pathway back to the very heart of ourselves. Summon your courage to navigate the infinite Escherian staircase of your soul, back to the radiant light of possibility.

ASCENDED MASTER HANUMAN ON LOVE AND DEVOTION

The Ascended Master Hanuman, a Hindu deity often depicted as a monkey god, embodies an enlightened warrior who has emerged victorious from countless battles across the Cosmos. He often likens himself to a Shaolin Monk, gracefully moving with precision and skill. I have met him on the astral planes, and he is a wonderful teacher. He is thoughtful, quiet, possesses a calm demeanor, and is hawkishly observant. Instead of interfering with a student's spiritual journey, he encourages them to find their own way within the grand design of the universe; he respects their individual paths. His motto is: when the student is ready, the master appears. If you do seek his assistance, be prepared for him to push you beyond your comfort zone straight into the "I smell a rat" of your fears. Just like Archangel Michael, he will shove your face right in the dipshit of your fears and say, *"Would you like a poppadom with that?"* With his simian face and powerful, yet agile physique, he embodies the fusion of wisdom, love, inner strength, courage, devotion, and the boundless joy of embracing life's highs and lows.

Legends tell of Hanuman commanding his armies of *vanara* warriors (monkey-like beings that possess human-like intelligence and mystical powers). With his profound understanding of sacred texts, mastery of martial arts, and deep connection to the Divine, Hanuman would strategize and guide his armies to vanquish the malevolent forces that threatened the divine cosmic order.

Hanuman shows us that real enlightenment isn't about basking in the spotlight, racking up victories, or sipping from the oversized mug of a severely bloated ego, while patting ourselves on the back. True enlightenment comes from nurturing wisdom, compassion, and inner strength—and acting with unwavering devotion to a higher purpose.

RELATIONSHIPS AND LOVE

Hanuman encourages us to approach life with a playful heart, seeing the world as an experimental playground meant for experience and adventure, rather than a source of suffering. He wants us to let go of limiting beliefs and self-imposed restrictions, and to stop playing it safe within the confines of a small, fearful mindset. Instead, he urges us to open our hearts to love—for ourselves, for others, and for life itself. Like a child filled with wide-eyed wonder playing on the swings, he tells us to embrace the adventure of life, break free from the limitations of our own minds, and soar to new heights of consciousness. With faith and devotion, we can let him take us by the hand and guide us on a divine journey of self-discovery. The master reminds us that life is a gift meant to be lived fully, courageously, and with wholehearted participation— not half-arsed! Every experience—even moments of apparent darkness—provide opportunities for learning, growth, and awakening. Embrace Hanuman's wisdom to uncover those inner pearls of wisdom, strength, and loving devotion. Becoming your very own caped superhero on the playground of life, allowing your spirit to soar free. Hanuman says:

"I AM the Lord of love circling your playground, swirling around, creating playful bubbles in your realm of joy.

I AM the warm-hearted warmth to the void of fiery compassion you withhold for yourself.

I AM the devotion you so lack for the self-care of your body, mind, and soul.

I AM the courage to the incontinence of your weeing fear.

I AM the 'oui oui,' to your 'non non.'

I AM the dragon's breath to your crippled and pained warrior.

I AM the anchor to your weakened strength when you feel weary and beaten down by the worldly collusion that has cherry-bombed your mind.

I AM the intelligence that whispers for you to keep going, even when times have drenched you into the oblivion of the souped-up mind.

I AM the joy to the lathered-up soap in your head.

I AM the board to your Silver Surfer, helping you surf the seas of your mind.

RELATIONSHIPS AND LOVE

I AM the lost golden slipper to your slipped-up, twinkle toe soul.

I AM the 'arriba arriba andale' to your wiped-out Speedy Gonzalez.

I AM the Cupid to your lost-in-a-hole Self-Love.

I AM that sweet Quan Yin to your knocked-out self-compassion.

I AM the spinach to your bent-out-of-shape, sight-for-sorry-eyes Popeye.

I AM the wheel that keeps on turning, pulling you out of the stuck-in-the-mud mind of self.

I AM Hanuman, the monkey God, helping you to transform that monkey mind that got you 'monkeyed' in a tussle with your head-on collision experiences.

I AM the stop and stare at yourself, sowing the seeds of love in your heart.

I AM the honeydew to your overburdened chicken tikka masala.

I AM the hair of the dog to your drunken, whiskeyed-out mind.

I AM the love that you cannot yet see, but most divinely ARE!

I AM the undercover rescuer, here to aid and abet in recovering the covered mind to a state of uncovering, and to remind you of the light of love that you have always been.

I AM here to remind you to bow at the light of your own two beautiful feet, for you are a magnificent, universal wonder to behold.

I AM the cheetah to your speed-bumped, headbutting demon-turned-gazelle, for there is order in the divine chaos that has you kick-spun so out of control.

I AM the 'Hail Mary' to your capsized, sinking boat of a mind, a beacon in the dark to your Jell-o-turned thoughts, that have gotten your e-motions 'frozen-pead,' like a salted, out-of-the-box Jack Frost.

I AM that fuzzy, pink flamingo, farting bubbles of love in your worn-out, flustered, rain-on-me parade.

I AM the sun to your moon.

I AM the stars to your darkness.

I AM your way guide to the repairman of your mind, heart, health, and wellbeing.

I AM the cable to your unplugged, dehydrated, and starved-of-oxygen self.

I AM the compassion to your impaled sense of self.

I AM the cross you bear, for the winds of utmost change that knock you off your socks and feet, sweeping you up in the chaos of that deliciously twirling, leafy, divine glory.

BE not so harsh on yourself, pounding yourself like a gorilla, giving King Kong a run for his money. Stop cracking the whip, flagellating the hurt and deepening the bleeding of your wounds. Instead, bathe yourself in the gentle waters of compassion and self-awareness, of wisdom and understanding, releasing the caused pain and suffering, embracing the beautiful, divine spirit you are and have always been. Remember, you are love. Be love. Show love. Spread love and wrap yourself in the snuggly, warm embrace of that loving devotion."

—The Ascended Master Hanuman

St. Germain wraps up this chapter with a beautiful reminder that life is all about love—pure and simple. We're all on a quest to rediscover the endless love within us and surrounding us. This love gives our lives meaning, strengthens our connections, and propels us towards a purposeful existence. When we strip away the layers of ego, fear, and distractions, we realize that the key to life's mysteries lies in surrendering to the love that flows through everything. Love isn't something we chase after; it's something we embrace, embody, and cherish in every moment. It's the source of our true selves, the light that guides us, and the bond that unites us all. Despite life's complexities, St. Germain's wisdom cuts through the noise to reveal the simple truth at the heart of our human experience—that we are here to remember, to reconnect, and to revel in the infinite love that is our birthright and our destiny. In the end, this is all that truly matters; this is the alpha and omega, the beginning and the end of the journey we call life.

"Life is merely a return to love, nothing more, nothing less, so love yourself and love all that have crossed your path on this journey of life, regardless of the experiences that have been hurled your way and left you flat-out, twirling like a spun-out bowling pin. Slap that ditz out of your mind, and bow but graciously in gratitude, for what more can one ask than to bury the hatchet and feel but consciously enlightened? Rather that, than being in a forever tug-o-egotistical-war with oneself, lying entangled in a heap of frustrating, Stumper the Rabbit, gnarly, knotted Christmas lights, non?"

—The Ascended Master St. Germain

CHAPTER 16
SHATTERED REFLECTIONS: THE TWIN FLAME EXPERIENCE

I WAS RIDING SOLO TILL early June 2024, when I was suddenly caught off guard by the reappearance of my ex, Mark. Our reunion was like a whirlwind. After fifteen years apart, and despite the emotional scars, we chose to enter into a relationship again, fueled by the undeniable bond we had as twin flames.

The concept of twin flames has captured the imaginations of many, conjuring up notions of a mystical, destined soulmate connection that transcends the bounds of ordinary relationships. However, the reality of twin flames is often far more complex and nuanced than the fairytale-like depictions that have become popularized. Twin flames don't complete us—we have to do that ourselves—but they reflect our deepest wounds and insecurities, pushing us to confront our inner demons and embark on a journey of self-discovery. Mark and I embraced this, viewing our renewed relationship as an opportunity to heal and grow. We understood that the true love we sought resided not in each other, but within the flame that burned brightly in our souls. Twin flames often dive deep into trauma together, acting as each other's triggers. Think of it as a fast track to healing—if we embrace these experiences as chances to grow, we can transform our pain into power.

What started as a thrilling reunion with Mark quickly spiraled into a chaotic and unsettling ordeal. Initially, everything went smoothly, but soon cracks in the relationship began to surface. Mark would often boast about his self-love and humility, claiming he could handle anything that came his way. However, his actions painted a different picture. The clash of time zones and our conflicting work schedules led to misunderstandings and disagreements.

While I was getting a glass of water from the kitchen early one morning, I commented on the time and wondered why Mark had not yet come to bed. Suddenly, he exploded in anger, hurling insults and accusations at me and accusing me of being condescending. Even though I kept my cool, as shouting matches aren't my style, the sudden outburst threw me off balance. I retreated to my study, curling up under a blanket, feeling a wave of disappointment wash over me. Little did I know that this was just the beginning.

Mark had several more explosive moments, each followed by hollow apologies that failed to stop the same abusive patterns from repeating, fueling my growing fear of him. Skipping my meditation practice and regular meals in an attempt to cope resulted in unintended weight loss and a lack of motivation to exercise. Every morning before dawn, I would walk my dog and clean and tidy my house, seeking solace in the quiet solitude. Although I recognized that I was neglecting myself, the overwhelming sense of dread and the compulsive need to walk on eggshells around Mark made it nearly impossible for me to prioritize my own well-being, which only added to my growing frustration. Meanwhile, Mark continued a worrying self-medication routine, mixing ADHD medication, testosterone, peptides, vitamins, and the dangerous substance GBL, which he converted into the even more potent GBH. Despite my vehement objections, Mark brushed aside my concerns, leaving me feeling powerless and trapped in an increasingly volatile living situation.

I've been a fly on the wall during some of Mark's phone calls about his various ex-lovers—from claiming one was the best kisser on the planet, to gushing about the best sex he ever had, to shifting gears and raving about the best girl he ever lived with. To top it off, he even accused me of lying, leaving me feeling worthless and disrespected, like yesterday's forgotten leftover pizza. I made it clear that his hurtful behavior was unacceptable, but Mark appeared unfazed.

It felt like I was caught in a gaslighting circus act. One moment he was the charming showman, and the next, he was pointing fingers at me, claiming I was the one spinning tales. It was like a real-life Jekyll and Hyde situation. The weight of it all was suffocating, and I felt as though I was losing my grip on both my own health and the wellbeing of someone I cared about deeply.

Following a life-threatening bacterial infection the year prior, Mark became convinced that a unique "brain interface technology" implanted in his head had saved his life. This alleged "chip" bombarded him with more than ten distinct voices, all vying to steer his choices and influence his daily life. Not all these voices were on his side, forcing Mark to negotiate and engage with them like a seasoned diplomat. Paranoid that the powers that be were tracking his every move thanks to this invasive technology, he changed his cellphone and number more frequently than he changed his underwear.

Increasingly consumed by exploring the chip technology further, Mark even entertained the wild notion of using a powerful magnet to extract the device, come hell or high water. I had hoped for a simple, one-on-one connection with him, not the chaotic orchestra of voices performing a mental symphony inside his mind.

Eventually, he confessed to being tormented by suicidal thoughts, driven by the incessant voices echoing in his head. I suggested for him to give meditation a try, believing it could quiet the chatter in his mind, but he just chuckled, dismissing the idea like a bad punchline. It was painfully obvious that his obsession with this so-called "chip" in his brain had taken over his life, leaving no space for a genuine, healthy relationship. I was saddened to see him spiral further into the depths of his own personal turmoil, knowing that the man I once knew was slipping away into the labyrinth of his own fractured mind.

Living with him was like running a marathon in quicksand—exhausting and frustrating. He was hooked on vaping, and his manic and messy eating habits created a delightful disaster zone of stains and food spills, making laundry my constant companion as I navigated the aftermath of his culinary adventures. He was fidgety, and simply couldn't sit still, his body betraying the frenzied state of his tortured mind, unable to find a moment's peace. His focus was splintered into a thousand different directions at once, like confetti in the wind. It was an unrelenting mental dance, his brain leaping from one thought to the next with the agility of a nimble woodland creature, much like trying to nail jello to a wall. Impulse control? That was a foreign concept to him. His online shopping sprees piled up charges that his credit card could barely withstand. Budgeting? That was as alien to him as a distant planet. Completely unaware of my financial responsibilities, he often expected me to pick up the tab for his impulsive buys. Contributing to shared expenses was a rarity for him, leaving me to shoulder the financial burden on my own. Since he had failed to renew his driver's license, I was tasked with being his designated driver, using my own car which consumed more fuel than a thirsty camel in the desert, leaving my wallet feeling the burn of all those extra trips.

He was the king of marathon showers, that stretched for hours, insisting it was all about detoxing. Meanwhile, I was left dealing with the thriving mold garden on the ceiling, a souvenir of his "ritual." A simple grocery store trip quickly devolved into a chaotic escapade worthy of a Hollywood heist film. In my attempt to get back into my own house, I had to cat-burgle my way across the neighbor's roof terrace, as Mark was having a crisis of his own–stuck in the bathroom for hours after indulging in a mountain of egg whites and a questionable self-medication plan that turned into a marathon bathroom session. What was meant to be a routine errand had morphed into a veritable comedic odyssey, the product of Mark's gastrointestinal misadventures and my impromptu foray into a high-stakes home invasion.

Two weeks into his stay, we sat down for a candid conversation and agreed that to give this relationship a chance, it was time for him to move out. After fifteen years, we had both evolved, and my home was feeling a bit crowded. We both craved the freedom to breathe and grow. However, when he attempted to secure his own apartment, his application hit a snag; the universe threw a pie in his face—his application got denied because he couldn't prove he had enough income to keep the lights on and the fridge stocked. And let's not forget the cherry on top—he spectacularly forgot my 50th birthday, the one he promised would be unforgettable.

All this seemed to have a knock-on effect; it was as if an invisible switch had been flipped and he became a completely different person. The caring and loving man I thought I knew had disappeared, replaced by a distant and cold stranger.

Only days earlier, he had described me as marriage material, but out of the blue, he insisted there was no chemistry between us, abruptly dismissing the connection we had seemingly shared. He was as subtle as a sledgehammer, declaring his need for physical intimacy like it was a daily triple special on the menu. He was unable to connect with the deeper, more spiritual aspects of life that could truly nourish his spirit. Like many in today's world, he equated sex with love, but the truth is they are worlds apart. Love is a profound emotion, while sex is a biological act. It's a physical expression, but love is a deep ocean of vulnerability, empathy, and emotional connections that go far beyond just physical encounters. Dr. David R. Hawkins, a renowned psychiatrist and spiritual teacher, eloquently captured the essence of love in his enlightening work *"Eye of the I."* He said, "Love is misunderstood to be an emotion; actually, it is a state of awareness, a way of being in the world, a way of seeing oneself and others." Additionally, Mark had no interest in anything spiritual, preferring to focus solely on the material world. Given the crucial role that spirituality played in my own life, this disconnect was devastating. He complained that I didn't look at him the way he looked at me, but I realized this was more about his own insecurities than anything else. To make matters worse, he accused me of being controlling, claiming that staying with me would lead him back to using fentanyl. He claimed the "nicest he'd ever been" to me was when he was overmedicated on ADHD medication, consuming over ten times the prescribed dosage during a visit to the Saturday market.

In the span of a few short days, this relationship had unraveled, leaving me bewildered and heartbroken. The whiplash of his shifting sentiments, his rejection of my spiritual beliefs, and the baggage of his emotional and substance abuse created an insurmountable divide that I could no longer bridge. It was a devastating realization that the future we had once envisioned together was no longer attainable.

Overwhelmed by his erratic, unpredictable behavior, I found myself unsure of how to navigate the tumultuous situation that had taken over my home. My study became my sanctuary, the only place where I could live, breathe, sleep, and work to escape the unfolding chaos. Feeling trapped in my own home, this was a far cry from the life I had imagined.

Each time I left my study, I was met with the lingering tension and instability that had permeated every corner. The atmosphere was thick with tension, as if the walls might start closing in on me like a bad Freddy Krueger horror movie. My home had become a pressure cooker of chaos, and I was the main ingredient.

Burying myself in my work became my only lifeline, using productivity as a means to escape the unraveling situation that had consumed my living space.

Enduring nearly three weeks of this relentless turmoil had pushed me to my limit. I could no longer tolerate this maddening situation and knew it was time for him to leave, for both our sakes. I refused to continue living in such a toxic environment, trapped in his devastating cycle of DIY medicating and unresolved issues. It was time to reclaim my life, home, and sense of self—whatever it took, I was ready to break free from this self-imposed prison.

On that fateful day, he secured a hotel in Murcia, but instead of packing, he found himself caught in a web of procrastination, delaying this until the late hours. I sensed his reluctance to leave and I inquired about his distress, only to be met with tears and a sharp retort. He blamed me for his life spiraling out of control, saying he would be dead within hours as he planned to take his own life. I calmly told him that if he continued this threatening behavior, I would call emergency services. I reached out to a cab driver I trusted, prepaid for his journey to the hotel, and explained the dire circumstances.

As he stormed out, he hurled a final volley of biting remarks at me that cut like a knife. The palpable intensity of his rage, mixed with anger and resentment, echoed through the air as he slammed the cab door shut.

In the aftermath of his departure, my home was left in shambles, a testament to the destructive force of his uncontrolled emotions. Faced with a monumental cleanup, I resolved to tackle it the following morning, opting to sleep in my study for another night. As I lay there, the weight of the world felt as though it had come crashing down around me, leaving me utterly drained both physically and emotionally, the events of the day having taken a heavy toll.

The next morning, I consulted with my spirit guides, who suggested a creative alternative to traditional sage: a blend I dubbed *'vinsasa.'* This mixture combined distilled white vinegar, table salt, and sage essential oil steeped in hot water. If using it as a spray, opt for distilled water. The ritual was both practical and profoundly spiritual, the simple ingredients infused with a divine purpose to help restore that sweet balance and harmony to my home. After a grueling two-day deep cleanse, during which I discarded or donated everything he had used, the oppressive weight lifted, replaced by a renewed sense of lightness. Though the process was exhausting and emotionally draining, it was necessary to reclaim my living space and begin the process of moving on. Finally, I did a deep-sea salt body scrub to let go of the toxicity and heaviness that clung to me, allowing the light to breathe back into my body and soul.

A week later, I heard a knock at my door, and to my dismay, it was a gaunt and disheveled Mark. My heart sank faster than the Titanic. After he demanded I pay for the cab that had gotten him to my door, I firmly told Mark he couldn't crash at my place. His suitcase had been stolen after he spent two nights sleeping rough in a park, and he had burned through his remaining money in the space of a week. Despite his haggard appearance, he did not seem to be under the influence of drugs. He promised to leave after a shower and doing some laundry. I made it clear that mental health struggles are nothing to be ashamed of, but he needed to take responsibility and confront his deep-rooted issues. Mark had long struggled with self-destructive tendencies, repeatedly sabotaging the good things in his life. He was like the tenant of hell in his own body, tormenting himself with reckless, self-defeating behaviors. and needed to confront his deep-seated issues head-on. I arranged for Mark to stay at a local hostel, using his own funds, and drove him there to ensure he checked in.

A phone call from a virtual psychiatric clinic on my US number—the very one Mark had used—revealed an unexpected truth. Although they couldn't share any details due to patient confidentiality, I discovered that Mark had been quietly facing his own mental health challenges, a truth he had kept hidden from me.

The next day, Mark returned, knocking on my door. It was heartbreaking, but I stood my ground, unwilling to let him in. I reached out to security, uncertain if he had finally given up and gone away. To my surprise, he had not budged an inch, instead having seated himself on the steps by my front door, presumably waiting for me to come outside. Security advised me to call emergency services, and within ten minutes, the police arrived. Once I explained the situation the police warned Mark that if he reappeared, he would face being arrested. In the end, I believe the officers gave him a ride back to the hostel, ensuring the situation was resolved.

Despite not seeing Mark after the incident, I learned he stayed an extra week at the hostel. Some people in the US intervened, covering his expenses and arranging for his return flight home.

I compassionately reminded myself that mental health challenges can affect anyone, and it's important to reflect on what might be driving someone's actions and what past traumas they may be grappling with. Often, hurt people end up hurting others, even if it's not intentional. While this doesn't excuse harmful behavior, understanding the root causes can promote empathy and healing. The best response is to offer love and support, while also setting boundaries. Ultimately, each person's journey is unique, and we are all products of our circumstances.

I've spent years trying to make sense of Mark's choices, and realized I had to draw a line in the sand, as enabling him would only further his self-destruction. I've been his ride-or-die for almost two decades, even when he rotated in and out of jail. I've gone to great lengths to save his arse, yet in the process I lost myself and sacrificed my own peace. I used to be attracted to fixer-upper projects to avoid facing my own pain. It turns out that I had a habit of seeking out broken birds, all because of my self-worth issues. Through my journey with Mark, I learned that true growth comes from within. It's not about fixing others to avoid facing our own pain, but about recognizing our patterns and taking responsibility for our own healing. Mark's story is a reminder that we all have the power to break free from destructive cycles and create a new path for ourselves.

Months later, I stumbled upon a frosty email in a rarely checked inbox—no acknowledgment, no apology, just a masterclass in deflection. This guy flipped the script, casting me as the villain while portraying himself as the innocent party. He labeled me as unstable and demanded I never contact him again, a classic tactic to ease his own conscience about the mess he created and to avoid facing any genuine responsibility for his actions.

My experiences with Mark were shaped by my own unique perspective on how events unfolded. Though Mark and I may have observed the same scene, our distinct viewpoints are influenced by our individual experiences and beliefs. Even when standing in the same room, people can interpret reality differently, each forming their own mental interpretation. Truth be told, I hold no ill feelings towards him. Why would I? Carrying that emotional baggage serves no purpose. Yes, he took advantage of me and cost me dearly, because I allowed it, and yet I chose this journey. Ultimately it was I that had to take responsibility and take back my power. We are the heroes of our own lives, the light that guides our way back to the love within. I didn't see him as a villain, but as a catalyst for my own transformation. I could say he destroyed me, as I once told him, but the truth is no one can destroy another emotionally unless that person allows it. Instead, I am grateful for the elevated experience, the reflection that pushed me to dig deeper into my own being. Through the fire, I left the ashes of my former self behind—shedding tears and layers (yet again), of who I once knew myself to be. My heart is filled with nothing but love for him as he navigates the depths of his buried pain. I have faith that someday, when his is ready, he will embrace his lost inner child with love and compassion. I now understand the significance of the experience and how it had such a profound impact on me. It was necessary for me to finally close that chapter in order to move forward with the rest of my life. I have forgiven myself, and I have also forgiven him. It was an experience, neither good nor bad, but one that allowed me to reflect, grow and become stronger.

THE EFFECTS OF TRAUMA ON THE EARTH

When we go through trauma, the earth absorbs it. Trauma, whether it strikes at our hearts, bodies, or minds, doesn't just fade away like a bad dream. Instead, it burrows deep into the very essence of our surroundings, becoming one with the ground we tread upon. Our planet, Gaia, is not just a backdrop to our lives; it's a living breathing being that absorbs the collective anguish of humanity, taking on our unresolved hurts and unhealed wounds. Just as the earth nurtures and sustains us with the essentials for life, it also stands as a silent witness to the chaos we endure. The traumas we fail to process seep into the soil, the air, and the water, leaving traces of our struggles in the natural world.

But the earth is not merely a passive sponge for our suffering; she is a masterful alchemist. Gaia has the remarkable ability to transform our heaviest burdens into fertile ground for new beginnings. However, this magical process has its limits. If we trudge through life weighed down by our past, that heaviness will continue to pollute the very environment that nurtures us.

This is why it's vital to understand the deep connection between our personal healing and the health of our planet. By tending to our inner worlds and bravely facing our wounds, we not only lighten our own emotional load, but also Gaia's. It is a symbiotic relationship; a beautiful dance of interdependence, one in which the wellbeing of the individual and the wellbeing of the collective are inextricably linked. Only by recognizing and honoring this sacred bond can we truly begin to restore balance, both within ourselves and within the greater ecosystem of which we are a part of.

HELPING YOURSELF HEAL

I won't lie, the trauma hit me hard, it was like a hardcore punch in the gut. After my experience with Mark, I sought help with healing from my ordeal. As I've learned, there's no shame in reaching out when the weight becomes too heavy to bear. I was juggling debilitating acid reflux, persistent headaches that felt like tiny gremlins throwing a rave party on my upper back and shoulders, and a rib cage that had decided to throw its own inflammation fiesta. The pain hit me like a lightning bolt, and breathing, walking, and even talking became a Herculean task. Even though I was feeling rough, I wasn't about to give in. I kept pushing through, juggling work and life, until I finally decided to listen to my doctor's sage advice. Five days later, I embraced the relief that came with some much-needed anti-inflammatory meds. While trauma can manifest in diverse ways, internalizing it leads to ongoing dis-ease that may erupt physically or mentally. When you bottle it up, it's like shaking a soda can—eventually, it's going pop. My go-to healer has always been Louise Rhodes, a Light Language Healer who channels the wisdom of the Arcturians and other Intergalactic Beings. Thanks to her, I was able to shake off some heavy trauma and find my balance again. Of course, it's a team effort—I've got to keep putting in the work too. In Louise's sessions, the light language frequencies realign and rebalance people's energy systems, allowing them to release old patterns, access expanded consciousness, and integrate higher aspects of self—empowering them to more fully embrace their soul's purpose.

THE POWER OF LIGHT LANGUAGE HEALING

If you are unfamiliar with Light Language, it can be further defined as channeling energy in the form of sound. It is a non-comprehensive lingo on a conscious level, yet your soul understands the timbre of these cosmic healing codes just beautifully. These elongated light codes are high vibrational frequency of sound coming from the many multidimensional Light BEings, using the human voice box to transfer these downloads directly into the recipient's soul. They say:

"Light Language may seem like served-up scrambled eggs to the mind, but it is a sweet soothing 'scrumptilicious' nourishment for the soul. It is the added oomph, like an indulgent warm fuzzy creamy vanilla chocolate latte topped with a tinge of zesty lemon and mint, allowing for your soul to sync, glide and dance back into alignment like a Viennese Waltz with one's current physical essence, and thus it is the enlightened gift of a de-light that keeps on giving, illuminating one's path, blowing but light into the darkened darkness of one's mind. Light Language is the electrical buzz kick, the booyah to get you swinging like the Jungle Book's

SHATTERED REFLECTIONS: THE TWIN FLAME EXPERIENCE

King Louie, re-attuning you to a more wholesome soul frequency. Light Language heals on a soullular level, freeing the tethered soul. It is the remedy to the sprinkled pixie dust that has kept your mind in an eternal, you spin me round like a record la-la-land-fiesta in slumberland, having chained the self to the artificial grid of existence.

But it matters not how one chooses to heal, what matters is that pain is the remedy to the unfurling hurt, allowing one to walk through the trepid blockages of one's mind, ultimately learning the song and breath of one's own heart."

When we receive a transmission of Light Language, a deep shift takes place in our brain and consciousness. As we tune in to the graceful tones and fluid movements of these sacred codes, our brain waves shift into the expansive gamma state. This heightened frequency allows the right and left hemispheres of our brain to sync up in a harmonious way, much like the iconic C-3PO droid from Star Wars. In this heightened state of awareness, our memory, sensory perception, focus, processing speed, and creative abilities are greatly enhanced. We become more open to the insights, inspiration, and innate inner wisdom that resides within the depths of our being. Light Language codes hold an incredible power to unlock gifts and soul truths that have long been dormant, waiting ever so patiently to be awakened. By raising our vibration and consciousness, these radiant transmissions align us with the higher frequencies of love, wisdom, vitality, and wholeness. As layers of density and limitation are gently released, Light Language brings about profound healing and transformation on both a cellular and spiritual level. Through the grace and magic of these sacred languages, we are empowered to embody our highest potential and step into the fullest expression of who we are meant to be.

Archangel Michael describes it, as creating a "Light Language tonic," a tincture of codes for the client to 'drink in' for the betterment of the mind, body, and soul.

THE HO'OPONOPONO PRAYER

Repeating the Ho'oponopono prayer was another key factor in my healing journey. It's like a Hawaiian hug for your soul and it literally means 'to make right.' This simple yet powerful mantra ("I'm sorry. Please forgive me. Thank you. I love you.") is a practice of forgiveness and healing that aims to bring harmony with those around you, yourself, and the world. It is based on the belief that balance and harmony are crucial for overall wellbeing. By clearing the mind of negative thoughts and emotions, and addressing inner conflicts, you can create a positive impact on your external reality.

Experiencing trauma and skipping meals made me look like a walking clothes rack, and it was a struggle to put those lost pounds back on. To regain the lost muscle mass and kickstart my tired body, I dragged myself back to the gym which I had ghosted for several weeks. Thanks to Archangel Raphael, I managed to let go of the baggage and embrace forgiveness, allowing the winds of change to sweep through my whole being.

Underneath all the trauma, our souls are beautifully intact, like a perfectly preserved vintage car, while our minds are like a cluttered garage filled with old junk just waiting to blow up. We're basically stashing our unhealed trauma like a bunch of old pizza boxes in our overcrowded mental storage unit. Eventually, it's going to pop somewhere. And those demons? They're not looking for a fight; they're just screaming out for a little TLC and want to be acknowledged. Sit with them, listen to them, embrace the pain, heal it, and let it go.

Seeking to level up, I decided to start anew under the guidance of my former mentor, Alania Starhawk, who years ago supported my channeling journey. After going through a lot of healing herself in recent years, she has transformed into a truly beautiful divine powerhouse. She is not merely my mentor, but a soul sister. Alania is an Akashic Record Healer, Soul Empowerment Coach, and published author. Working with her has done wonders for me, and I'm making progress in moving forward with my life, improving my meditation practice, rediscovering the power of deep breathing, and realigning my focus on achieving my goals. I am now embracing the truth: *I am deserving*.

2024 has indeed been a year of reckoning for many, as old wounds have resurfaced and forced us to confront unresolved issues from our past. For some, like myself, this has manifested in the reemergence of a powerful connection with a twin flame. In my case, Mark *"checkmated"* himself out of my life. It was a bittersweet chapter; a painful but necessary part of my journey of self-discovery and spiritual evolution. This year had been a poignant reminder that some connections, no matter how tempting, can't blossom without any commitment to healing and wholeness.

The painful situation I went through highlights the immense challenges faced by those grappling with persistent mental health and substance abuse issues—challenges that can feel insurmountable and all-consuming. Overcoming these disorders requires immense courage, commitment to treatment, a support system, and above all, strength from within. The devastating consequences of ignoring these struggles is a heartbreaking reality, and I hope that sharing Mark's story has highlighted the need for greater empathy, resources, and accessible routes to lasting recovery.

CHAPTER 17
KARMA AND PAST LIVES

"I AM the Light that you cannot yet see, and yet you are that dazzling, cosmic superstar, gliding across the starlit heavens, cloaked like that sweet little red riding hood, walking along your merry way in the earthly realms of that dense forest, trying to find your way in the dark, back to the I AM Light that you are, and most certainly have always been."

—Lord Maha Chohan

WHAT IS KARMA?

THE "KARMA HOTEL" WELCOMES you ever so gracefully into its warm, loving embrace. Understand that here, mirrors don't lie and the truth hits hard. Check in anytime you like, but your baggage can never leave. We've reserved a luxury suite just for you—come see yourself through someone else's eyes. Our concierge service will ensure you get *exactly what you deserve*. Enjoy your staycation!

Like the description above, I like to think of karma as something inescapable. Karma is like tossing a pebble into a quiet pond—*plop!*—while ripples spread out in all directions. What goes around comes around—that's what you call the Law of Cause and Effect. Karma's the whole "you reap what you sow" thing. Plant pumpkin seeds, you get pumpkins. Plant dandelions, you get weeds. The same goes for our human lives.

If you send out good vibes, you'll be swimming in "warm fuzzies." Send out bad vibes, and good luck digging yourself out of that hot-chili-cheese-sandwich of a mess. If you plant seeds of kindness, you'll reap the sweet fruits of compassion. Sow seeds of hatred, and you'll find yourself lost in a thicket of resentment. Karma simply means every little thing we do matters. Our words, deeds, and even our thoughts send out waves into the universe. The smallest acts send out reverberations that will return to us, for better or worse. Be mindful of the seeds you scatter each day. Tend to your inner garden with care. The blossoms you'll see tomorrow depend on what you plant today.

KARMIC GUIDANCE FROM LORD MAHA CHOHAN AND MASTER DK

The mysterious name "Maha Chohan" comes from two fascinating linguistic roots. "Maha" springs from ancient Sanskrit, meaning "great" or "supreme". It has often been attached to enlightened teachers and heavyweight "spiritual VIPs." The word "Chohan" hails from old-school Tibetan, meaning "lord" or "master". It was also often used as a nod to spiritual guides with some serious wisdom in their field. Put these terms together and you get "Great Lord" or "Supreme Master"—worthy labels for someone uber-wise and with insider knowledge of all cosmic laws.

When someone is dubbed a "Maha Chohan," you know they've got an enlightened handle on the inner workings of the universe. The title signals a spiritual all-star who makes existence click. So, here's hoping he does that for you with his innate, enfolded wisdom compressed into a nutshell of what he's all about.

"I AM Lord Maha Chohan, Divine Director and Orchestrator of the Blessed 7 Rays of Light, shining forth like a beacon upon the Earthly

KARMA AND PAST LIVES

grids and pouring Love and Light into the heart of Gaia and humanity, to the enlightenment of Conscious Evolution.

Having hopscotched, stumbled and fallen into various human incarnations, of a once upon a time humble versifier, transcribing much ancient, intrinsic wisdom into the written poetic verse, many of which mankind took time to find a soluble resonation with whilst others remained confused within the dome of their minds, questioning the seeker time and again in the search for answers to the very enlightenment of the soul that was oh-so-heavily cloaked within that puff-cream-pastry of an armor of that human embodiment.

I have lived countless lives here on this plane and many other planes within the cosmic grid of eternal existence. One may have heard my human names pass through the earthly corridors one has the pleasure of wandering through; from an illustrious poor peasant to becoming a mere illustrious poet, by the name of Virgil the Italian. I was honored to be Homer the blind, having to sense and learn to see from within, for the eyes failed me to the see the beauty of the world without, and yet it gave me the opportunity to ignite the breath of the Cosmic Flame of the Holy Spirit back into the very essence of my inner BEing, realizing that we are all connected, and that I needed not eyes to see the world for I saw the world from the inside out. I conjured forth into the incarnation as Orpheus the Seer, the founder of the Mystery Schools, teaching the spiritual union with the Divine, that 'cosmology pot of oneness,' teaching humanity through the art of the written word on the higher planes of consciousness, with many of my Ascended Brothers opting to learn upon incarnating; yet many were seen as imposters, for duality taught man to be judgmental and cynical of heart, choosing to live one's life through the separation of the heart and mind in many a conditioned scenario. Yet that did not deter us into standing with stance in our beliefs in the hope that one day Man would awaken to see that one needs merely to bridge the heart and mind back to the God Consciousness of Self.

CHILD OF THE SUN

I lived as a shepherd in the hills and lush but yet ruggedness of India, becoming the chalice for the Flame of the Holy Spirit to flow back forth the Love of pureness into the heart of Gaia, being a conduit for Master Sanat Kumara.

I AM the Lord of that swirling, often-icy Karma cream, restoring balance and equilibrium in the tit-for-tat, eternal game of ping pong one seems to be rattling each other with, understanding that wonderful feat of living in that steaming, 'coffeed' duality, causing one another pain through the sheer, sharp, lashing-out of blades of not understanding the light within. It is the haphazard of those deserved consequential experiences so that one may learn to understand and forgive others for their reflections cast upon you. The corresponding element to the Holy Spirit equates to the chemical formulation of 'Oxy-gen', of 'flowing oxy' into the veins of the Mother to keep her sustained against the forces holding her hostage. The Holy Spirit always seeks to 'unblemish' the blemishes brought on through the destruction of mankind, that is merely in place due to the EGO requiring satisfaction through that barnyard competition with one another, living with one's head cut off, clucking and pecking each other to get ahead in the race of life. Everything seems solid. Everything seems separate. All skate but happily on the surface of themselves. Yet be not fooled, for all of you are interwoven and connected by that fine, woven thread of invisible light, with each soul having (rather willfully, I might add) incarnated, holding the Wisdom and Purity of the Threefold Flame within the sacredness of their hearts, waiting to be reactivated, and reawakened, once the key fits the clock to one's sleeping soul, to shine forth the light of love within themselves as much as into the cradling bosom of Gaia. Be gentle with her nature as she is gentle with yours.

Remove the beer goggles of that third-dimensional consciousness, and allow for your exasperated EGO to float out the door, with your mind detoxing from the intake of all it had to bear. It is an unnecessary qualm that gives the heart many misgivings, and to what end, may I ask? See ye not, my Child, that this cold coffee karma is the cosmic law of cause and effect? Energy does not lie. Energy does not discriminate. Energy merely welcomes those to that enigmatic karma café when your number is up, and you are duly called upon to collect your karmic concoction.

You make mud puddles in someone else's life, then those mud spatters will be flung back at you, with the exact same velocity you sent it to others, muddying the waters of your very own cosmic little existence. A like for like, an equal trade-off seems only fair, non?"

As the Ascended Master DK continues:

"Dharma equates to one's 'life wheel' rolling on back onto its soul path, with all unfolding in divine order according to the very rhythm of one's chosen life.

K(h)arma is the '(h)arm of the ka'; it is the harming of the soul through one's actions, reverting back to the user like a proverbial boomerang, with the same intensity it was sent out. It is the cycle of the 'quid pro quo, back to you,' for what is cast out to others is ever so willfully cast back to you by the law of cause and effect.

Surrendering in the embrace of love and forgiveness equates to compassion, for it is the way back to the heart of the lotus of openness and understanding. Without compassion, one would be a rather poor meme of insoluble and a perplexity of insults and shame pertaining to the self, which is merely a created feat of the mind, for all thoughts commence with a seed planted fervently within the mind, to sprout according to one's watered mantras of thoughts, exhibiting its traits into the materialization of one's outer world.

This constant feeding-the-ego craving is nothing more than an addiction, serving as a deviation of ever loving yourself. Why would you need a constant fix to keep you on that high of feeling worthy and valued? Stop diluting yourself to a sly, devious, 'Kaa the snake' fixture in your own head, constricting your mind because your ego is a maverick-wrecking dust ball, causing nothing but a dust-up of whirling sand clouds, projecting this onto others, only to be slapped back in your face like a wee bouncing banana ball."

Finally, as Sadhguru says, *"Nothing is accidental here. The whole physical existence is happening between cause and consequence."*

Karma: what goes around, comes around. This crazy cosmic dance between one another is just a big game of ping pong between cause and effect. We're all paddling around in this vast ocean of karma, laughing when we splash others, but not so much when we get splashed back. The universe has a wicked sense of humor when it comes to kismet, setting up elaborate and scheming "Rube Goldberg machines." Think of those crazy gadgets that accomplish something simple in the most complicated way possible. Those things with funky gears, levers, pulleys, and springs that turn easy jobs into hilarious spectacles; that's pretty much the karmic universe.

Next time you spot a contraption that takes twenty convoluted moves just to crack an egg, remember, that's karma knocking on your door and giving you the slip—all because you once treated someone else the same way. Everything you do comes back to you. And let's not forget the wise words of Savage Garden: "I believe in karma, what you give is what you get returned," and the universe certainly has a knack for delivering cosmic punchlines.

THE DEATH AND REBIRTH CYCLE

Does karma really shape our destiny? Our past actions must balance out before we are reborn. Once we enter this world again, the cycle continues. With each choice we make, good or bad, we spin the wheel of karma anew. There is hope amidst this endless turning, though it does depend on how you decide to act in life. Mindfulness helps opens the door to walking a wiser path. By living with compassion, we can gently untangle the knots of karma and discover that peaceful freedom at the center of the wheel.

KARMA AND PAST LIVES

I have died a thousand deaths, and I will die a thousand more until I ascend in continuance of my soul's evolution elsewhere. (Although, mind you, I've been to "St. Elsewhere," and incarnated many times onto different "elsewhere" planes and planets, and I will continue to do so. In my first book, *BE-com-ing Authentically Me*, I shared glimpses of my journeys across both earthly and galactic realms, revealing the rich tapestry of experiences that have shaped who I am today).

I've been here since the dawn of time—if ever such a thing existed—and I've lived more lives than a cat has hairs on its back. I must surely love it here! I've incarnated as a man and as a woman. I've flipped that coin so many times I've lost count. Each round trip of life has taught me something new about this crazy planet we call Earth, and during each of my lives I've had to try and figure out why the heck I incarnated back here in the first place! We simply keep spinning that wheel, living, learning, and coming to understand the core, secret ingredient of who we are: pure, unconditional love.

When I tap into the memories of my past lives, I feel like I'm stepping into a cinematic experience. One moment I'm in the present, and the next moment I'm immersed in the sights, sounds, and feelings of another era. The words just start flowing through me in the voice of that life. It's wild! I'll be speaking all proper and poetic from an 1800s past life, then snap into a totally radical, long-lost-civilization vibe from another life even further back in time. It's a trip navigating different times, places, and perspectives. But I'm embracing my inner time traveler and speaking in the tongues of lifetimes gone by, learning so much along the way. While I'm still learning to harness my current physical form that my soul has been suited and booted in (sometimes feeling rather rigid and limited, like a clunky robot trying to dance), I try to smile and remember to appreciate the gift of my human experiences.

Like the Cookie Monster from *Sesame Street*, devouring yummy, cookie-cut, created experiences, I am also embracing all my experiences. I accept them all, voraciously consuming each one. The sweet, doughy moments nourish me, while the bitter ones challenge me to grow. I'm the chef in my own kitchen of life, whipping up my own soul food with the ingredients of my choosing. I take full responsibility for blending and concocting all my experiences together into something new. Every step leads me closer to myself, and every breath fills me with the joy of being truly alive. This body, this lifetime, these experiences—they are gifts, allowing me to savor the flavors that comprise the banquet of my being. I cannot be anything other than grateful for the opportunity to alchemize it all into these sprouting seedlings of wisdom and understanding.

LEARNING FROM MY PAST LIVES

In a past life, in the lands of what was once Ancient India, I embraced the role of a humble healer. I embodied the essence of a man who resided alongside the magnificent Brahmaputra River, right where the flowing water gracefully forks in two. I was surrounded by countless souls seeking healing and guidance for both their physical and spiritual ailments. My existence was one of simplicity and devotion to humanity, and I led a resolute and celibate life. Nature was my closest companion, and I found solace in the tranquil stillness that enveloped me. Sitting in silence, I would immerse myself in the symphony of life, listening to the harmonious melodies that resonated from the depths of the earth. My attire was modest, adorned with nothing more than a dyed cloth, my long hair was neatly tied, and my body served as my humble abode. I often traversed the earth barefoot, relying on the generosity and kindness of those I encountered on my life's journey. I dedicated myself to the study of herbs, imparting knowledge and wisdom to the minds and hearts of the people. It was my mission to enlighten the world about the incredible healing properties that nature so generously bestowed upon us. In those days, India was a sanctuary of unparalleled beauty, and a natural haven for nature's wonders to evolve, untouched

KARMA AND PAST LIVES

by the ravages of man that we witness today. To lead a life dedicated to nurturing the body's vitality and expanding the horizons of the mind brought me immense joy. It was a life of simplicity, yet one filled with profound gratitude. Eventually, my body aged and I transitioned into the realm of light. I had become an elderly figure, relying on a long stick to support my weary steps. My time as a healer in India was a testament to the power of compassion in service to others, but also of enhancing the body's longevity and expanding the mind, a beautiful cultivation of inner joy. This was a life that I cherished deeply, for it allowed me to touch the lives of many and leave behind a legacy of healing and love.

In a lifetime even further back, I was what one would call a sacrificial human lamb led to slaughter in the steamy jungles of South America. The native people bound my limbs with rope and encased me in a metal cage. As drums pounded and chants echoed through the trees, I was lowered, inch by inch, into a bubbling pit of molten lava. The heat seared my skin and melted my flesh before I even touched the lava's surface. I could feel my life slipping away bit by bit as the lava consumed me. The agony I experienced was indescribable. It was a slow, and excruciatingly painful death that I wouldn't wish upon my worst enemy. Though it may have been considered an honor to be sacrificed, no honor can erase the pure agony of being burned alive. My screams echoed through the air, but brought me no salvation. The lava embraced me completely, and my vision went black. Though the sacrifice is a distant memory now, I can still feel the pain of that experience.

Centuries ago, during an era when humanity had severed its divine connection with their "inner god-self, I was reborn as a towering, muscular Aztec warrior in the Southern Americas. Fueled by a zeal that knew no mercy," I ruthlessly sacrificed countless innocent folks for the sacrificial good of the lands and the heavens like they were piñatas at a birthday party. My agile movements only amplified the grim efficiency with which I wielded my blade, leaving a trail of death in my wake. I followed every command of the Divine ruler who reigned over us. I fought and killed without hesitation, believing it was my duty, until one day, I had a change of heart. My conscience returned to me, and I refused to slay anymore—causing me to be hunted and killed for disobeying orders. Having to kill so many for sacrificial gain is what I was taught from a young age. It was an honorable way of life.

Long before my descent into this Earthly Aztec incarnation, many Galactic emissaries came and docked on the created 'landings-temples'. These "landing temples" were architecturally designed to reflect a profound understanding of celestial mechanics and the rhythms of the cosmos, serving as physical evidence of humanity's ancient connection to the greater galactic community. Interactions with these otherworldly visitors gave ancient civilizations transformative insights that altered the very fabric of their societies, expanding their worldview, illuminating the truth that they were part of a much larger, awe-inspiring cosmos, forever changing their understanding of life and their role within it. They came with love in their hearts. Yet, when the selfishness of man came to light with the brewing of a darkness in their hearts, the once Atlantean region ruled by Casimir Poseidon and the many other Ascended Masters retreated, and we as a tribe lost touch with our divine essence, having fallen from grace, descending into the seas of chaos fueled by ego and war. The art of living within the sacred geometrical divine grid lost in the 'noise' we reciprocated, causing nothing but an epic distortion in our ways. My people were once so in tune with their sacred divine heart of selves and the stars, but lost themselves along the way with an instilled wind that crept in their once warm hearts turning them but to an icy fragility of a bickering with the senses. Thus, when I chose to be born, we had long descended into a structured chaos of existence, driven by the EGO within our hearts and a true separation from the whole.

The ancient tradition of a blood sport was a feast of skilled athleticism and skill, where participants ran and scored using a heavy ball for the mere sake of sacrifice. It embodied the spirit of the warrior, and yet it was a dismal display of debauchery, killing for the love of the Gods and the Divine Ruler who willed it so. In the quiet of my mind, I could not discount the wails and the agonizing screams of those whose blood I had spilt and offered as sacrificial lambs to the celestial heavens, to appease the Gods, letting their blood flow to feed and sustain the lands so that the harvests could continue to flourish. For just as one nurtured the Gods, the Gods would, in turn, grant us that same favor of nurturing us. Thus, as I lived by the sword, turning my back on the inflicting of pain, I surely so died by the sword of disobedience towards the Divine ruler. All too gladly, I walked back into the warmth of the Light Eternal, for my soul untethered and unbound, could bask in the Divine I AM Presence in the embracement of love and forgiveness.

As a 16th century inquisitor in the Americas, I was a cruel, thieving scum—not my finest moment. Having set foot in the Americas in full armor, wading through the water and sand—an almost impossible feat due to the sheer heaviness, leaving me feeling clobbered. I spoke both Portuguese and Spanish and I had dark, shoulder-length hair and a beard. I was shown the western side of the Americas, along the coastline of Peru and Ecuador, and given the word "conquistadores," meaning "conquerors" in Spanish. The Inquisition worked in many different ways. I wore a hood to conceal my identity as an inquisitor, which allowed me to roam freely amongst the native people and betray those that refused the doctrine of the Catholic Church. My Guides gave me the word "enquisicado," which in Portuguese means "queried," indicating that I questioned the motives of those brought before me. (During my exploration of this lifetime, I was bombarded with Spanish phrases. Since I speak very little Spanish in my current lifetime, I had to rely on Google Translate to understand this former aspect of myself).

The Inca mines were plundered of gold and many of the indigenous people were put to work in the exploited salt mines further south. The Inquisition was cruel, and more often than not, anyone accused of dissenting was either sentenced to death or enslaved into other arduous labor. I saw myself chopping people's hands off—it was horrendous to hear their screams. Women were subjected to gang rape, homes were set ablaze, and individuals were burned at the stake. We used waterboarding techniques, pouring water down their throats, causing immense suffering. If we didn't burn them at the stake, we drowned them in the lakes, or hung them upside down, causing seizures and eventual death due to the blood pooling in their heads. I kept a native woman as a servant in my home, exploiting her for both labor and sexual gratification.

Despite trading my armor for lighter cotton clothing, mosquitoes tormented me in the sweltering, unbearable heat, their bites a constant annoyance to my infected skin. Ironically, I succumbed to malaria fever, an illness that the very people I tortured and decimated could have cured using quinine from the cinchona tree bark. Looking back, I deeply regret that brutal lifetime of violence against the Incas. I now recoil from such cruelty, having experienced both sides of the coin of tyranny. My actions as an Inquisitor represent one of the darkest chapters in my soul's journey. (And don't even get me started on those Middle Age nuns who beat me senseless. I was a scrawny orphan who dared to communicate with my celestial guides whilst scrubbing the floors and the pews).

But it hasn't all been blood and gore. I found real purpose as a revered Chinese general during the Tang Dynasty, even if I did meet my end in battle—as did thousands of my comrades who I led into war. Yet, my lifetime as a priestess of the goddess Isis were spent in peaceful devotion.

Through the ups and the many, many downs, I've slowly uncovered the lessons of this insanely wild ride we call life. I've experienced joyous highs that made me feel like I was flying and crushing lows that felt like endless free-falls into darkness. Yet, through those graph-like peaks and valleys, triumphs and tribulations, I've gradually discovered profound teachings hidden within this exhilarating journey. The human experience is characterized by these dancing lights of duality; the dance of opposites, the power of empathy, the magic of love, the liberation of forgiveness, the strength of patience, the dedication to purpose, and the art of living in the present moment. My numerous lifetimes have bestowed upon me invaluable experiences, whilst the many lessons I've learned tell me this human experience is an opportunity to transcend our pain and evolve as souls, embracing the love we are, always have been, and will always hold within.

CHAPTER 18
NADI ASTROLOGY

WHAT IS NADI ASTROLOGY?

While in the mystical land of India, I was fascinated to discover the ancient art of Nadi astrology, also known as "palm leaf astrology." Its origins lie in prophecies from ancient texts, written on palm leaves, thousands of years ago. These cryptic manuscripts were allegedly authored by exalted figures such as Agasthiya, the revered Vedic sage; Bhrigu, father of Hindu astrology; Shukra, son of Bhrigu and guru to the gods; Kaushika, a courageous warrior and descendant of the great Kusha. Other sages like Koumara, Bhoga, Vashista and Vishwamitra also contributed their wisdom to these texts.

Delving into the past, the Nadi leaves were kept in the Sarasvati Mahal Library in Tanjore, Tamilnadu, nestled within the walls of Thanjavur's palace. I've never been, but I'd love to explore its hallowed halls someday. This treasure trove dates back to the 16th century Nayak dynasty, when Thanjavur's rulers first gathered a magnificent collection of Sanskrit manuscripts and texts. Later, the Maratha king Raja Serfoji expanded the library's offerings to include works in other languages, turning it into a true storehouse of knowledge. As Thanjavur's most prized historical site, this library offers a glimpse into the rich cultural legacy of long-gone kings. Its rare manuscripts and regal atmosphere transport you to the pinnacle of Thanjavur's royal prestige, a time when art, literature, and learning were cherished above all else.

In 1918, it came under the control of the Tamil Nadu Government, and the name of the library was changed to the Thanjavur Maharaja Serfoji's Sarasvati Mahal Library. The new name honored Maharaja Serfoji, who expanded the collection during his reign. The Modi script manuscripts in the archives reveal the history and culture of Thanjavur's Maratha rulers, offering a glimpse into the past. The Nadi leaves have endured, safeguarding ancestral wisdom for generations, despite facing destruction by the Moghuls and exploitation by the British.

The mystical seers of Nadi astrology claim they can unveil one's destiny, as it has been recorded on the ancient palm leaves. But can our fates really be set thousands of years in advance? Much mystery and misconception shrouds this ancient art. You must gaze upon the ancient leaves yourself to know if their prophecies hold meaning for you. As the reader interprets the ancient symbols, the ancient leaves seem to come alive, whispering their cryptic messages from across thousands of years. I was amazed to think these leaves had foretold the fates of generations long passed and was eager to know more.

Subramanyam scored me an appointment with a legit Nadi astrologer in Bangalore. I'd been "geeking out" over Nadi astrology online, and I'd read reviews that ranged from amazingly insightful, to dodgy, to flat-out fake. But to pass judgement without firsthand experience is to judge a book by its cover. To truly appreciate the ancient art of Nadi, one must learn its history, respect its devotees, and open one's mind to the unknown. I was excited to find out what my leaves could possibly reveal about my destiny. This was my chance to get the 4-1-1 on my future, straight from an ancient Tamil text written just for me. "Nadi" a word from the Tamil language, is translated as *"to come in search of"*—and that's exactly what people do when they visit a Nadi astrologer. These mystical palm leaf readers can unravel your past, present and future simply by examining your thumbprint. They don't read just anyone's leaves—your life must be predestined to be recorded on these ancient scripts. These ancient predictions are written in Vatteluttu, an obscure, ancient verse that only a seasoned Nadi reader can interpret. With a glance at your thumb, the astrologer locates your personal leaves amongst the thousands stored in their libraries. Like unravelling a beautiful tapestry, each thread of a person's fate is interwoven into poetic verses. A skilled Nadi expert can interpret the leaves, translating the archaic verse and decoding life's mysteries. They can reveal pivotal moments from your past, insight into your present, and glimpses of what's to come. For believers, it's proof that the universe moves in mysterious ways, intertwining our fates and futures.

It was not easy to find this renowned Nadi astrologer. After asking around for Sri Sivakumar Nayanar, we finally located his humble abode, tucked away in the maze of backstreets off a main road in Bangalore which seemed to go on forever. As we drove down the dusty roads, a cow and a skinny stray dog caught my eye, both rummaging side by side through a massive pile of garbage, scavenging for their next meal. My heart went out to these poor souls, they were so skinny, you could see their ribs—yet they seemed to find a sense of solidarity in their shared struggle for survival. It was a beautiful yet sobering scene, the kind you rarely come across in the big cities of the West. When we arrived, I was ushered into a small room by an elderly man to have my thumbprint taken. The print from the left thumb is used for men, and from the right thumb for women. After inking my thumb, I pressed it onto a piece of paper four times, leaving clear imprints. I also wrote down my name, phone number, and details of my birth.

The man disappeared through a side door, and I asked my colleague what would happen next. He explained they would now search the rooms upstairs for my palm leaf, on which my destiny over lifetimes had been inscribed by ancient sages. The ancient Nadi leaves, fragile yet enduring manuscripts, emerged after what seemed like an eternity.

As Sri Sivakumar carefully unfurled the yellowed documents, the tiny script upon them proved their medieval origins. We sat there in silence, knowing we were privileged witnesses to the unveiling of knowledge from ages past.

Sri Sivakumar asked me a series of rapid-fire questions based on the ancient verses etched on the palm leaves in order to find my match. I'll admit, I was a little apprehensive about this whole process at first. I learned that the questions asked could only be answered with a simple "yes" or "no" response. He asked if my work was clerical (no), if my father was still alive (no), if I was born at 10 a.m. on a Tuesday (yes), if I had an older sister (no, older half-sister only), is your mother remarried (no), does your sister have health problems (yes), are you studying (no), do you have a person in mind you want to marry (no), do you travel a lot (yes). There were many more personal questions about my family and life. I was intrigued. But then he mentioned the names of my parents, Iris and Roland, and I had to stop him there. Those were not my mum and dad's names at all! He suggested some first letters of their first names, but they were also incorrect. My heart sank a little. Sadly, this was not my leaf.

I was gutted, but the Nadi reader kindly invited me to return in a couple days. He would need more time to locate my personal palm leaf among the thousands in his library. Sadly, my leaf was never located. Though I was disappointed, I remain fascinated by the art of Nadi astrology.

HOW DOES PALM LEAF READING WORK?

Agasthya and his dedicated followers recognized the sixteen essential elements that form the intricate tapestry of human life. These elements, known as "Kandams" in Nadi Astrology, symbolize the true essence of existence. Think of them as the various "Chapters" that shape the unique journey of each individual from birth to death. Each of these components represents a key aspect of the human experience, from the beginning of life to the profound moments and significant events, leading up to the ultimate transition into the great unknown. Together, these sixteen chapters provide a detailed portrayal of a person's path, capturing the essence of life's ups and downs, successes and struggles, joys and sorrows. Just like the chapters of a captivating novel, these elements intertwine seamlessly, creating a narrative that is both personal and universally relatable. By understanding and honoring these sixteen Kandams, we gain profound insight into the very essence of what it means to be alive–to be human in all its complexity, beauty, and mystery.

The Sixteen Kandams

- Kandam 1 offers glimpses into marriage, career, family ties, health, and more.
- Kandam 2 unveils education, communication, and intuition.
- Kandam 3 reveals siblings and relationships.
- Kandam 4 shows motherly comforts and assets like land and vehicles.
- Kandam 5 discloses children, births, and their lifestyles.
- Kandam 6 indicates hardships from disease, surgery, enemies, and legal issues.
- Kandam 7 unveils marriage timing, spouse name, and remedies for obstacles.
- Kandam 8 reveals lifespan, accidents, and place of death.
- Kandam 9 shows the father's fortune, travels, and social life.
- Kandam 10 highlights career, profession, and business predictions.
- Kandam 11 indicates secret relationships and profits.
- Kandam 12 reveals expenditures, overseas journeys, rebirth, and salvation.

- Kandam 13 Shanti Pariharam reveals the soul's journey—how many lives remain, the final birth, past karma, rituals to overcome previous misdeeds.
- Kandam 14 Deeksha Kandam unlocks methods for Mantra Raksha, shielding from envy, ensuring success, initiating the soul's power through ceremony.
- Kandam 15 Avushada Kandam holds medicinal wisdom—prescriptions for chronic sufferers, proper administration for healing.
- Kandam 16 Disabukhti illuminates planetary periods and influences.

The first reading only touches the surface of what the palm leaves have to share. Should you wish to delve deeper into any area—be it career, relationships, or destiny—then the leaves of wisdom can continue to be explored. There are always more insights to uncover.

KARMA AND DESTINY

It's important to remember that any rituals the leaves prescribe are merely guidance, not requirements. You walk your own path. Though sometimes rituals help align us to more fortunate energies, the ultimate power lies within us. So, take the advice as you will, ideally with an open and discerning mind. The leaves aim to inform, not control.

Nadi astrology often attracts those facing turmoil. The ancient leaves outline one's karma, both past and future. According to ancient Nadi astrology, our karma must resolve before we can be reborn. Once born, new karma accumulates based on how we live. The practice also prescribes rituals to counter the bad karma and restore balance. One such ritual remedy to bad karma is "dakshina," or "donation," which often raises eyebrows. But in times of distress, we grasp for solutions, even cryptic ones. However, if we continue to focus on the pain, we remain in that energetic state of suffering; if we focus on the lesson held within the experience, then we opt to progress and grow. The leaves promise to decode karmic quandaries and provide the exact Puja to restore balance, getting rid of the bad. While modern sensibilities may hesitate, Nadi astrology has an undeniable allure for its definitive answers on life's problems. The prescribed resolutions offer hope, however enigmatic. When staring down the barrel of a gun called struggle, who can blame those suffering for seeking solace in these ancient leaves? For believers, Nadi astrology illuminates the path out of darkness through ritual and sacrifice.

I am sure many people are stunned by the accuracy of a Nadi reader if the correct leaf is read, but does it actually lead them to a more spiritual path? If everything is predestined, then what about the concept of free will? What is the point of living?

I believe the key is balance. Certain life points may be mapped out, and destiny may guide us, but it is our beliefs and actions that shape who we become. The spiritual path beckons not to fatalism, but to awakening; to realizing that we are not helpless actors in some cosmic soap drama, but creator beings with the power to transform our lives. We walk this path to unlock our highest potential, but also to reignite the spark of returning to that loving nature of ourselves.

MANIFESTATION

By following our inner wisdom, we can manifest the life we envision. But what does "manifestation" even mean? Manifesting is all about realizing that you have the power to shape your reality through your thoughts, words, and actions. Although you can't control every single outcome, you can control the energy you emit out into the universe. By channeling the radio waves of your inner positivity, consciously acting upon the thought intention, and speaking your desires into existence, you harness the spiritual energy you hold within and tap into your innate ability to create the life you want.

For the longest time, I sucked balls at manifestation. I was stuck in my own stinking trauma. However, the key lies in letting go and fully embracing our emotions. The process involves acknowledging our current circumstances, taking actionable steps toward healing, realigning our focus, and visualizing the outcome we wish to achieve. We must then take tangible steps toward that manifested goal, rather than merely stating "I want to become…" or "I want to move…". Instead, try saying "I am successful," or "I moved to my dream house," or "I travel the world," etc. Envision it in the present tense, and take steps towards it now. Don't just *want* it someday, *live* it today. You may not be able to control the outcome, but you can control your thoughts, actions, and words.

"The sum of all equations of your life are held within the palm of your very own mushy-pea, hue-man hands, not in the hands of another, unless you decide to eloquently give away your own I AM power, then indeed you have been slammed sideways, lost control of your Mario-soul-kart, being the brazen obstacle block you are and hurtled yourself into the thorny bushes, limping like a cracked, 'limp bizkit' through life, because you adamantly shake your head into oblivion, coming to that place of an 'aha' acceptance that all accountability lies solely with the perpetrator, being most humbly yourself."

—The Ascended Master Ganesha

EMBRACE THE PLAN OF THE UNIVERSE

Psychic mediums and spiritual counsellors may guide us, but we alone can shape our destiny. The power lies within each of us to create the life we want. No matter how dark our lives may at times become, as my father used to say, "There is always light at the end of the tunnel." By focusing on the positive, we attract the energy we need to manifest the reality we desire. All we need do is trust in ourselves and in the brightness that lies ahead, waiting for us to reach for it.

It can be hard to feel and be positive when the road seems like a melted, rocky chocolate bar. Rather than indulging in the overbearing trickle of sinking deeper into toffee pudding, we must learn to open our hearts to the whispers of our feelings. Walk hand-in-hand with your emotions through the shadows, seeking to understand the hurt. Ask how you can bring light to these pains, soothing them with the pink, cotton candy balm of self-love. Keep believing in your own radiance, and the candy corn sweetness of growth. With patience and care, we can heal our hurts and gain more space to breathe within the environment of our lives.

Truly feeling your emotions is like drinking your daily smoothie: it nourishes your emotional health from the inside out. Suppressing difficult emotions is like trying to live on fatty donuts and coffee alone—you'll end up nutritionally deficient. Treat your feelings as preventative medicine for the soul. Give them space to be felt fully, without judgment. Let your emotions flow through you like a cleansing tidal wave, rinsing away what no longer serves you. As St Germain says, *"Much like Tide laundry detergent, that stain and odor-fighting power for all your unlaundered experiences."* Difficult feelings won't kill you, but avoiding them might. Feel it all—the joy, the sorrow, the anger, the bliss, the *blurgh*—because in the end, your heart will thank you for it.

For so long, my Guides told me to flow with the universe. Their words made sense, but to truly feel the "flow" energetically was another matter entirely. Being the slow-moving turtle I am, I didn't fully grasp it until 2024. The truth is, you and the universe are dance partners, gliding together across life's grand ballroom. Forget Billy Idol and "dancing with myself," instead dance but ever so gracefully and joyously, with peals of laughter, across the magnificent cosmic dance floor, with your partner the universe, creating a symphony of swirly frequencies that will have your life blossoming in no time. Your essence is woven from the same bursts of stardust particles that formed the cosmos. All you have to do is feel the rhythm of the universe's movements as she guides you through each step, swaying to the melody of existence. Let her take the lead when the music swells, trusting the surety of her steps. You are but a feather floating along in her cosmic currents, a dinghy drifting down the winding river of tick-tock time. When challenges arise, see them as dips and lifts, each spin bringing the next graceful turn. Don't grasp or cling—simply let go and move as she does. Though life's song contains both crescendos and diminuendos, learn to quickstep through it all, carried by the grace that flows between you and your cosmic dance partner. No aggressive kung fu fighting here—just a graceful waltz through the stars. The universe and you—connected yet separate, leading yet following—spinning through space and time. The inner self and the outer cosmos unite through movement. You are one with all, and all is one with you. Your dance is an intimate embrace between the infinite and the finite, the eternal and the ephemeral. As you sway, the boundaries between "self" and "other" dissolve. You are no longer just dance partners—you are the dance itself. If you can do this, you'll find the freedom of a flawless dance and the natural rhythm and alignment of life's blissful choreography.

It all sounds great, right? So why is it that even when we write everything down, make a plan, and create a vision board, we still seem to falter? This is a question I asked St. Germain, and his response was as follows:

"You falter because your energy is out of whack, having landed in those hairy whiskers of limbo land. You are sacred geometry. You are frequency. Fine-tune yourself! Cough up the ole dust stuck like a tickle in yer throat, leaving you staggering, like a bleary-eyed cowboy who's been staring down into the bottom of a whiskey glass for too long. You live too much in a deviation outside of yourself and not in the divine eternal truth of your I AM. Tell me; do you live in the truth of your nature of being your authentic self? Or are you a mastermind, smooth-talking, criminal wannabe of trying to fit into the worldly garments one has been given

to wear to play but this wordily whack-me-jack cloak and dagger with the self through the participation of the EGO? You fail not for a want of trying, but for a lack of understanding. You are trying to create from without, trippin' miserably and ending up bruised and boiler bunny badgered, rather than learning to create from the heart space within. Everything comes from within. Does one's soul not sit within one's body? If it sat without, you'd have lost your outer garment to the decay of the earth, and flown Chitty-Chitty-Bang-Bang home, landing among the stars of the celestial heavens—in other words, you'd be 'dead', non? You merely need to sit in the very breath of the stillness of yourself, connecting and anchoring yourself to the I AM Presence of your beautiful, divine self, appreciating and embracing that very light pulsating within, planting a seed in the soil of your fertile heart, nurturing this 'seed' and learning to expand your goals and aspirations from within to expand without—it can be no other way.

Your I AM Presence is the gateway to mastering the self in all that you do, unwrapping that snaked up and strangled, beautiful mind of yours in the process; for being in the hold of a boa constrictor of your unlearn-ed experiences will get you nowhere indeed, but for living a chosen, exasperated life of flailing around and gasping for air oh so endlessly. Master the mind to master the inner hearth of your soul, emerging from the crystal clear and divine waters of self, in turn blossoming in the outer warmth of duly unfolding and expressing yourself in the world just beautifully.

Always remember, your thoughts are the architects to the creation of your destiny—you will into creation according to the thought of your mind. You are the genie in your own 'bottle' and all those wonderful thoughts, words and feelings you choose to put out into the stratosphere, soundingly comes back to you in kind—because you are the Alchemist of yours truly, your very own creation."

The Nadi leaves that may have held my destiny had eluded me, but perhaps it was never meant to be read. I've weathered far worse storms since then. More trials and tribulations awaited, with more traumatic shit that was flung my way that I couldn't have foreseen or altered. (If I'd known what was coming, who knows how I might have changed the course of my life. The universe works on its own schedule, not mine). Still, I wouldn't trade the woman I've become, through all the chili-flavored experiences, for anything. I am who I am because of the sticky, gooey, messy hurt and growing pains I went through. While the Nadi leaves remain a mystery, the journey itself was worthwhile. I'm still becoming, growing stronger and a little wiser through each storm, with my story still beautifully unfolding.

If you seek guidance amid the maze of Nadi astrologers, I recommend going straight to the source—the Sarasvati Mahal Library. There you may discern the real from the counterfeit and find truthful answers from learned advisors. Tread carefully, but don't abandon hope. With an open mind and a sensible eye, you may yet find the reading you seek!

CHAPTER 19
HEALING WITH AYURVEDA

"Health is not just the mere absence of disease. Health is the dynamic expression of life."

—*Gurudev Sri Sri Ravi Shankar*

THE MIND, BODY, AND SPIRIT CONNECTION

WE ARE MORE THAN just flesh and bone. We are body, mind, and spirit—all intricately connected. When illness strikes the physical form, it's tempting to treat just the symptoms, but true healing requires looking deeper. Our body's movements are like a mirror, reflecting the inner workings of our mind. There is an intricate connection between our thoughts and our physical expression. Our mind holds memories and mental wounds that can manifest as physical disease. Our spirit longs for alignment, yet can be pulled out of sync. Each cell in our body listens intently, hanging on to our every word, every syllable we utter, akin to a curious rabbit with perked-up ears, eavesdropping on the chatter of our inner dialogue. To fully restore wellness, we must nurture all facets of our being. With self-awareness and compassion, we can mend the mind and realign the spirit, allowing the body to joyfully return to harmony.

Pain and illness do not come out of nowhere. They are born from the gnarly feelings we bury deep inside of us, like squirrels burying nuts, and they are the result of trapped emotions. When we lock these "demons" in the dungeon of our hearts and swallow the key, their dark energy festers and poisons our body, rotting our organs, and withering our limbs. The only cure is to break open the rusted lock with courage, raise the portcullis, and storm the keep, releasing those villainous emotions, dragging out those stinky bedraggled kicking and screaming hyenas, that have been laughing at our own expense. Only by confronting ourselves can we heal. Only then will the clouds lift and the body mend, breathing a sigh of relief.

Sadly, Western medicine tends to discount the importance of the mind, body, and spirit connection entirely. I'm not a "Big Pharma" fan— truth be told, they've pulled a fast one on us all. This two-hundred-year-old industry wants us to believe its lab-made potions are the only "real" medicine. But true healing flows from the earth herself, not some chemical lab. They've gotten us hooked on quick fixes and Band-Aid solutions that mask the real issues instead of promoting true healing. We pop a pill to numb the pain rather than looking inward and doing the real work to heal the root cause. We grab an aspirin rather than asking what caused the ache. Feeling depressed? Swallow an antidepressant and ignore the discord within. Big Pharma bombards us with quick chemical fixes that subdue our emotions without addressing the root cause. They've messed with our heads, convincing us that healing is complicated and requires expensive medication. The truth is, our bodies know how to heal themselves if we get out of their way. Rather than pumping ourselves full of pharmaceutical laden chemicals, we could turn to Mother Earth's natural medicines. Her remedies don't just suppress our feelings; they realign our energies and heal us from within. The difference is night and day— earth's aspirin (willow bark) or Big Pharma's? Healing holistically to wholeness or having a hole where your soul should be? The choice is yours.

Pain is the crucible from which creation is forged–the intense heat and pressure that forces us to confront our deepest wounds and vulnerabilities, shaping us into something new and more resilient. It is through the fire of our suffering that we are transformed, emerging as stronger, more authentic versions of ourselves. True healing comes not from suppressing or concealing this pain, but in confronting it head-on with the power of forgiveness. Forgiveness is the alchemy that transmutes our hurts into wisdom, our anger into compassion, and our brokenness into wholeness. When we have the courage to face our pain, to really feel it and understand its roots, we open the door to a profound healing that goes beyond merely treating the symptoms. It is in this sacred space of self-reflection and self-acceptance that we find the wellspring of true, lasting change—not a quick fix or a superficial bandage, but a deep, abiding transformation that allows us to move forward with greater clarity, purpose, and grace. The journey may be arduous, but the rewards of this inner work are immeasurable. For in embracing our pain as the fertile soil of our growth, we unlock the door to a life of greater authenticity, deeper connection, and unfettered joy. Pain may be the crucible, but love is the alchemical elixir that transmutes it into our greatest strength. True healing is simple if we tune into our bodies and souls. Big Pharma doesn't want us to know that. They profit when we remain dependent on their drugs and disconnected from our inner power to heal. That does not mean I discount traditional medicine completely, as I believe both can go hand in hand. Holistic healthcare is a remarkable approach to medicine that embraces the concept of treating the "whole person," holistically. It goes beyond merely addressing physical symptoms and delves into the realms of emotions, spirituality, and mental wellbeing. Conventional Western medicine primarily focuses on alleviating pain or curing illnesses, whereas holistic healthcare takes a proactive stance by getting to the root cause of the problem, emphasizing both treatment and prevention. By considering all aspects of an individual's health, a holistic approach aims to foster overall wellbeing and harmony.

> *"The greatest medicine of all is teaching people how not to need it."*
>
> *—Hippocrates*

The National Health Service (NHS) in the UK was once a pillar of compassionate care, but has sadly become a bit of a joke. Getting an appointment with your General Practitioner (GP) is nearly impossible these days. Even if you manage to see someone, they'll dismiss your symptoms as "all in your head" because you're "too old" or "too young" to really be sick. While phone-based diagnoses may be convenient, they also carry significant risks. In-person consultations with healthcare providers are essential and can be life-saving. Sadly, many individuals are suffering fatal consequences from incorrect or postponed diagnoses. These days, GPs often diagnose patients by Googling their symptoms instead of listening compassionately. It's unfortunate that the sacred art of healing has been reduced to quick searches on the internet. While technology can be useful, we must not lose sight of the human touch in medicine. The doctor-patient relationship is built on trust, empathy, and truly hearing the patient's experience. Rushing to plug symptoms into a search engine is not health care, and it can lead to misdiagnoses and a lack of deeper understanding. Unfortunately, patient care has taken a backseat to business interests.

The healthcare system was built to care for people, not profits. Those days feel long gone as individuals are treated more like revenue streams than human beings. Today, people often feel like little more than numbers in an increasingly broken and impersonal system that has strayed far from its original purpose. Patients deserve a healthcare experience that restores the caring, person-centered approach it was meant to embody.

> *"There is a divine purpose behind every physical calamity."*
>
> —Mahatma Ghandhi

WHAT IS AYURVEDA?

I didn't have a clue what Ayurveda was until I experienced it firsthand. The word itself offers some insight to its meaning: "Ayurveda" combines the Sanskrit words *"ayus"* (life) and *"veda"* (science or knowledge). So, at its core, Ayurveda is the "science of life," an ancient system of health and wellbeing.

This system of healing has its roots in India, with records dating back to 3000 B.C. While its exact origins may be shrouded in the mists of time, one thing is certain: this time-honored practice is all about promoting an overall state of health and happiness. More than just medicine, Ayurveda is a science of joyful living. It's about rediscovering your unique vitality and meeting life's challenges with renewed energy.

Unlike Western medicine's focus on treating disease, Ayurveda emphasizes balance in how we live. It's a holistic approach, integrating mind, body, and spirit. The goal is to maintain your optimal health, no matter what life brings you.

Ayurveda includes specific, tailored recommendations about your lifestyle. What foods align with your constitution? How should you exercise and reduce stress? Ayurvedic practitioners personalize treatments, like massage and herbal remedies, to restore your unique, personal balance.

During the Advanced Course, I learned that the human body is incredibly complex. Dr. Pinkita, from the renowned Panchakarma Clinic, illuminated this truth as she explained the wondrous intricacies of Ayurvedic medicine. She said that while we may all be similar in a lot of ways, each of us is biologically unique—much like a fingerprint. What provides relief for one person may not help another. The clinic's wise founder, Sri Sri Ravi Shankar, sums it up beautifully: "Health is the dynamic expression of life." Ayurveda recognizes we each have a distinctive constitution and unique imbalances. Panchakarma's holistic therapies don't take a one-size-fits-all approach. Instead, through personalized care and time-tested wisdom, the clinic helps reveal and honor the magnificence of your individual body's vital energies.

I had my "nadi" (pulse diagnosis) done by an Ayurvedic doctor, followed by several Ayurvedic treatments done for my back. Let me tell you, lying on a hard, wooden massage table brings the user no joy. But the nadi reading itself was fascinating! The doctor felt my pulse and could instantly tell things about my body, mind, and spirit.

"Nadi" is an ancient Ayurvedic technique for assessing someone's health holistically. During the consultation, the doctor prescribes dietary guidelines tailored to your specific body type. He tells you which foods to embrace and which to avoid based on your unique needs.

I mean, look at most of us today—we're not even conscious of how much junk and processed stuff we shove into our mouths each day. We are neglecting our health in an alarming way. It has gotten worse as time goes on. We let our bodies run down like abandoned shacks, and treat our stomachs like garbage disposals. Just look at the kids today–When I was in school, I'd pack a homemade sandwich, an apple, and a drink. But today's kids have enough money to eat whatever they want. I've seen the lines at KFC, McDonald's, and other fast-food joints. Growing up in the 80s, going to McDonald's was a real treat for me! But for today's kids, the novelty has worn off. It's their daily fuel, and unhealthy eating leads to unhealthy living.

> *"To ensure good health: eat lightly, breathe deeply, live moderately, cultivate cheerfulness, and maintain an interest in life"*
>
> —William Londen

Our bodies are living miracles in how they function. My dad always said, "Your body is a temple, treat it as such." And you know what? He was so right. A temple is a special, holy place. It's where people go to connect with the divine, to worship, and to just be present with something greater than themselves. In the same way, our body is a sacred space—literally the temple of our spirit. It houses our inner light, our essence, our soul. Our body deserves to be honored, cared for, and respected. It allows us to move through this world, to learn, love, and just be ourselves. Be mindful of how you treat your bodily temple. Nourish it with healthy foods, move it with joy, speak kindly to it, and rest it when it's tired. Keep it as a clean, serene space for your spirit to shine through. Your body is your temple. A one-of-a-kind, work of art. Treat it that way, and it will serve you well.

As Terry Guillemets said, "Health is a relationship between you and your body." If you choose to eat junk, processed foods, and chemicals, then your health will suffer immensely. If we're being honest, most of us probably aren't as due diligent about nutrition as we should be. How many of us skip exercising regularly, eat poorly, don't get enough rest, and deal with constant stress? The logic is straightforward: if you don't put the right fuel in your car, it won't run properly. How often do we ensure we're giving our body the movement it needs to stay in tip-top shape? A car functions the same way. If you never drive it, neglect its maintenance, and ignore its need for gas and oil, it will soon sputter, cough, and leave you stranded when you need it most. Our body is no different. We must use it consistently. The more we use it, the better it performs.

The ancient science of Ayurveda teaches us how to maintain health by understanding our unique body types. As Sri Sri Ravi Shankar said, "Ayurveda provides us with knowledge to prevent disease and eliminate its root causes." Ayurveda offers time-tested wisdom on protecting our bodily gardens from the pests of illness. With greater awareness and positive habits, our vitality can blossom.

LISTENING TO YOUR BODY

Your body and mind are BFFs, looking out for each other like peas in a pod. When you nourish that bond with self-care and compassion, your spirit feels exhilarated and snuggly at home in its own skin. But let toxic people or situations "rain on your parade," and your whole system can short-circuit. I learned this the hard way. When I was being treated very badly in a relationship, I became ill—I was literally sick to my stomach. For months, I dragged myself to work but couldn't "stomach" anything. My GP thought it might be a strain of IBS, but I knew in my heart that I'd let someone else's darkness dim my own light. I had allowed myself to become disempowered.

Having studied holistic nutrition and definitely not wanting a camera shoved up my butt, I slowly but surely listened to what my body needed to repair itself: tons of mangos, bananas, yogurts, and soothing soups. I shed weight faster than a snake sheds its skin and absolutely hated the way I looked. It was frustrating, and the real win didn't come until later in life, when I finally learned to let go of the things I could not control. I stopped letting other people's drama and "emotional blackmail" bring me down. I realized I needed to treat myself with the love and respect I deserved. After all, you treat people the same way you treat yourself.

Your body's got your back always, but are you listening to what it's telling you?

"When an illness arises, it comes first in thought form, then in sound form, and then light form, which is in the aura. It is only then that the illness manifests in the body. With the practice of Ayurveda, the illness can be nipped in the bud."

—*Gurudev Sri Sri Ravi Shankar*

If you don't worship your own body, who will? Your body, believe it or not, holds the answers you seek, if only you quiet your mind and listen. Your body is your most trusted guide, always leading you towards healing and wholeness. Your body is the *real* doctor, and the most sophisticated pharmacy in the world lives within your very own being, having a cure for every 'dis-ease' already housed within your physique. When fatigue weighs you down, your body speaks to you to rest, renew, and reconnect. When hunger gnaws at your stomach, it says: Nourish me, sustain me, fuel me. When your body sounds the alarm with an ache, a pain, or a discomfort, it's telling you something vital is lacking; seek and you shall find. It's screaming at you for help.

There have been times when I ignored my body's cries and screams, refusing to hear all that hardcore yelling, telling my body to "zip it!" My body was saying, *"We're supposed to be a team. We're in this together. I'm your ride or die, and you seem to be speeding up the process of wanting to die, treating me like I'm some sort of disposable diaper! I'm not replaceable! Once my 'live-o-meter' has been used up, you go on forever, but I don't! We're in this thing called 'life' together, so a little bit more respect, a little more love, hugs, kisses, and care would be appreciated, thank you."* Your body is a gift, so cherish it, nourish it, worship it. If you neglect this living sanctuary, who else will uplift it?

Our health depends on the flow of "chi," our vital life energy, through the body. Chi is the mystical force that makes us "tick" and determines if we sink or soar. When our chi gets clogged, it's usually because of our thoughts, emotions, or even the foods we eat. As the saying goes, *"What you thinketh, so will you becometh."* If your chi is out of whack, practices like tai chi, meditation, gentle yoga, and focused breathing can get your energy flowing again. Well, that and a healthy diet full of superfoods like leafy greens, berries, and omega-3s. These handy tricks nourish your chakras, your body's sacred energy hubs, and bring you back into alignment.

"Yoga and Ayurveda purify the body, knowledge purifies the intellect, meditation purifies the soul, and service purifies our karma."

—Sri Sri Ravi Shankar

THE THREE DOSHAS: VATA, PITTA, AND KAPHA

At the core of Ayurveda are the five elements—earth, ether, air, fire, and water. These represent different energies and forces in nature, not the literal substances. How they combine determines the three doshas (or

CHILD OF THE SUN

tridoshas): Vata, Pitta, and Kapha. These doshas are the vital energies that make up every living being. We each have a unique mix of doshas that shape our physical, mental, and emotional temperament. From an Ayurvedic perspective, each individual's constitution is determined by the state of their parents' doshas at the time of conception. Upon birth, a person has the levels of the three doshas that is right for them. Life and all its forces can cause the doshas to become unbalanced as time goes on, which can lead to ill health.

When the doshas are balanced, life is "groovy," as we experience vitality and wellbeing. But life's stresses can knock us on our arse and in turn, knock our doshas out of whack. One dosha may become dominant and cause problems. Fiery Pitta revving too high? You may battle heartburn, anger issues, and inflammation. When airy Vata flies out of control, anxiety, insomnia, and cramps can flare up. Kapha in excess? There's a tendency toward lethargy, weight gain, and congestion.

VATA

Vata is the mover and shaker, made up of air and space. This fickle dosha governs movement in the body and mind, from the flow of nerve impulses to the flitting of thoughts. When Vata is balanced, you feel energetic and creative. When it is off, you may struggle with anxiety, insomnia and digestive issues

PITTA

Pitta is the fiery transformer, combining the elements of fire and water. This intense dosha rules metabolism, digestions, and enzymes—all the processes that break things down and convert them to energy. Balanced Pitta promotes intellect and contentment. Out of whack, Pitta can stir up inflammation, irritability, and even ulcers.

KAPHA

Kapha is the grounding force, made of earth and water. This stable dosha governs structure, strength, and immunity. When Kapha is in sync, you feel calm, steady, and secure. Imbalanced Kapha can lead to fatigue, weight gain and congestion.

The *kapha dosha* is also known as the chilled-out dosha. This mellow element is a smooth blend of water mixed with the grounded strength of earth. Like the earth, kapha promotes muscle growth, immunity, and supports our frame. Kapha keeps things together, holding space like a loving hug, providing the well-greased wheels we need to flow through life with ease. It's the energy of structure and stability, keeping us grounded and helping us feel satisfied. Kapha dosha is all about building strength, nourishing the body, promoting growth, and providing lubrication for our joints. It gives us endurance and the ability to keep going through life's marathon. But too much kapha throws us off balance, making us feel heavy, sluggish, and about as motivated as a sloth. The mind gets foggy and all we want to do is sleep. The key is balance—just enough kapha for solid foundations, but not so much that we're glued in place.

The *vata dosha*, light and airy, is the force behind all movement in mind and body. With its breezy nature, vata is the force that makes you flexible, both mentally and physically. It's the prana, the life breath, that animates your body and mind. Vata stirs your nervous system into action, keeps your bones strong, and sharpens your senses of touch and hearing. This airy dosha helps you adapt gracefully to all of life's changes. But when vata is out of balance, too much wind makes you jittery and ungrounded. You may struggle with anxiety, insomnia, dry skin, and a racing mind. The key is to keep vata dosha in check with grounding routines. Slow down, nourish your body, and spend time in nature.

The *pitta dosha* is the heat that drives your inner fire. It's a powerful blend of fire and water elements that drives metabolism, emotions, and intellect. Pitta allows us to "digest" life experiences and break them down into nutrients for the soul. It also rules appetite and literal digestion, turning food into cellular fuel through enzymes, hormones, and acids. In essence, pitta provides the heat and fluidity to transform everything we take in. It converts sensations into understanding, food into energy, and ideas into passion. When balanced, pitta fills you with courage, charisma, and clarity of mind. But beware, for an overabundance of pitta's fire brings anger, jealousy, a wolfish hunger, and inflamed skin. Like a phoenix rising from the ashes, harness the power of pitta, but find balance in the fires of transformation that burn within you.

By understanding these three elemental doshas and listening to our bodies, we gain wisdom into our nature. Ayurveda offers time-tested wisdom for bringing your doshas back into harmony through diet, herbs, yoga, meditation, and other holistic solutions. With some "TLC," you can nurture your unique mind-body constitution and realign with your deepest state of health.

MY VISIT TO AN AYURVEDIC DOCTOR

"We are energy, so the body does know how to heal itself if the soul-healer within understands not the passage to healing the wound of the mind itself"

—*The Divine*

I can only speak from my own experience with Ayurveda, though I know practitioners around the world likely use many different methods. The Panchakarma clinic at the Art of Living Center itself was a serene oasis with lush gardens bursting with vibrant green shrubs and flowers, the gentle trickle of a fountain, and bamboo curtains swaying lightly in the breeze. After paying 250 rupees (about $3 USD) for my consultation, I splashed the cool fountain water on my face and neck to beat the intense heat and humidity.

The reception area was nestled under a bamboo and grass roof supported by bamboo poles, and it was open on all sides to allow the fresh air to flow through. I headed to the shoe rack, took off my flip flops, and crossed the quaint little bridge to the cozy waiting area. The walls here were hand-painted with two holy beings—one male, one female.

On the other side was a small shrine to Krishna, adorned with flowers, that visitors could pay their respects to upon arriving. Out of respect, I refrained from photographing the shrine up close, but took in its beauty as I awaited my pulse reading. Though more costly for foreigners, the 250 rupees allowed me to experience the oasis of calm and connection that the clinic provided. For the Indian people, the cost is 150 Rupees (about $1.80 USD). Just like when paying for the courses at the ashram, the "domestic green grass policy" applied.

The little side table held two different sticky, colored substances: a red and yellow paste to be smeared on the forehead. This was bindi paste, and dots of it are applied on the forehead, adorning many Indian people's faces. It is either made up of red turmeric or zinc oxide and dye. To my untrained eye, the bindi looked like melted French cheese, thick and gooey. But its significance, of course, ran deeper than dairy. For thousands of years, the bindi marks a major nerve point called the "third eye" or "ajna," which is the seat of concealed wisdom within the body. By decorating this spot, the bindi is said to maintain the energy within the human body and help focus the mind.

The red bindi is also the symbol of marriage and is believed to lead to prosperity, making women the guardians of family welfare and the offspring. Now I understood why Indian wives wore these red and yellow dots. It's an important symbol. These days, the bindi has also become a fashion statement. Women match the color to their saris, and some add sparkling beads or "diamonds" above the bindi for extra glamour. However it's worn, the bindi is beautiful. This dollop of culture on the forehead tells a rich history of spiritual meaning.

I waited for about ten minutes before I was told to go upstairs and wait there. As advised, I made sure not to eat anything for at least two to three hours beforehand, so my stomach would be completely empty. This, I was told, is crucial for an accurate reading.

Once upstairs, I had to wait another fifteen minutes or so, where the sun's rays flooded the open space.

I noticed a young man with the most mesmerizing green eyes I had ever seen, waiting patiently for a consultation. His worn shirt and faded blue pants were torn and tattered, yet he sat there with a quiet grace. It was clear he did not have much, and I felt a tinge of sadness within my heart for this soul. I wondered who he was and what had brought him here.

When it was finally my turn to see Dr Padmalocham, a kind and elderly gentleman, I asked him about the identity of the young man, and offered to cover any medical expenses he might require. His face lit up with appreciation at my offer, but he gently declined, explaining that the young man was actually an employee of the Art of Living Center. Though he appeared downtrodden, the doctor reassured me he was well cared for and told me not to worry.

During the examination, the doctor placed three fingers on my wrist, and closed his eyes in concentration. A minute passed in silence before he remarked on my back problems, which I'd struggled with for years. He could tell just from my nadi that stress caused weakness in two spots along my spine. One up high on the left, the other down low, where nerves often got pinched. It made perfect sense. He also picked up on the imbalance of fire and air (vata and pitta), in my spirit, which made me a creative person, but also one suffering from "restless spirit syndrome," always on the go, and with thoughts racing like a relentless roadrunner. He could tell that I suffered from cold hands and feet, often overworked myself, and had issues with my metabolism. He warned me that my back pain would worsen if I didn't slow down. I had previously been advised by my GP in the West to have injections in my lower back, but I declined, eager to explore finding relief in a more natural and holistic way.

The nadi doctor saw my history of stabbing headaches that for many years had been my unwelcome companion. The headaches struck daily, like clockwork. They'd trigger acid reflux, causing me to throw up, leaving a nasty taste in my mouth. This acid reflux also caused heartburn, and together these unwanted tenants zig-zagged within my body, spreading their toxicity wherever they pleased. I allowed it, because the energy of my unhealed trauma that I kept stuffed in the overflowing archives of my mind was all too happily redirected their way. I used to pop ibuprofens like Tic Tacs—three or four a day, sometimes more—just to keep going, learning to push through the pain. The headaches eased after learning the Sudarshan Kriya, which improved my circulation. But even this was a temporary fix, and it took many more crappy experiences and healing to overcome all the pain I carried. The doctor emphasized the importance of listening to my body and not ignoring its signals. After all, taking ibuprofen only temporarily numbs the pain before it resurfaces again.

He provided me with information about my dietary needs, including what foods I should and shouldn't consume. Additionally, he explained the three herbal remedies and treatments recommended for my back issues:

- **Kati Vasti,** a therapy where medicated oil is gently pooled over the lower back, allowing its nourishing warmth to stimulate the nerves and muscles, providing relief from pain and numbness.
- **Greevavasti**, which targeted the neck by soothing its achy vertebrae and discs with more warm oil on the affected areas, alleviating any pain and stiffness.
- **Uzhichil,** a full body, deep-muscle massage with medicated oil to improve overall circulation and energy flow.

(I've had similar benefits from AromaTouch Therapy with DoTerra oils, and I eventually became a certified therapist. This synthesis of ancient wisdom and essential oils is deeply healing).

I'm grateful for plant medicines that treat gently and holistically. These therapies nourish both body and soul, and act as a deep healing balm for modern life.

MY EXPERIENCE WITH AYURVEDIC TREATMENTS

The doctor had advised me to wait until the end of the Advanced Course at the ashram before beginning the recommended ayurvedic therapies, when they could more fully and accurately assess the state of my doshas. I trusted their expertise and finished the course before receiving a customized treatment plan.

As I entered the treatment room for the first time, I was greeted by the sweet aromas of herbs, oils, and spices, which immediately put me at ease. Beena, my petite Indian massage therapist (who spoke limited English but had a heart of gold), greeted me with a warm smile. The ambiance was tranquil and inviting.

I noticed a unique wooden steam cabinet in one corner and a rudimentary massage table in the other. The thought of lying face down on a hard, wooden surface for over an hour filled me with dread, as it didn't look too comfortable.

Beena handed me a basic cloth to tie around my waist. (It looked like a loincloth, to be honest, and I felt like some Amazonian jungle warrior ready for battle). She propped my head up with a towel, but lying face-down on that unforgiving table for over an hour was absolute torture. Rather than being able to drift off and relax, I was trying to breathe through the pain on that rock-hard Flintstone table. If only her victims—I mean "clients"—knew the true suffering that awaited on this so-called "massage table." When I treat my own clients, they lie on a comfortable table with padding, usually made of high-density foam and covered with either vinyl or leather. There was no such luck for me.

Beena started off with the Greevavasti treatment, asking me which side the pain was on. As I lay face down, unable to see what Beena was doing, I felt a cold, doughy sensation as she pressed something onto my upper back, near my neck. It smelled heavenly, and when I asked what it was, she revealed it was chapatti dough shaped into a circle to "fasten" to the painful spot. I breathed in the aromatic scent—the dough must have been infused with herbs.

In the corner of the room was a bubbling pot of warm, medicated oil. Beena carefully poured the soothing lukewarm liquid over the dough, bringing sweet relief to my aching back. Every few minutes, she would use a sponge to dab up any excess oil before repeating the process several more times. She explained that the oils were absorbed through the pores and penetrated deep into the muscles and nerves.

Once finished, she removed the chapatti dough and wiped away any remnants. I was fascinated by this unique treatment and how the dough and fragrant oils worked together to ease my pain. The Greevavasti technique proved to be an interesting and effective method.

Next was Kati Vasti, targeting my lower back and using the same dough ring technique and medicated oil. By the end, I was overjoyed to finally turn over after gritting my teeth through that agonizing hour on that rigid wooden table.

I finished with the Uzhichil oil massage, and it was pure bliss. Beena worked wonders on my achy muscles. When the massage was over, she slipped some cozy slippers on my feet and helped me up from the table. I was as slippery as an eel from the oils! Then came the real treat—the wooden steam cabin. I'd never experienced one before. She closed me into the compact space, which felt like a sanctuary even as it quickly became piping hot. Only my head stuck out as the medicated oils and herbs enveloped my body in their steamy and warm embrace. With each breath, I could feel the oxygen circulating through my body while the steam coaxed my pores open. She left me to sweat it out for five to ten minutes while she cleaned the massage table with water and soap and tidied up. The heat and steam were great for detoxification. It reminded me of Native American sweat lodges, those dome-shaped huts that get scorching hot from steaming, heated rocks placed inside. I've tried them before—you come out absolutely drenched in sweat! It's an ancient ritual for cleansing mind, body, and spirit that appears in many cultures. This steam cabin worked wonders on my pores and I left me feeling oily, but refreshed.

After being steamed, and still dripping with oil, Beena led me to the bathroom with a bucket of water to rinse off. "Hot or cold?" I enquired, looking at the water.

"Hot," she replied.

"Is the tap water hot, too?" I asked.

She nodded. "As hot as you need. Use as much as you like."

For the first time in nearly two weeks, I was granted the luxury of hot water. I was ecstatic and over the moon! This simple comfort felt like a godsend after enduring ice-cold showers for nearly two weeks. I could have jumped for joy, though I probably would have slipped like a klutz on the slick tiles.

These time-honored, ayurvedic treatments work to restore imbalanced doshas back to their natural state, but it often requires several sessions to achieve the full effect. I was only able to undergo three days of treatments before I had to catch my flight back home. Despite the abbreviated treatments, I did feel some relief. My frozen left shoulder regained some mobility and my lower back pain had subsided to a dull ache. While not cured, I was deeply grateful, and I left feeling refreshed and optimistic after these authentic Ayurvedic healing treatments.

I was lucky enough to see Dr. Pinkita herself on my last day of treatment. My stomach was still churning, I'd dropped weight, and those dry Marie biscuits were the bane of my existence. She motioned me over, saying many doing the Advanced Course get upset stomachs as toxins flush out. She prescribed some herbal medication to soothe the pain, and to my relief, they did work.

I asked Dr. Pinkita about a good friend of mine at the time, Janny, who had fallen ill after swimming in a lake in the UK that was polluted by chemical pesticides. This had caused her many serious health issues, and I wondered if Dr. Pinkita had any advice. With wisdom and compassion, Dr. Pinkita read Janny's nadi through me. She held my wrist and asked me to close my eyes and simply focus on her. Dr. Pinkita saw right into her soul, and her insights were eerily accurate as she spoke of

Janny's health struggles. I wasn't thinking of specifics, yet she knew. It was truly mind-blowing how she described her condition in detail even, though they were worlds apart and had never met.

Dr. Pinkita prescribed Ayurvedic medications for Janny, but warned that they might clash with her current prescription medications. As it turns out, that's precisely what Janny's doctor back home in the UK said, too! She'd have to wait three months before considering any of the Ayurvedic remedies. And even though my friend couldn't take those natural cures in the end, it warmed my heart to try to help her. The experience showed me there are mystical forces at play we don't fully understand. I'll never forget the nadi reader's amazingly accurate insights that day, and I'm grateful I got to glimpse my friend's spirit through the nadi reading before she passed in the summer of 2023. She was a true fighter, and even though her physical body was worn to the max and she is no longer with us, her radiant spirit lives on, dancing carefree in the light. Her beautiful soul has crossed over to a place where she is now free of pain, filled with joy and happiness, and in a simple state of peace. Her gentle presence still surrounds us, reminding us that love never dies. Her memory will forever live on within our hearts while her untethered spirit celebrates her love from above. The beautiful message she conveyed to me from beyond resonates with a profound truth and poetic grace.

"You've got to dance with life, and even though our physical essence is a temple to bow down to in gratitude, we often forget in our human form that we are our own worst nemesis, through those poisoned apples we feed our minds, thus intoxicating our own healing process within that process. There is no right or wrong in how you choose to heal— there is only your way, and what you believe is the best course of action for you. My body was withered and weathered, and I healed myself to the best of my human abilities, being a repeat customer to the hospital, knowing full well from where I am now, that there was still trauma to be

healed, causing my energy to be short-circuited more times than I would have liked. The trick is to make the unconscious conscious, rather than keeping that conditioned brick, bricked in place, ignoring the triggers and signs of your fatigued soul, held within that beautiful suit that you have been given to walk this earth. Just experience the experiment of life, experimenting with your experiences, making sure to take care of what you feed your mind, because what you allow in, forms your belief system. Quieten the mind to listen to the heart, body, and soul, and know that there is nothing that cannot be healed; there is nothing that cannot be altered; as above, so below, we are all energy and energy can be woven and molded according to the whims of how you decide to manifest this into the boon of your very earthly existence, rather than the bane of it."

—Janny

GRATITUDE FOR THE EXPERIENCE

I was overwhelmed with a downpour of Ayurvedic medications. It was more than my body could handle without becoming a total herbal pill popper. I never actually took all of the remedies given to me, as it would've had me higher than the Himalayas! Instead, I tuned into my body's inner wisdom, which told me plainly to "chill" and take it easy, as there was no need for that much herbal stuff to course through my veins. I listened, skipping the supplements that would've had me "tripping." My body knew best, so I followed its lead, and I still do to this day.

I had asked for a tour of the new Panchakarma wing before it opened to patients and Dr Pinkita graciously led me through the connecting doors on the first floor. We walked through a little walkway that opened up into a picturesque courtyard. Though unfinished, I could imagine patients finding Zen amongst the calm and tranquility here. The simple woodwork gave it a peaceful vibe, even though just around the corner was a lake with warnings to beware of crocodiles!

I learned the clinic could accommodate about thirty-two in-house patients. Some rooms were still empty but would soon have ensuite bathrooms. Outside, workers were planting palm trees in the dug-up dirt. The trees would eventually form a lush oasis, like the front of the current building. The spacious new facilities had a large kitchen in addition to the reception area and treatment rooms. With its beautiful architecture and serene scenery, the new wing would definitely provide a relaxing, healing environment to escape the hustle and bustle of the city. There was respite awaiting in this eco-friendly wellness sanctuary. The devoted team of volunteers, called 'sevaks,' served those at the clinic with presence and intuition cultivated through meditation, pranayama, and the Sudarshan Kriya. They're simply there to hold space for those wanting to heal and transform themselves, bringing them back home to their own inner radiance, their own inner light of selves.

The whole Ayurveda experience was like stepping into a magical world where body, mind, and spirit are all interconnected. I was in awe as the doctor analyzed my pulse, uncovering deep insights about my physical, mental, and spiritual wellbeing with just a touch. Despite the uncomfortable treatments on a hard wooden table, the holistic healing journey was truly enlightening. My back pain resurfaced eventually, but I left with a newfound admiration for Ayurveda's wholistic approach to wellness. The sanctuary within the Art of Living ashram was a sacred space for rejuvenation and reconnecting with myself. It was the perfect spot for a transformative retreat, blending traditional Ayurvedic therapies with spiritual introspection. The staff's expertise and compassion made this clinic a gem of Ayurvedic excellence. I have since fully embraced a wholistic approach to my health and wellbeing rather than quick fixes and superficial solutions.

CHAPTER 20
CONCLUSION: THE ROAD TO BETTER TOMORROWS

"Life can be a bit of a dosa toss-up, either reveling in the sweet aroma of a bed of roses, with petals gently caressing your skin or landing on a gnarly bed of nails, puncturing the bruis-ed ego in the hope of waking you up to the lessons held within your experiences. The choice is yours for the making; twist and shout or dunk that funk?

Love is the breath eternal that you are and always have been, so walk back oh so gloriously to the very home of the loving self, that you have so abandoned, becoming aware of the 'medicine' held within each created and encountered experience. Live a life extraordinaire, filled with love, with hope and a slap on the bottom for you to take risks, to start living rather than being lived."

—*The Ascended Master St. Germain*

THE PAST FEW YEARS have truly been a whirlwind of experiences for me. After working tirelessly in my high-pressure corporate oil and gas job, rarely even taking a weekend off to recharge, I found myself utterly exhausted and on the verge of a complete burnout. I refused to listen to the warning signs of my body and persisted in my demanding role, simultaneously pouring my limited free time into my true passions of spiritual work by promoting my published book and writing another. I was burning the candle at both ends and feeling utterly exhausted. With prices quadrupling in the UK, the universe nudged me to plot my escape, so I made the bold decision to move to Spain.

Despite feeling like I'm stranded in a spiritual wasteland, surrounded by folks barely scratching the surface of who they truly are and splashing around in their shallow puddles of existence, which is perfectly fine, my Guides insist that this is the ideal place for me to focus on self-healing, growth, protecting my energy, and unleashing my creativity. So, for now, I'm just gonna chill here until the universe nudges me to pack my bags and go elsewhere in the world.

Delving deep into my thoughts and feelings, and reconnecting with my inner self despite the challenges, has actually turned out to be a hidden gem. Yoga has become my sanctuary, exercise my release, meditation my solace, and running my freedom.

Did Sri Sri wave a magic wand and make everything perfect? Nope, not quite. Maybe he sent some healing vibes to those in need, but let's be real, nobody can wave a wand and fix us. We cannot simply rely on charismatic gurus or enlightened beings to swoop in and make everything perfect—that responsibility ultimately lies with each of us as the guardians of our souls. The infinite galaxy within, filled with both light and shadow, is ours to navigate and tend to, especially when it comes to the deeply personal work of healing our deepest wounds and traumas. We have to roll up our sleeves, confront our shadows, process our pain, and piece ourselves back together. It's a lifelong journey of self-discovery, self-acceptance, and self-empowerment as we take charge of our inner worlds. There are no quick fixes or magic solutions, we've got to sift through our crap, confront our pain, and realize that the power to heal ourselves lies within. But it is through this very process that we find the greatest gifts of healing, growth, and transformation. We're the only

CONCLUSION: THE ROAD TO BETTER TOMORROWS

ones who can save the day, fix what's broken, and mend our own hearts. Sure, folks have said to have faith and trust in Sri Sri, but honestly, I don't buy it. We can't rely on someone else to swoop in and save us. We've got to put on our own superhero cape and be our own damn saviors.

The warm Spanish sunshine did little to alleviate my exhaustion. By the close of 2023, I felt like a deflated balloon that had lost its joyous party spirit, with my health taking a hit from the never-ending hours. Those regular paychecks were like a warm hug, but the toll on my well-being was way too high. In just one year, I had cranked out the equivalent of seventeen months of work, only to be rewarded with a bonus that felt more like a shriveled cherry on a sad little cupcake. As my work life threatened to snap like an overcooked spaghetti noodle, I decided it was time to change the narrative, take a deep breath, and embrace a more positive outlook.

Never give up on your dreams no matter what, even if you feel like you're stuck in a job that's as exciting as watching paint dry. You've been given this one life, it's too precious to waste on something that doesn't set your soul on fire. And don't ever settle for a job that forces you to be someone you're not just to blend in. Never allow your true self to be stifled and gagged. Speak up and let your voice be heard.

My true purpose lies beyond the limits of a traditional career. This may require me to wade through the challenges and growing pains of the corporate jungle, dodging office politics and sidestepping the drama like it's a game of Twister, but deep down, I know I'm here to sprinkle a little magic and inspire positive change in the lives of those I meet. This phase of my life is merely a temporary stop on my journey, a springboard for my spiritual work to empower others to lead more fulfilling lives. I find joy in helping others, and through my voice and quirky light language codes, I humbly serve as a cosmic GPS nudging people to remember their own superpowers to heal, improve, and transform their lives from the inside out. We all possess this incredible force within us—the choice to either unleash our highest potential and soar to dazzling new heights, or, you know, to hit the self-destruct button and essentially "nuke" ourselves into oblivion. My mission? To help others recognize and harness that light, reclaim their divine sovereignty, and step into the extraordinary beings they were always meant to be. Besides healing, I find a little slice of happiness in channeling and writing, with the aim to plant seeds of awakening. My hope is that those unfurling petals of self-love will blossom into positive change and a subtle stirring out of that long slumber within the soul. I'm simply here to spark that inner fire and encourage others to *live life* rather than being *lived by it*.

Life is about pursuing our passions, whatever they may be. It's about embracing all of who we are, living with intent, finding joy, driving positive change in our own lives, and spreading that positivity to the world around us. I believe that when we follow our hearts, embrace our humanity, and freely share our gifts with the world, we discover the true meaning and beauty of this amazing human journey.

Upon incarnating into this world, my sister chose a challenging journey, she clearly signed up for the ultimate obstacle course. Yet, she is more like a determined tortoise in a world full of speedy hares. Those first twenty years were a ride or die of trials. Yet, she emerged as a gentle, caring, and fiercely protective spirit. My sister, bless her heart, has been on a spiritual treadmill for years—running in place but never really getting anywhere. She thrived on stress like it was her morning coffee, thinking it made her feel "alive." Spoiler alert: it didn't. This obnoxious, yet feisty little firecracker had a knack for battling every little injustice, which is both her superpower and her kryptonite. She has lost her bearings plenty of times, given her power away, like free promotional samples at a grocery store, and battled those little gremlins of doubt and insecurity. She has now learned to tap into her inner reservoir of strength to overcome her created "storms in a teacup." By letting go of those cloudy meatballs of heaviness, diving deep into her own heart, and welcoming the little flicker of her inner brilliance, she's on a fabulous journey to unearth those precious gems of self-love, beauty, and forgiveness and her

CONCLUSION: THE ROAD TO BETTER TOMORROWS

spirit is feeling lighter and more balanced than ever. Today, she joyfully declares, "I am a happy, flappy soul... always growing and glowing!"

My sister is an amazing intuitive reader. Her readings which include Theban, (angelic language) are consistently accurate, offering her clients profound clarity and direction as they navigate the complexities of their life journeys. Those who seek her counsel emerge with a renewed sense of purpose, their paths illuminated by the wisdom she imparts. I love my sister, and I know eventually her brilliance will shine brighter than ever.

Though I make it my mission to help others, I also make time to help myself. I am a constant work in progress. I stumble, fall, and make mistakes because, like you, I'm only human. But I'm fully aware of every step I take, even those automated patterns I sometimes fall into. And you know what? Imperfection is perfectly okay. Building self-awareness is the key to healing, shifting our mindset, and transforming our lives. When we catch ourselves replaying those old mental tapes, we have the power to choose a different response. It takes practice, but we can rewire our neural pathways away from those tired, painful, knee-jerk reactions. Eventually, we'll become the absolute best version of ourselves. Change is a lifelong process, not a destination. As long as we keep showing up for life and hitting our traumatic experiences out of the ballpark with a beautiful, unfolding, and open heart, we're moving in the right direction. Don't be too hard on yourself, like I used to be (I'm a pro at that, trust me), and I still have my moments. Be gentle and be kind to yourself.

I know that trauma can feel like this insistent, pesky visitor that keeps haunting us, knocking on our door, and urging us to confront the bleeding wounds of our past experiences. Even when we make a conscious choice to heal, trauma can boomerang back to the hand that threw it, circling back until we catch it, listen to it, and learn from it. At the same time, it's also a reminder that we have the power to break free from the cycle of pain and suffering. Remember that suffering isn't a meaningless intruder. It's our hidden compass, guiding us to become more whole within ourselves. All we have to do is follow its lead. Just as a phoenix rises from its ashes, we too can emerge stronger and wiser from our struggles. By acknowledging our pain, we take the first step toward healing and transformation, embracing the journey of self-discovery.

"Remember opportunities to the new are waiting to knock on your door, but they will only open if you are ready to do the internal work to support them. Until then, opportunity will halt, and you will be silently listening on the other end of the closed door as much as opportunity will silently sit and wait on the other end, until you decide to get up and do the work to open that door."

—*The Ascended Master St. Germain*

In the rush of everyday life, it's easy to let the present moment slip away. Instead, strive to embrace each passing moment—let it guide you, heal you, inspire you, and strengthen you. Too often, our days blur together in a mindless routine, and we find ourselves constantly worrying about the future rather than living in the now. The key is to make a conscious effort to find joy and meaning in the small, fleeting moments of each day. Rather than always deferring happiness to "someday," choose to be fully present and engaged with your life as it unfolds before you.

As I write this, the golden rays of the rising sun cast a warm glow over the sleepy Spanish urbanization around me. There is still quiet and calm in these early hours before the bustle of the day begins. As I sip my ginger-infused herbal tea on the balcony, I find my mind drifting back through the years, remembering all of the difficult times and the characters who challenged me, taught me, and helped shape me into the person I am today. There were painful moments of adversity, confusion, and doubt; times when I burned and blistered my arse through the hellish trials of my own making. But those hardships now seem worth it for the insights they brought. The wisdom imparted to me by the many master teachers, mentors, guides, and enlightened souls along the way has proven invaluable, with their lessons etched into my spirit. With-

CONCLUSION: THE ROAD TO BETTER TOMORROWS

out those experiences, both bitter and sweet, I would not have grown into the more contemplative, compassionate, and spiritually-centered being I am today. Given the chance, I would gladly walk that same rocky road again, even with all those false starts and backtracks, knowing that the journey itself holds meaning and purpose. Our struggles teach us, our failures strengthen us, and the eclectic souls we meet are mere reflections, granting us new perspectives.

The story of my time in India and the lessons I learned there isn't "gospel" or a set of rules to live by. It isn't a manual for life. Instead, the lessons incurred were like a spicy curry for the soul—full of flavor, teachings, and a whole lot of heart. It was a symphony of growth for my soul. By sharing my journey, I hope to stir something within your own soul and sprinkle a little magic, leading you to reconnect with your inner light and the ever-unfolding story of your life. If my words strike a chord, then I'm honored to be a part of your journey. Take what resonates, leave what doesn't—it's all part of the buffet of life.

Sri Sri's teachings at the Art of Living Center were a soothing balm for my spirit, guiding me to find peace in life's storms. And let me tell you, meditation is like a daily dose of magic for the soul. It's much like a beauty skin care routine—the more you use it, the better you feel from the inside out. Even in the midst of all the pain and chaos, it's crucial to remain calm and centered. Just as Buddha taught, "the mind is like water—when it's turbulent, it's difficult to see, but when it's calm, everything becomes clear."

I may have visited India years ago, but my story needed time to simmer and marinate before it was ready to be served. It needed time to age and mature before my words could be uncorked. I had a lot more life experiences to rack up, fears to face, struggles to overcome, and had to learn to dance with my demons before I was ready to spill my ink onto paper..

Observing periods of silence was particularly reflective, as it encouraged me to turn inward rather than outward. Taking a moment to shut up and listen to the sound of your own thoughts can be pretty enlightening. It's like a little vacation for the mind, a chance to cozy up with your own thoughts and feelings. Silence was that secret ingredient that helped me reconnect with my true self.

My story is not one of seeking perfection, but of a flawed journey navigated with courage, compassion, and an unwavering belief that better days lie ahead. I hope that the words within these pages dare you to hope and dream once more, and to find the strength to take the first step towards healing and growth, even when the road ahead seems dark. In sharing my story, I hope it serves as a lighthouse for those who need it most, and that it will illuminate and inspire. We are not alone in our struggles, but part of a tapestry of human experiences woven together by our shared capacity for hope and love.

There's no one-size-fits-all approach to life. You have the power to carve your own path and create your own future. No matter where you find yourself right now, cherish the breath and the gift of life, embracing the full spectrum of the human experience. The highs and lows, the triumphs and tribulations, the moments of joy and sorrow—they have shaped you into the remarkable person you are today. And while endings can feel daunting, it's important to remember that they are not truly an end, but rather the shaping of new beginnings. Like a dear friend, welcome these transitions, for they hold the potential to open doors to uncharted territories and help you evolve into a more wholesome version of yourself. Always stay true to yourself, instead of conforming to society's expectations. With time and reflection, you'll come to realize that every single step you've taken on your journey—whether faltering or confident, whether celebrated or challenged—has led you inexorably to the person you were destined to become. Never compromise your true essence by bending to the desires and demands of others. Sing your own song, even if your voice falters or goes against the chorus around you. You alone have the power to shape your purpose and pave your own way. Embrace the darkness and the light, for without the shadows, even the stars could never shine so bright.

—Birgitta Visser, 22 September 2024, Orihuela Costa, Spain

RESOURCES

Art of Living Centre
https://www.artofliving.org/in-en

The Art of Living's Global Matrimony Platforms
http://www.artoflivingmatrimony.org

The Art of Living–Making Life A Celebration–Sri Sri Panchakarma Clinic
https://www.artofliving.org/in-en/ayurveda/remedies/sri-sri-ayurveda-panchakarma

Care For Children - Art of Living Free Schools
https://www.careforchildren.org/index.html

The Art of Living's Global Matrimony Platforms
https://www.artoflivingmatrimony.org/

Nadi Astrology–Dr Sri Sivakumar Nayana.
https://nadiastrology.net/

Integrated Positive Astrology–Dr Shivakumar Nayanar
https://www.staripa.com/

Louise Rhodes–Light Language Channel & Energy Healer
http://www.louiserhodes.co.uk/

Alania Starhawk Divine Channel & Spiritual Mentor
https://alaniastarhawk.com/

Power Soul Healing–Work with Barbara
https://www.powersoulhealing.com/work-with-barbara

Visser, B. (2022a) BE-com-ing authentically Me. London: Light Warriors Press.

Nic Nierrias Holistic Lifestyle
https://thenicnierraswholisticlifestyle.com/

Davidji–mindbody health & wellness expert, mindful performance trainer, meditation teacher & author
https://davidji.com/

Caroline McCready Meditation Practitioner
https://www.carolinemccready.com/

Opheana & Sikaal Sheehan–Divine Light Meditation Teachers
https://www.opheanasikaal.com/

Whispers of the Wild Meditations & Holistic Healing & Spiritual Retreats, with Nature &
Animals–https://www.katiewyatt.love/

ABOUT THE AUTHOR

BIRGITTA VISSER IS AN author, speaker, and a modern-day mystic, guiding others on a journey of self-discovery and empowerment. As a Soul Empowerment Coach and Divine Channel, she taps into higher realms of consciousness to channel transformative messages and light codes from a wide array of celestial guides and master teachers. With her gift for Light Language Healing, she weaves intricate tapestries of light codes that catalyze deep shifts and alignment within those seeking to reconnect with their soul's true purpose. Through her books, including *BE-coming Authentically Me* and the collaborative works, *Become Empowered, Echoes of Grace and Strength* and *I'm So Glad You Left Me*, Birgitta has shared her profound insights and teachings with readers worldwide, inspiring them to awaken to their own limitless possibilities. Her work shines like a beacon of hope and inspiration, illuminating the way for all of us to realize our own potential for growth and empowerment. Her unwavering honesty and vulnerability remind us that even in our darkest moments, we have the power to heal, overcome, and embrace our true selves. She is currently based in Southern Spain where she lives with her rescued Floridian mutt Myra.

www.ingramcontent.com/pod-product-compliance
Lightning Source LLC
Chambersburg PA
CBHW072147070526
44585CB00015B/1032